CHURCHES AND SOCIAL ISSUES IN TWENTIETH-CENTURY BRITAIN

Churches and Social Issues in Twentieth-Century Britain

G. I. T. MACHIN

CLARENDON PRESS · OXFORD
1998

Oxford University Press, Great Clarendon Street, Oxford OX2 6DP
Oxford New York
Athens Auckland Bangkok Bogota Bombay
Buenos Aires Calcutta Cape Town Dar es Salaam
Delhi Florence Hong Kong Istanbul Karachi
Kuala Lumpur Madras Madrid Melbourne
Mexico City Nairobi Paris Singapore
Taipei Tokyo Toronto Warsaw

and associated companies in
Berlin Ibadan

Oxford is a trade mark of Oxford University Press

Published in the United States by
Oxford University Press Inc., New York

British Library Cataloguing in Publication Data
Data available

Library of Congress Cataloging in Publication Data
Machin, G. I. T.
Churches and social issues in twentieth-century Britain / G. I. T. Machin.
p. cm.
Includes bibliographical references and index.
1. Church and social problems—Great Britain—History—20th century. 2. Christianity and culture—Great Britain—History—20th century. 3. Social change—Great Britain—History—20th century. 4. Great Britain—Church history—20th century. 5. Great Britain—Social conditions—20th century. 6. Great Britain—Moral conditions. I. Title.
GN39.G7M24 1997
261.8'3'09410704—dc21 97-33040

ISBN 0-19-821780-3

1 3 5 7 9 10 8 6 4 2

Typeset by Best-set Typesetter Ltd., Hong Kong
Printed in Great Britain by
Bookcraft Ltd., Midsomer Norton,
Nr. Bath, Somerset

To Jane and 'The Boys'

PREFACE AND ACKNOWLEDGEMENTS

Churches are primarily religious and doctrinal organizations, but social attitudes, policy, and practice have always and inescapably been a large part of their concerns.

Christianity is mainly organized by means of Churches, in Britain no less than in any other country. Churches represent Christianity in the way each believes to be the best and most appropriate. Churches share with each other the basic Christian doctrines of the existence and activity of God and the incarnation and redemption of Christ, but beyond these beliefs their doctrinal systems are diverse. Also diverse are the organization and liturgy of Churches and their attitudes to control of religion by the State.

Towards mankind in general, Churches lay their chief emphasis on conversion and repentance as routes to salvation. Men and women must be persuaded to improve themselves in order to increase their fitness to receive the benefit of the saving grace of Jesus Christ. Hence morality has always been a major part of Christian teaching, and from this springs a desire to supervise and improve the whole range of personal behaviour demonstrated by mankind.

Extension from personal morality to public policy is inevitable in the case of Christian intentions and activity. Government actions as well as personal behaviour are seen as shaping the individual, and personal morality is seen as partly a product of public policy. So the Christian is often deeply interested in social policy and its workings. Personal quietism and disinterest in the affairs of the world have, of course, always been, and remain, very significant strands in Christianity. The extent to which Christians should forsake the spiritual cloister and go forth to save the material world was sometimes a matter of anxious dilemma and dispute. But the outgoing desire to improve the state of man through the influence of Christian morality on public policy and action has proved, since the early nineteenth century at least, to be a more powerful force than spiritual seclusion. Christianity has indeed been the main cultural influence on the changing social policies of Britain. There is a great deal of consensus between Churches on social questions, both private and public, despite the differences over theology and liturgy which mark these Churches (or groups within Churches). But there is also clear diversity between Churches on some social matters (for example, artificial birth control, divorce, and women's ordination), and a good deal of diversity on social matters in general between members of each Church. Christian thought has largely produced the whole variety of approaches to social policy in twentieth-century Britain, from Keir Hardie to Margaret Thatcher.

The purpose of this book is not to present another useful social investigation of the church-membership and church-going habits of the population or of the role of denominations in the social structure. The purpose is rather to examine the attitudes of Churches and their members and adherents to social issues, including both public policy and personal morals and behaviour.

The book does not address the question whether a Church's social attitudes differ from one area of the country to another, depending on habits and viewpoints prevailing in each area. This question is probably too complicated and many-sided to answer satisfactorily—at the very least, there would be exceptions in any geographical area from a general 'norm' of behaviour. In any case, it is probable that such differences in regard to locality have diminished as the century has progressed, because of the increasing extent and influence of the mass media and mass forms of entertainment, and because of the increasing mobility of the population. Certain Churches, particularly the Free Church of Scotland, have been associated mainly with one area (in the case of that Church, the Western Highlands and Islands), but there has always been the presence in the area of rival Churches with different attitudes towards some social matters. It has probably been a case of members of a Church being influenced in their social behaviour by the organization in whatever area they happened to live, rather than Churches moulding their own approach to that prevailing in a particular area.

Most of the research for the book was done on the period from 1918 to 1970. The first chapter, dealing with the years from the opening of the century to 1918, is rather broad and introductory compared with the bulk of the work. The concluding chapter, on the years since 1970, is a general survey rather than a detailed treatment. It is hoped that a future historian will deal fully with the subject in the last thirty years of the century (and extending into the years beyond), when more of the important sources are available for study and the period can be placed in satisfactory historical perspective.

The question of the Churches in relation to education has not been given the detailed and consistent attention it deserves in this book, as this is a specialized subject which would be more satisfactorily handled in a separate study.

The manuscript and typed correspondence sources I have used have been the ones which seemed the most appropriate and potentially useful of those to which I was allowed access. I have not attempted to utilize any oral history records, but have used the correspondence columns of a wide range of religious newspapers as providing more instantaneous examples of individual opinions on issues at the times they appeared. Apart from letters either in collections or in newspapers, the main primary sources have been information and articles in newspapers and the records of a broad range of Church assemblies and committees, and of societies supported by Churches.

With regard to the use of sources and other matters, I am most grateful for the help of many people, especially R. W. Ambler, David Bebbington, Clyde Binfield, Michael Brock, Deryck Lovegrove, Edward Luscombe, John Rowett, Reginald Ward; the staffs of the British Library, the National Library of Scotland, Lambeth Palace Library, Dundee University Library, Dr Williams's Library; and Tony Morris, Anna Illingworth, Hilary Walford, and their colleagues at the Clarendon Press. I am also most grateful for grants in aid of research from the British Academy, the Twenty-Seven Foundation, and the Department of Modern History at the University of Dundee; and for the invaluable secretarial help of Helen Carmichael and Sara Reid.

Ian Machin

CONTENTS

ABBREVIATIONS

AID	artificial insemination by a donor
AIH	artificial insemination by a husband
BH	*Baptist Handbook*
BP	Bell Papers
BT	*Baptist Times*
BW	*British Weekly*
CCC	*Chronicle of the Convocation of Canterbury*
CEN	*Church of England Newspaper*
Copec	Conference on Christian Politics, Economics, and Citizenship
CRAC	Central Religious Advisory Committee
CT	*Church Times*
CYB	*Congregational Year Book*
DP	Davidson Papers
FCFC	Free Church Federal Council
FP	Fisher Papers
G.	*Guardian* (a Church of England newspaper)
ICF	Industrial Christian Fellowship
LP	Lang Papers
LW	*Life and Work: The Church of Scotland Magazine and Mission Record*
MR	*Methodist Recorder*
NCCI	National Committee for Commonwealth Immigrants
NFCC	National Free Church Council
PAGAFCS	*Principal Acts of the General Assembly of the Free Church of Scotland*
PMC	Public Morality Council
RGACS	*Reports to the General Assembly of the Church of Scotland*
RP	Ramsey Papers
SP	Stopes Papers
SU	*Scottish Universe*
T.	*Tablet*

TCCC	Temperance Council of the Christian Churches of England and Wales
TP	William Temple Papers
U.	*Universe*
YJC	*York Journal of Convocation*

God is not so much denied as merely crowded out.

Broadcast by Archbishop Lang, Dec. 1936

What is the good of giving new houses, refrigerators and full domestic equipment, when we lack the central heating that only the Church can supply?

Speech of Dr John White in General Assembly of Church of Scotland, May 1945

Introduction

This book attempts to chart the reactions of the British Churches to a succession of social and moral change that was unprecedented within a single century. During the twentieth century not only did State collectivism establish itself as the central means of initiating and administering social policy, but so many changes took place in personal behaviour (some of them sanctioned and encouraged by legislation) that a virtual social revolution of a non-political variety took place. This was especially the case in the 1960s and the subsequent years which were affected by the multifarious changes of that decade. In the realm of social policy the twentieth-century watershed was the 1940s, when the Welfare State was established. In regard to personal morality and behaviour, the century's watershed was the 1960s, after which a markedly different climate prevailed in these matters than had previously been the case.

In some respects the Churches, as the moulders of British civilization, can be said to have initiated or at least encouraged many of the social changes that took place. In other respects, however, change was caused or encouraged by scientific invention (as in the case of the contraceptive pill) over which the Churches had little or no control; or, on the basis of freedom of speech, freedom of publication, or freedom of display, change was pressed to an extent that the Churches could not sanction. Whatever the extent to which the Churches had helped to provide the original climate of thought in which twentieth-century social changes came to flourish, the Churches were clearly challenged to defend or modify their traditional attitudes as the changes developed. Considerable controversy and division were caused both between and within Churches as they struggled either to repel or to absorb the changes.

The Churches were bound to regard all social developments from the viewpoint of Christian morality. The reactions of individual members of Churches to these developments were, or should have been, based on whether they believed the changes could be reconciled with Christian morality—or, conversely, whether Christian morality could be modified sufficiently to accommodate them.

Although modifications of Christian moral attitudes had frequently occurred in the past, Churches were sometimes reluctant to make these changes lest they be accused of inconsistently reversing long-held standpoints.

Over both public social policy and personal behaviour there were similar attitudes and diverse attitudes to be found both within a Church and between the Churches. Over public policy, for example, 'individualists' and 'collectivists' were found sharing membership, pew, and communion in the same Church. Over personal morality and behaviour it is also shown in the book that there was much agreement between the attitudes and injunctions of the various Churches, however pronounced their theological differences. But there were also marked differences in certain social respects, notably over the Roman Catholic attitudes to birth control, divorce, and women's ordination, which became more pronounced marks of divergence as the century progressed.

The Churches have been influential bodies in Britain throughout the twentieth century, but in general their influence in society has declined from one end of the century to the other. There is no direct and exclusive correlation between the declining church-membership and attendance figures and declining influence in society, but there is undoubtedly some connection between these tendencies. It is sometimes claimed that the Churches are ending the century with an upward flourish, but a good deal of investigation would need to be done before much could be asserted on this question.

Whether or not the Churches are ending the century in decline, it is clear that religion in Britain can no longer be equated almost wholly with Christianity. This was still the case in the first half of the century, when the Christian monopoly was broken only by a relatively small number of Jews and a very light sprinkling of people of other faiths. But since the 1950s, immigration from ex-colonies has added large numbers of Muslims, Hindus, and Buddhists to the population. These now form a substantial minority, and future comprehensive studies of religion in this country will have to take account of them. This book, however, restricts itself to the social attitudes of the Churches, their assemblies, members, and adherents—still the chief manifestation of Christianity, and indeed of religion, in this country at the present time.

I
Churches and Social Questions, c.1900–1918

A study of the social concerns of Churches in twentieth-century Britain begins at a time when both the Churches and the question of social reform were of great importance in that country. Already, however, while the Roman Catholics continued to grow apace, membership and attendance figures in the Protestant Churches were a lot less healthy, certainly when membership assessments are compared with the size of population. Around 1906 the major Nonconformist denominations in England and Wales began to experience numerical decline in membership, and the Church of England was having fewer attendances at Easter Day services. But in Scotland the Protestant Churches were not yet affected by numerical decline, and as in England the Roman Catholic Church continued to advance steadily.[1] The Churches as a whole had so far lost little of the active presence and influence they had gained so notably since the later eighteenth century.

Part of the Churches' continuing influence lay in their contributions to the current growth of interest in social reform. Questions of widespread poverty and poor housing, and of the physical disability and weakness of many in the population, seriously worried the richest and most powerful country in the world. This was particularly the case when many of the recruits to fight in the Boer War had to be rejected because of unfitness. A previous wave of intense concern to enact social reform through government intervention, in the 1830s and 1840s, had deeply involved religious opinion. Though waning somewhat thereafter, this concern had continued in the appearance of the first 'Christian socialist' movement in the 1850s. From the 1870s, desire to effect social improvement grew strongly

[1] For these developments, see the figures in R. Currie, A. Gilbert, and L. Horsley (eds.), *Churches and Churchgoers: Patterns of Church Growth in the British Isles since 1700* (Oxford, 1977), 31.

again in the country, and the Churches made a notable contribution to it.[2] Sometimes this interest took effect through specifically Christian channels such as the Christian Social Union, founded by Anglicans in 1889, and the similar Scottish Christian Social Union founded by Presbyterians in 1901.[3] The papal encyclical *Rerum Novarum* of 1891, among other published expressions of papal opinion at this time, was an encouragement to moderate social reform by a basically conservative Supreme Pontiff. A number of Christians attached themselves to Socialism, and denominational socialist societies were formed by Anglicans, Nonconformists, and Roman Catholics in the first decade of the twentieth century. Some clergy and ministers supported the socialist Independent Labour Party. A few even supported the Marxist 'clean sweep' recommended by the Social Democratic Federation and the later British Communist Party. The young William Temple's advocacy of the nationalization of industry was endorsed by his membership of the Labour Party from 1918, which he seems to have continued to hold in spirit even after he cancelled his subscription on becoming Bishop of Manchester in 1921 (on the grounds that a bishop should be officially non-partisan).

Some Anglo-Catholics espoused a belief in 'sacramental socialism' as a product of their sacramental faith, and the Catholic Social Guild was formed by the Roman Catholic Church in 1909.[4] The annual Church Congress of the Church of England devoted one of its sessions to social questions in nearly every year from 1880 to 1900. The National Free Church Council appointed a Commission of Enquiry into Christianity and the Social Order in 1909. The Quaker B. Seebohm Rowntree in York was among those who

[2] J. Harris, *Private Lives, Public Spirit: A Social History of Britain, 1870–1914* (Oxford, 1993), 220 ff.

[3] For a comprehensive review of growing Church support for social reform, covering the major denominations in England, see K. S. Inglis, *Churches and the Working Classes in Victorian England* (London, 1963), 250–321 (chapter on 'The Churches and Social Reform'). See also D. W. Bebbington, *The Nonconformist Conscience: Chapel and Politics, 1870–1914* (London, 1982), 38 ff.; also, for Scotland, D. J. Withrington, 'The Churches in Scotland, *c.*1870–1900: Towards a New Social Conscience?', *Records of the Scottish Church History Society*, 19 (1975–7), 155–68; W. W. Knox, 'Religion and the Scottish Labour movement, *c.*1900–39', *Journal of Contemporary History*, 23 (1988), 613–15.

[4] G. I. T. Machin, *Politics and the Churches in Great Britain, 1869 to 1921* (Oxford, 1987), 280; C. C. Clump, *A Catholic's Guide to Social and Political Action* (Catholic Social Guild Year Book, Oxford, 1939).

conducted local investigations into the extent of poverty, commencing in the later 1890s.

The Scottish Christian Social Union embraced members from what were the two main Presbyterian Churches in Scotland from 1900, the Church of Scotland and the United Free Church. The new association soon established local branches and a summer school (concerned with questions of child welfare, slum housing, and unemployment), and influenced the formation of a Social Work Committee in the Church of Scotland in 1904 and a Social Problems Committee in the United Free Church. The Church of Scotland also emphasized its social reform interests by giving them a central place in four National Church Congresses from 1899 to 1907, and later by establishing a Church and Nation Committee of the General Assembly in 1919 to give a continuing critical review of economic, social, and political issues. More radical than the Scottish establishment in social criticism before the First World War was the United Free Church. At the 1908 General Assembly of this Church, heated argument took place between progressives and conservatives, 'between those who wished the Church to work for a reformation of the social and economic structures of society in order to achieve a more Christian social order, and those who held that the Church's only task was to preach the Gospel to individuals, leaving it to redeemed individuals to create a more Christian society'. This General Assembly instructed its Life and Work Committee to consider a variety of social questions, including the matter of relating Christianity to the Labour movement and forming links with employers and trade unions. The 1910 General Assembly of the United Free Church established a Special Committee on Social Problems on a permanent basis, the first permanent committee formed on this subject by a Scottish Church. In 1911 the same Church held a large three-day congress on social questions and a Labour Week, the latter being organized by the Social Problems Committee and addressed by Labour politicians.[5]

Christians frequently adopted the attitude of one political party or another towards social reform, though this was a matter for individual and not for Church decision. Christians who were Liberals ardently welcomed the introduction of old age pensions in 1908

[5] The information in this paragraph, including the quotation, is from D. C. Smith, *Passive Obedience and Prophetic Protest: Social Criticism in the Scottish Church, 1830–1945* (New York, 1987), 332–54.

and the passing of the National Insurance Act in 1911. Church leaders often detached themselves from an overt party position, though most of them advocated a general liberal, reforming approach to social problems. This attitude did not endear them to those politicians who believed that their particular viewpoint should receive official religious sanction.[6] The Churches' social message often appeared bland and ephemeral at a time, especially in the first four decades of the twentieth century, when the concept of class was especially prominent and rival social doctrines were very much to the fore.

The diverse views of Christians on social policy have been reflected in the different reforming plans adopted by Governments in the course of the twentieth century. Much less straightforward has been the development of personal morality and social behaviour in comparison with Christian attitudes at the beginning of the century. Christians held, and continue to hold, differing opinions on these matters. By 1900 a liberalizing tendency in Christian attitudes on these questions was in conflict with a conservative emphasis on upholding the laws of the early and mid-nineteenth century which tightened morals. A great many members of different Churches supported the evolution of democracy. The aspiration for a democratic society promoted the desire to exercise more and more personal choice in the realms of morals and behaviour. By the early twentieth century there were demands for divorce to be granted on grounds additional to those permitted by law, for abortion to be made legal, for censorship of stage productions to be removed, and for more leisure activities to be enjoyed on Sundays.

Thus, puritanical attitudes in social life were coming increasingly under criticism. The moral discipline of some Churches—for example, the role of Church of Scotland kirk sessions in this respect—was breaking down by the end of the nineteenth century.[7] But puritan conventions were still flourishing, and their decline was not yet in sight. A strong interdenominational campaign for social purity had obtained in 1886 the repeal of the Contagious Diseases Acts, which were held by many to give official countenance to

[6] e.g. R. A. Bray, *Labour and the Churches* (London, 1912), 71, 101–12.

[7] S. J. Brown, 'The Decline and Fall of Kirk-Session Discipline in Presbyterian Scotland, *c.*1830–1930' (unpublished conference paper, Association of Scottish Historical Studies, 1991), 1–22; K. M. Boyd, *Scottish Church Attitudes to Sex, Marriage, and the Family, 1850–1914* (Edinburgh, 1980), 157–8.

prostitution. A National Vigilance Association, formed in 1885, gave rise to many local bodies with the aims of countering public breaches of accepted morality. This Association pressed successfully for a variety of legislative enactments on moral issues.[8] The Public Morality Council was an interdenominational body founded in 1899 primarily to try and reduce prostitution in London; it later extended its ambit to the surveillance of plays, films, and literature sold publicly in the capital. The National Vigilance Association sponsored the National Purity Crusade, which campaigned actively in 1901 and 1908 against prostitution; its secretary and director was James Marchant, a Presbyterian minister. In 1909 the Crusade became known on a more permanent basis as the National Council of Public Morals. This was supported by a wide range of Protestant denominational leaders, ranging from the Church of England to the Salvation Army.[9] The development of liberal social tendencies—which in some ways began to achieve legislative success in the 1920s and 1930s, but in others not until the 1960s—challenged the morality and behaviour which was strongly defended by these bodies. The liberalizing tendencies eventually gained success largely because they obtained support from many Christians.

The twentieth century thus commenced with questions of social reform absorbing an increasing amount of attention in Britain.[10] This was by no means necessarily at the expense of concern with religion, which continued to be influential and flourishing, if decreasingly so. But concern with religion, at least in the sense of formal attachment to Churches, has declined in the course of the twentieth century—for reasons largely though not exclusively distinct from growing interest in social questions—whereas concern with social matters has remained at a high level. The extent of the influence of the Churches over social attitudes and behaviour has declined; though the opinions and advice expressed by Church leaders and assemblies on these matters continue to be influential amongst their own followers, and sometimes amongst a wider public.

[8] S. Petrow, *Policing Morals: The Metropolitan Police and the Home Office, 1870–1914* (Oxford, 1994), 117–26.

[9] S. Hynes, *The Edwardian Turn of Mind* (Princeton, 1968), 279–93, 296–306.

[10] Cf. E. R. Norman, *Church and Society in England, 1770–1970* (Oxford, 1976), 220ff.

Of the issues concerning personal behaviour which were of clear concern to the Churches in the opening years of the century, the well-established social activities of drinking and gambling headed the list. All Churches were opposed to the excessive consumption of alcohol, though none made teetotallism, or even a commitment to moderate drinking, a condition of membership. Rather more emphasis was given to anti-drink resolutions in the Nonconformist Churches than in other Churches; sharp party political disputes over licensing questions in the first decade of the century no doubt strengthened this difference.

The Churches had their own temperance societies, overlapping with the work of many national organizations. The Church of England Temperance Society had over 150,000 members by 1900; while the more extreme United Kingdom Alliance, committed to teetotallism, had only about 20,000.[11] After the example of Cardinal Manning, of whom it was said that 'his greatest work for the poor was in the field of temperance', temperance campaigns were conducted under the auspices of the Roman Catholic League of the Cross. A series of these campaigns was successfully conducted by priests and Capuchin monks in south London in the summer of 1911.[12]

Consumption of alcohol generally became more moderate from the 1870s, and arrests for drunkenness decreased, probably as a result of the restriction of opening of public houses and other provisions of the Licensing Act of 1872. But later government legislation was not always seen as being friendly to the cause of temperance. The Unionist Government's Licensing Act of 1904, granting compensation for the loss of licences under this measure, was opposed partly on religious grounds. A Liberal bill of 1908, trying to reverse this provision, was rejected by the House of Lords. But some restrictions on drink sales were introduced in Lloyd George's Budget of 1909 (initially rejected by the Lords but accepted by them the following year after a general election on the Budget issue). In 1913 a Temperance Bill was passed for Scotland, to come into effect in 1920, allowing 'local option', a range of choices regarding the regulation of drink sales, to be arrived at by means of a vote of the ratepayers. Temperance

[11] Petrow, *Policing Morals*, 180. Cf. G. T. Brake, *Drink: Ups and Downs of Methodist Attitudes to Temperance* (London, 1974).

[12] *T.*, 19 Aug. 1911, p. 299.

opinion hoped this would lead to the adoption of local option throughout the UK. Significant temperance gains had thus been made by 1914. Temperance opinion, which had the increasingly powerful figure of the Baptist Lloyd George on its side, was influential and buoyant.[13] Further drink restrictions introduced in the First World War considerably encouraged this confidence.

If drinking was slowly lessening, gambling seemed to be expanding. The Churches had a common opposition to excessive indulgence in gambling, just as they did in the case of excessive drinking, though Christians had differing opinions about moderate participation in either activity.

The National Anti-Gambling League, founded in 1890, received support from clergy and ministers of different denominations, and it was in that year that the Wesleyan Conference issued its first Declaration on Gambling.[14] The report of a House of Lords Select Committee appointed in 1902—the only parliamentary inquiry into gambling between 1870 and 1914—suggested that the placing of small bets, often away from the racecourse and on the streets, was increasing; that betting had spread from horse racing to football pools; and that advertising in newspapers was furthering the practice of betting. Restrictions on 'off-the-course' betting already existed, and they soon increased. Betting 'houses' or shops were prohibited by an Act of 1853. Betting on the steets was forbidden by an Act of 1906. Betting on credit—for example, placing a bet by telephone and paying later—was now the only form of 'off-course' betting which was legally permitted, and this practice tended to exclude the working-class gambler. But street betting continued as an illegal popular pursuit, flourishing on the willingness of the police to turn a blind eye.[15]

Matters of birth limitation were of pressing concern to many families, particularly poor ones. Abortion was first made illegal by

[13] N. D. Denny, 'Temperance and the Scottish Churches, 1870–1914', *Records of the Scottish Church History Society*, 23/2 (1988), 233–4.

[14] Petrow, *Policing Morals*, 240; D. P. Campbell, 'Methodism and Social Problems in the Inter-War Period, 1918–39', M.Litt. thesis (Oxford, 1987), 105–6.

[15] Petrow, *Policing Morals*, 239, 257. Cf. B. S. Rowntree (ed.), *Betting and Gambling: A National Evil* (London, 1905); R. McKibbin, 'Working-Class Gambling in Britain, 1880–1939', in R. McKibbin (ed.), *The Ideologies of Class: Social Relations in Britain, 1880–1950* (Oxford, 1991), 101–38; A. Davies, 'The Police and the People: Gambling in Salford, 1900–39', *Historical Journal*, 34 (1991), 88–91.

an Act of 1803, the prohibition being reinforced by a further measure of 1861. But abortion was none the less much used as a secret, back-street practice which, if discovered, could bring severe penalties on the doctors who performed it. Medical preventatives were also employed: evidence of the use of abortifacients was growing, claimed a Yorkshire medical officer at an Infantile Mortality Conference in 1906.[16] The number of defendants tried for procuring abortion doubled between 1900 and 1910, and doubled again between 1910 and 1930.[17]

Artificial birth control was not illegal but was frowned on by respectable opinion and was opposed by national purity organizations and campaigns. Knowledge of the available methods spread none the less, and they were increasingly in use by the late nineteenth century. By 1900 artificial contraception was spreading widely among the middle classes.[18] The working classes, it is generally believed, relied less on the practice until after 1918, following the wide extension of contraceptive methods among soldiers in the First World War—as a protection against venereal disease—through government action. No doubt because of the increasing use of contraception, the birth rate was declining. Church reactions were rather indecisive. Nonconformist Churches, while by no means liking or openly advocating the practice, were generally prepared to leave the use of artificial contraception to individual judgement. This was also the attitude of the Church of Scotland, though its General Assembly did not pronounce fully and decisively on the matter until as late as 1960. The Church of England also acted slowly. The international Lambeth Conference of Anglican bishops in 1920 pronounced clearly against the practice; but the next conference in 1930 gave a very hesitating concession that private judgement might decide, provided there was strong justification.

Among other matters of great concern to families, divorce reform was an increasingly prominent issue between 1900 and 1914, not least because it was advocated in the plays of George Bernard Shaw. A Society for Promoting Reforms in the Marriage and Divorce Laws of England was founded in 1903, and in 1906 this body merged with another association to form the Divorce Law Reform

[16] B. Brookes, *Abortion in England, 1900–67* (London, 1988), 2, 23.
[17] Ibid. 28.
[18] Hynes, *The Edwardian Turn of Mind*, 198–9.

Union; Sir Arthur Conan Doyle was president until 1916.[19] Divorce was thoroughly investigated by a Royal Commission on Divorce and Matrimonial Causes, which was appointed in 1909 and produced its report in 1912. This recommended that the legal grounds for divorce in England and Wales be extended to include desertion, cruelty, insanity, habitual drunkenness, and imprisonment under a commuted death sentence. In Scotland the law had permitted divorce for desertion as well as adultery since 1573. In England and Wales the Matrimonial Causes Act of 1857 had permitted divorce for adultery on the suit of a husband, but for adultery only if it were accompanied by cruelty on the suit of a wife. The 1912 report recommended that men and women should be treated equally through removal of the special condition imposed on a wife. An attempt was immediately made to pass appropriate legislation, but no bill was enacted until 1923, when the conditions for men and women were equalized. The grounds for divorce were further extended by Acts of 1937 and 1938, causing ecclesiastical disturbance and response. Church opinion was divided on questions of divorce reform, reflecting the different interpretations which could be obtained from the Scriptures on the subject. The Roman Catholic Church did not countenance divorce, but was prepared to annul marriage in approved cases. Most other Christians probably found the Commission's main recommendations in 1912 too radical, and needed considerable time to consider such wide proposals to extend divorce opportunities.

New developments in popular entertainment gave cinematograph shows an increasing role in the 1890s and the succeeding decade. These shows continued to spread during the First World War and gradually ousted the music hall as the leading popular entertainment outside the home. As the Home Secretary declined to provide an official censor of cinema films, the British Board of Film Censors was established in 1912 by the cinema trade itself. The first president of the Board, who held the post for many years, was the Catholic T. P. O'Connor, a journalist who was Irish Home Rule MP for the Scotland division of Liverpool. The members of the Board were appointed by the cinema proprietors, who thereby sought respectability for the films they showed. Censorship was thus being extended rather than abolished. Many writers would

[19] Ibid. 192 ff.

have preferred abolition. Throughout Great Britain the duty of censoring plays rested, in rather archaic fashion, with the Lord Chamberlain, an official of the royal household who was not accountable to Parliament. His powers had been decided by the Theatres Act of 1843. The actual reading and judging of plays were performed by an assistant to the Lord Chamberlain, the Examiner of Plays. The Examiner from 1895 to 1911 was G. A. Redford, who was later appointed to a similar role by the British Board of Film Censors. Redford forbade the discussion of sex, religion, and politics on the public stage. He did permit some sexual material—as in French farces and Aristophanes' *Lysistrata*—when he considered it innocuous foolery, but a version of the Oberammergau Passion Play was refused a licence on account of its religious theme.

In 1907 seventy-one writers—including Barrie, Conrad, Galsworthy, Hardy, Maugham, Meredith, Shaw, Swinburne, Synge, Wells, and Yeats—protested against the continuing 'autocratic' powers of the Lord Chamberlain. They demanded the end of the licensing of plays, saying that sufficient protection for the public lay in the requirement that theatres be licensed annually. A private member's bill to abolish censorship in theatres and music halls was brought into the House of Commons in April 1909, and soon afterwards the Prime Minister (Asquith) agreed to appoint a committee of both Houses to consider this desire. The committee, chaired by Herbert Samuel, heard nearly fifty witnesses, including representatives of the Church of England and the Roman Catholic Church. The Anglican Bishop of Southwark (E. S. Talbot) defended freedom of conscience, but most witnesses favoured the retention of censorship. The committee's report in November 1909 recommended retention, but also advised that it should be optional to submit a play for licensing; an unlicensed play could be prosecuted for indecency. Optional submission was allowed, but this made little difference to actual practice. A licence from the Lord Chamberlain was usually sought as before for the sake of respectability and protection from prosecution. The Lord Chamberlain retained his position as censor of plays until 1968.[20]

During the First World War government social policy did a good deal to encourage those who wanted more collective State inter-

[20] Hynes, *The Edwardian Turn of Mind*, 212–53

vention. The State greatly increased its powers and regulations, though in nearly all cases these were emergency provisions and there was little hope that they would be continued after victory in the armed conflict had been secured. But it was hoped by many, including the increasing number of Church leaders who advocated the growth of State intervention, that the Government would build on the pre-war base of social reforms to extend collectivism in peacetime. Lloyd George's election speeches in 1918 emphasized that a reconstructed and improved society was an aim equal to that of a just and lasting peace. The war (like the Boer War before it) had revealed the poor physique of many recruits, and foremost among State policies should come better health and housing for the people.[21] His tone was echoed by fellow-Baptists and Nonconformists, among others. Scott Lidgett, a leading Wesleyan minister who was Secretary of the National Free Church Council, influenced the adoption by that body of a pre-election declaration stating that:

> the nation is summoned to undertake the vast task of Reconstruction in a spirit that shall be worthy of the heroic devotion by which the victory has been won . . . (the Churches) should summon the people of all classes to a united effort of comradeship and self-sacrifice in order that Britain may become a truly Christian commonwealth.[22]

The Church of Scotland Commission on the War had already, in 1917, expressed a similar view that the war was a divine call to brotherhood and cooperation, and hoped that 'the people who have nobly borne the burden and patiently endured the calamities of the war may find recompense in a worthier social environment'.[23] A committee of the United Free Church, which was now moving towards union with the Church of Scotland, called for cooperation with the latter Church for the establishment of a better social order in the years after the war. The two Churches jointly sponsored conferences in 1917 and 1918 to discuss reforms suggested by the Government's new Committee on Reconstruction, and the Church of Scotland General Assembly established its permanent Church and Nation Committee in 1919 to

[21] *BW*, 14 Nov. 1918, p. 98.
[22] NFCC, Minutes of Executive Committee, 29 Nov. 1918, bk. 4, p. 200.
[23] Smith, *Passive Obedience*, 357–8; S. J. Brown, 'The Social Vision of Scottish Presbyterianism and the Union of 1929', *Records of the Scottish Church History Society*, 24/1 (1990), 84.

apply moral and spiritual considerations to political and social developments.[24]

The Quaker Yearly Meeting in 1915 appointed a War and Social Order Committee of thirty-six persons. A conference held on the initiative of this Committee in 1916 produced 'Seven Points of a True Social Order', and these were adopted (after revision) as 'Foundations' of an improved society by the Yearly Meeting in 1918. They advocated the communal ownership of most property and the democratic control of industry, and included the following statement: 'We should seek for a way of living that will free us from the bondage of material things and mere conventions, that will raise no barrier between man and man, and will put no excessive burden of labour upon any by reason of our superfluous demands.'[25]

The high religious hopes of a better society withered through the Coalition Government's failure, under the pressures of sharp economic recession from 1920, to fulfil its large promises of social provision. It was incorrect to say that 'the policy of *laissez-faire* is ended', as Bernard Snell, Chairman of the Congregational Union of England and Wales, announced at the Autumn Assembly of the Union in October 1917.[26] Collectivism might have been far more influential in the Governments of the 1920s and 1930s if the economy had been healthy. But depression drove Ministers back into traditional orthodoxy, and *laissez-faire* far exceeded collectivism in the government policies of the inter-war period. The First World War was a formidable watershed in a political sense, but it was not 'the watershed of the ages', as the next Chairman of the Congregational Union, E. Griffith-Jones, declared it was in May 1918. It did not prove to be the case, as he prophesied, that 'future historians will divide history into two sections—that before the war and that after the war'.[27] This speaker enthusiastically asked: 'we have fought hard for purity and for temperance, but how shall these battles ever be won unless we strike at their root in the conditions that make vice and drunkenness almost inevitable?'[28] But these

[24] Brown, 'The Social Vision', 85. Cf. *LW* (Feb. 1918), 20.

[25] *A Brief Record of the War and Social Order Committee* (London, n.d. [1922]), 1–5.

[26] *CYB* (1918), 34.

[27] Ibid. (1919), 32.

[28] Ibid. 39.

hopes for large social reform depended on the presence of a favourable economic climate as well as on sustained government willingness to act.

The most thorough religious contribution to the wartime plea for social improvement through collectivism came from the Church of England. Anglican demands of this kind originated in different quarters. In 1917 the 'Collegium' discussion group, over which William Temple presided, published a book entitled *Competition: A Study in Human Motive*, which advocated a collectivist approach.[29] But a few clerics wanted social revolution as well as collectivism. Conrad Noel, an Anglo-Catholic and Marxist who was Vicar of Thaxted (Essex), told a gathering in his parish in the revolutionary year of 1917 that 'reconstruction without revolution is evil'. He founded at Thaxted in April 1918 'the Catholic Crusade of the Servants of the Precious Blood to transform the Kingdoms of the world into the Commonwealth of God', which ran in parallel rivalry to the more moderate Church (of England) Socialist League and its later permutations.[30] At a more official level, the Lower House of the Convocation of Canterbury (consisting of all clerical representatives except diocesan bishops) passed in 1918 by forty-nine votes to two a resolution for a minimum wage and improved methods of unemployment relief. The National Mission of Repentance and Hope, initiated in 1916 by the Archbishops of Canterbury and York (Randall Davidson and Cosmo Lang), gave rise to five Anglican committees of inquiry into various aspects of religious concern relating to the nation, with a view to advocating post-war reform and reconstruction.[31] A report was issued by each of these committees in 1918. The Fifth Report, *Christianity and Industrial Problems*, was severely attacked by Arthur Headlam, Regius Professor of Divinity at Oxford and later Bishop of Gloucester, as 'one of the most harmful documents that has been issued in the name of Christianity since the Stuart divines taught the doctrine of the Divine Right of Kings'. It seemed to him to proclaim that 'State Socialism is an integral part of

[29] A. Wilkinson, *The Church of England and the First World War* (London, 1978), 282; Norman, *Church and Society*, 240–1.

[30] I. Goodfellow, 'The Church Socialist League, 1906–23', Ph.D. thesis (Durham, 1983), 321, 330–1.

[31] D. O. Wagner, *The Church of England and Social Reform since 1854* (New York, 1930), 291–5.

Christian teaching'.[32] Supporters of collectivism, who now included much of the Anglican leadership, generally had no quarrel with the wide-ranging and constructive document. But the document was insufficiently socialist for George Lansbury, Labour MP, President of the Church Socialist League, and a member of the committee which had issued the report. He and Richard Tawney, he declared, were the only Socialists on the committee.[33]

The Fifth Report was central in a strand of collectivist thought which was coming to occupy a dominant place in the Church of England. Intensely critical of the social system, it had given rise to its own vocal critics, who defended the values and benefits of individualism and competition—Professor Headlam; Hensley Henson, Bishop of Hereford and later of Durham; W. R. Inge, Dean of St Paul's; William Cunningham, Archdeacon of Ely; and J. C. Pringle, Secretary of the Charity Organization Society. Headlam referred to the report's 'teaching of an erroneous and dangerous character', its 'crude and half-thought-out opinions', its 'doubtful economic history', its 'confused thinking and hazardous politics'. It was not the Church's business, he wrote, 'to discuss economic questions, or to attempt to solve difficult economic problems. It is not its business as a rule, directly to be concerned with political questions.'[34] Archdeacon Cunningham published the opinion that:

> material progress and private gain are not necessarily evil things, they become evil if an exclusive importance is attached to them; there is no need of a revolution and of reconstituting society on a moral rather than on a material basis, if pains are taken that material progress shall be directed to public interests.[35]

Many other clergy and ministers must have defended, silently or otherwise, the individualist and *laissez-faire* tradition, and it is difficult to say how far collectivist ideas spread in clerical ranks. Among Church leaders, however, these ideas were becoming al-

[32] *Christianity and Industrial Problems, Being the Report of the Archbishops' Fifth Committee of Inquiry* (London, 1918); J. Oliver, *The Church and Social Order: Social Thought in the Church of England, 1918–39* (London, 1968), 48–54; Goodfellow, 'The Church Socialist League', 322; Norman, *Church and Society*, 241–4.

[33] Wagner, *The Church of England*, 298.

[34] A. C. Headlam, *The Church and Industrial Questions: A Sermon Preached before the University of Cambridge* (London, 1919), 4–20.

[35] W. Cunningham, *Personal Ideals and Social Principles: Some Comments on the Report of the Archbishops' Committee on Christianity and Industrial Problems* (London, 1919), 8.

most an orthodoxy—their chief Anglican clerical proponents included Temple (Bishop of Manchester from 1921), Charles Gore (Bishop of Oxford until 1919), Archbishop Lang, F. T. Woods (Bishop of Peterborough and later of Winchester), J. A. Kempthorne (Bishop of Lichfield), J. E. Watts-Ditchfield (Bishop of Chelmsford), and Cyril Garbett (Bishop of Southwark and later of Winchester). Archbishop Davidson appeared in a more detached role as a cautious sympathizer. The Fifth Report was prominent in a growing spate of publications and conferences which culminated in the vast interdenominational Conference on Christian Politics, Economics, and Citizenship (Copec) of 1924. This produced its own very extensive literature and encouraged the holding of further conferences and the conduct of further surveys.

As far as Church opinion regarding personal behaviour during the war was concerned, there was some encouragement for the cause of temperance. The Temperance Committee of the Congregational Union referred to 'enormous gains',[36] but these were far from amounting to a temperance revolution. The membership of temperance organizations declined during the war, probably because of the departure of many members to fight in the trenches. A memorial to the Government from the National Temperance Federation tried unsuccessfully to build on the passage of the Scottish Temperance Bill in 1913, in order to persuade Ministers to introduce a similar provision for local option in England and Wales.[37] But Church efforts to spread the temperance message advanced through interdenominational cooperation and other means at a juncture when wartime responsibilities were thought to require more stringent controls over drinking. The Lower House of the Convocation of York in April 1915 passed a resolution in support of an interdenominational appeal for abstinence from drink during the war, though it defeated a motion for Sunday closing in England (Sunday closing was statutory in Wales and Scotland).[38] Also in April 1915 took place the formation of the Temperance Council of the Christian Churches (TCCC) of England and Wales. This was organized by Henry Carter, a Wesleyan minister and Secretary of the Wesleyan Temperance Committee, and represented eleven

[36] *CYB* (1917), 22.

[37] G. P. Williams and G. T. Brake, *Drink in Great Britain, 1900–79* (London, 1980), 45.

[38] *YJC* (Apr.–July 1915), 222–9.

denominational temperance bodies. Four joint presidents were elected: Archbishop Davidson, Cardinal Bourne (Archbishop of Westminster), W. B. Selbie (a leading Congregationalist), and General Bramwell Booth of the Salvation Army.[39]

The bodies forming the TCCC gave their support to proposed reforms. These took the form of Nine Points, including reduced opening hours, Sunday closing, fewer licences, and local option on drink sales. The Government was urged by denominational bodies to ban the sale of drink during the armed conflict and post-war demobilization. This attempt was not successful. But Lloyd George did say that 'we are fighting Germany, Austria and Drink, and the greatest of these deadly foes is Drink';[40] and King George V, in an influential example, took the pledge of abstinence. In 1915 the Government created a Central Liquor Control Board, which shortened opening hours, increased the excise duty on drink (which greatly increased the price), reduced the strength of its alcohol content, and took complete control of licensed premises in areas where there were important munitions factories and naval establishments.

With the exceptions of reduced hours of opening and the implementation of the Scottish Act, however, the restrictions did not extend far into peacetime, despite the hopes of the temperance movement. The Central Control Board was disbanded in 1921. The US Government adopted prohibition in 1918, and in the previous year the Wesleyan Conference called for this policy to be espoused in Britain.[41] This proved an unrealistic hope, but there was comfort for temperance advocates in the large reduction in drink sales which occurred during the war, and the comparatively modest consumption which persisted for some fifteen years after its conclusion.

A proposal by Lloyd George that the State should purchase and assume monopoly control of the liquor trade was condemned at a National Temperance Convention representing numerous local

[39] *Official Handbook of the Presbyterian Church of England* (1917–18), p. xv, (1918–19), 2; *BH* (1918), 46; *CYB* (1919), 8; *New Campaigner: Being the Official Organ of the Temperance Council of the Christian Churches of England and Wales* (2nd quarter, 1936), 13–14.

[40] Quoted in J. Stevenson, *British Society, 1914–45* (Harmondsworth, 1984), 71. Cf. G. J. De Groot, *Blighty: British Society in the Era of the Great War* (London, 1996), 237–8.

[41] Campbell, 'Methodism', 35.

and denominational bodies, held at Manchester on 13 November 1918, just after the end of armed hostilities.[42] The Church of England Temperance Society was tentatively favourable to the scheme, but one of the numerous opponents of the plan said that, if the trade became government property, 'temperance agitation will be looked upon as disloyalty to the State'.[43]

No other social question of special concern to the Churches aroused as much debate as temperance during the war. But anti-gambling opinion (in which the Wesleyan Church was again prominent, the leadership of Benson Perkins providing a parallel to that of Henry Carter in the temperance field) was gratified when the Government accepted a Select Committee recommendation in January 1918 to avoid introducing premium bonds.[44] But it seemed likely that other issues would come forward after the war, including divorce reform and plans to extend the use of artificial contraception. In regard to the former, Lord Hugh Cecil, a strong defender of the lifelong marriage bond, was concerned enough to urge Archbishop Davidson that the Church of England should 'formulate a complete and intellectually coherent theory of marriage on Christian principles . . . there is a tendency to shirk the crucial issues in all authoritative Anglican teaching that I have seen'.[45] The Church of Scotland magazine, *Life and Work*, also warned that 'the instincts of religious people revolt' against extended divorce provision, which would be 'an encouragement of the desire for divorce, and an assault upon the most sacred bulwarks of society'.[46]

Dr Marie Stopes, a Quaker palaeobotanist who was becoming a foremost advocate of artificial methods of birth control, published her controversial book *Married Love* on this subject in March 1918. Clergy and ministers of different Protestant Churches, including Dean Inge (in a markedly qualified manner), sent her congratulations on the publication.[47] But there began to appear signs of

[42] *National Temperance Convention* (London, 1918).
[43] G. Davies, *The Churches and State Purchase* (repr. from *The Welsh Outlook*, 1918); *The Rt. Hon. H. H. Asquith, MP., for Local Veto and against State Purchase* (leaflet, London, 1918). Cf. Manifesto of United Kingdom Alliance in general election of 1918; *BW*, 28 Nov. 1918.
[44] *LW* (Aug. 1923), 171.
[45] Cecil to Davidson, 20 Aug. 1917, DP 417, fo. 102.
[46] *LW* (Feb. 1918), 20.
[47] Inge to Stopes, 26 Jan. 1918, SP BL Add. MS 58548, fos. 128–9; also ibid. 58548, fo. 7, and 58554, fos. 1, 3, 17.

conflict with the Roman Catholic Church, which utterly refused to support her views. A Jesuit, Father Stanislaus St John, wrote to her about the book:

> As a piece of writing I find it admirable all through . . . no one could have expressed your theme in more beautiful language or with a truer ring of sympathy . . . but our ways part when you treat of preventives . . . To my mind, it is not the destruction of one spermatozoon that is the question, but the deliberate prevention of an eternal existence which . . . would result from its life . . . we (as Catholics) do not believe that man may directly frustrate the divine end.[48]

Questions of greater emancipation for women were naturally expected to follow the grant of the vote early in 1918. Before this occurred, a matter of central concern to the Churches—the ordination of women—received its first official encouragement when Constance Todd (Coltman from her marriage on the following day) became an ordained minister in the Congregational Church on 17 September 1917.[49] It was far too premature to say, as was announced by the ordaining minister at this service, that 'the old civilization in which woman was the subordinate of man has come to an ignominious end'.[50] At least, however, the example of female ordination was followed at different times by other Nonconformist denominations—though the established Churches held off for decades, the Church of Scotland until 1968 and the Church of England until 1992.

Growing encroachments on Sunday observance were worrying to many in the Churches. This was not only in connection with decline in church attendance, which was affecting most Protestant Churches, but also in relation to increased opportunities for leisure, some of which were seen as harmful. Lord Salisbury had told Queen Victoria in 1899 that strict observance of the Sabbath had long been waning.[51] But there was plenty of resistance to this trend. In October 1918, for example, the Edinburgh presbytery of the

[48] St John to Stopes, 11 Dec. 1917, ibid. 58553 (unfoliated when seen); R. A. Soloway, *Birth Control and the Population Question in England, 1877–1930* (Chapel Hill, NC, 1982), 233 ff.

[49] E. Kaye, 'Constance Coltman, a Forgotten Pioneer', *Journal of the United Reformed Church History Society*, 4/2 (1988), 134–46.

[50] Ibid. 134.

[51] G. E. Buckle (ed.), *The Letters of Queen Victoria, third series, 1886–1901* (3 vols.; London, 1930–2), iii. 368.

Church of Scotland asked its Committee on Observance of the Lord's Day to take suitable action in regard to 'the increased and increasing number of encroachments on the rightful observance of the Lord's Day', and to 'co-operate with other Churches for common action'.[52] One of the threatened encroachments was pressure from the cinema industry to show films on Sundays. By 1914 there were already about 3,000 cinematograph theatres in Britain (small in size compared with the purpose-built 'picture palaces' of the inter-war years). By 1919 it was estimated that half the population was going to the cinema twice a week[53] (this was at least twice as many as were attending church once a week). With leisure of other kinds already encroaching on the Sabbath, it was most unlikely that so popular a pastime as 'the pictures' would remain content with weekday functioning.

When the war ended, the British Churches still appeared as a very large, flourishing, and influential group of organizations. But how strong actually were the Churches in 1918 and the immediately succeeding years? The Churches' fortunes did not experience any dramatic adverse effects from the recent conflict, and membership remained on something like a statistical plateau in the 1920s, holding up well and increasing somewhat before there was more of a decline in the 1930s.[54] Nor, however, did the conflict reverse the longer-term declining position of the Churches, taken as a whole. But in this matter it was difficult to take the Churches as a whole; there were too many differences in fortune among them. The Roman Catholic Church stood out notably as an expanding force until 1970, in contrast to nearly all Protestant Churches; and the Scottish Protestant Churches, unlike the English, were still preserving a consistently growing membership. In 1947 it was estimated that 56 per cent of the adult population in Scotland were members of a church, compared with 23 per cent in England and Wales.[55] Generalizations about the decline in membership and influence of the British Churches have more validity in the years after the 1950s than they had before that central decade of the century.

[52] Church of Scotland Edinburgh Presbytery Minutes, 30 Oct. 1918, CH2/121/36, pp. 69–70.

[53] J. Walvin, *Leisure and Society, 1830–1950* (London, 1978), 133.

[54] Figures in Currie *et al.* (eds.), *Churches*, 31.

[55] Knox, 'Religion', 610.

The Churches, moreover, showed signs of increased strength, in terms of their independence and unity, in the fifteen years or so after the end of the war. William Temple's Life and Liberty movement obtained success in the passing of the Enabling Bill by Parliament in 1919. This allowed the Church of England a larger self-governing role in regard to formulating its own regulations. These were still liable to parliamentary veto, but the Church was in effect rendered much freer from the delays and frustrations of the parliamentary timetable. It so happened that in 1927 and 1928 Parliament rejected a revised Prayer Book approved by the new National Assembly of the Church, but this occurred because of exceptional circumstances arising from strong objections to the reforms proposed rather than because of Parliament's desire to reverse its concessionary attitude of 1919. Parliament also passed the Church of Scotland Act in 1921, affirming the right of self-government to the Scottish establishment and thereby paving the way for the union of the majority of the largest Scottish dissenting body, the United Free Church, with the Church of Scotland in 1929. Other ecumenical discussions were also in evidence in the 1920s—between Anglicans and Nonconformists, Anglicans and Roman Catholics—though a different feeling was apparent in the revival of active anti-Catholicism in Scotland in the inter-war years. A National Free Church Federation was formed as a coordinating body for England and Wales in 1919, and in 1932 the successful urge towards Methodist union culminated in the formation of the Methodist Church of Great Britain.

After Welsh disestablishment had been implemented in 1920, British Churches were no longer much divided by the question of maintaining established Churches. A comment made by a leading Labour politician and Methodist, Lord Snowden, in 1934 indicated that disestablishment was practically dead as an issue.[56] It was not in fact completely defunct, but it showed only momentary flickers of life in later years. The issue of denominational education remained much more alive as a matter of ecclesiastical controversy. The intensely disputed Education Act of 1902, which had encouraged denominational provision, survived Liberal efforts to change it and remained

[56] Philip, Viscount Snowden, *An Autobiography* (2 vols.; London, 1934), i. 41–2.

effective after the First World War. Despite numerous resolutions of protest in the inter-war years, the provisions of the Act continued, and were unaltered by the Butler Education Act of 1944.

2
Churches and Social Policy, 1918–1939

Having won the war, the Lloyd George Coalition wished also to win the peace—that is, to provide the much better social conditions which government ministers had extolled as the anticipated fruits of both armed and electoral victory. In similar vein, the Archbishop of Canterbury, Randall Davidson, called for a 'new birth' in April 1918.[1] But the highly indebted state of the country and depressing economic developments soon reduced these hopes. A brief post-war boom ended by late 1920, and was replaced by recession and rising unemployment. Rather than raise taxes at a time when industry was struggling to recover, the Government curtailed its social programme. An important Unemployment Assurance Bill got through in 1920, but other intended reforms were cut short or shelved. Moreover, industrial contraction caused bitter disputes between employers and the greatly expanded trade unions over reductions in pay and longer hours of work. The recession lasted, with fluctuations, throughout the inter-war years, and improved social conditions came about much more slowly and sporadically than had been hoped in 1918.

Many Church leaders, though by no means all, advocated the improvement of social conditions and more equality in society by means of increased State intervention. But few of them took what still appeared to be the fairly extreme line of Socialism—and far fewer supported the other extreme of Fascism—in order to urge this development. There were committed Socialists among Christians in all denominations. This was despite the much-disputed opinion of one Lavernia Scargill, writing to the Church of England *Guardian* newspaper, that 'earnest churchmen who strive to take up the Socialist point of view are attempting something that is absolutely incompatible with their beliefs. One of the points of the

[1] A. Wilkinson, *The Church of England and the First World War* (London, 1978), 281.

proletarian creed insists on the preaching of the "class war". How is a Christian to reconcile himself to that?'[2] The usual approach among Church leaders who advocated State intervention was the moderate one of 'new Liberalism' or Fabian Socialism. A study of the attitudes of the Methodist Churches to social problems in the inter-war years has suggested that 'the principles and ideals of inter-war Methodism were largely the same as those of the "New Liberals" of the pre-1914 era'.[3] This approach was intent on improving the conditions of the poorer sections of the population by State intervention without altering the free working of the capitalist economy, and it avoided the concept of class war. An approach of this kind appealed to most clerics and other spokesmen for the Churches, who tended to feel above or beyond the battleground of politicians, and were commentators and persuaders rather than political activists. Nor were they technical experts on economic and social questions. Their position as non-specialized commentators deterred Church leaders from formulating their own distinct programme of economic and social reform. References were quite frequent among them to the need to establish 'the Kingdom of God' in earthly living conditions and relationships; but the nature of the Kingdom of God—so far as humanity could conceive it—was in the eye of the individual beholder, and therefore had a confusing number of mansions. In 1923 the Church Socialist League was reconstituted as the League of the Kingdom of God, but it did not flourish under this name and became associated with other, mainly Anglo-Catholic, reformers in the Christendom Group. This later merged, in 1957, with the Industrial Christian Fellowship. The pronounced Anglo-Catholic strand in social reform in this period was shown by the holding of the Anglo-Catholic Summer School of Sociology, which first met at Oxford in 1925. The vast and enthusiastic Anglo-Catholic Congresses held in the 1920s and 1930s also demonstrated that this century-old religious movement was now at a peak of confidence.[4]

While there were some clear exceptions, the main tendency among Christians regarding the question of social change was to

[2] *G.*, 21 Mar. 1924, p. 240; ibid., 28 Mar. 1924, p. 263.

[3] D. P. Campbell, 'Methodism and Social Problems in the Inter-War Period, 1918–39', M.Litt. thesis (Oxford, 1987), 2.

[4] W. S. F. Pickering, *Anglo-Catholicism: A Study in Religious ambiguity* (London, 1991), 32–4, 48–64.

keep to the general, the moderate, and the non-partisan in their expressions. 'There is nothing in the Church's gospel which enables her to settle vexed questions of wages and hours of labour and systems of production . . . she is the Church of no party and no class', said the Church of Scotland magazine *Life and Work* in 1921.[5] This approach limited the Churches' role in social policy to that of advisers. They hoped that the politicians who devised and executed social policy would pay heed to their advice. Politicians sometimes implied that the Churches should support their particular party and preach their propaganda, but they could show a sensitive awareness of the Churches' position with regard to politics. Arthur Henderson, leader of the Labour Party and a Wesleyan lay preacher, showed sympathy with this position when he wrote in 1919: 'The Church is the one institution left in the world to-day that must not be allowed to take sides, but must stand "above the battle" and interpret the secular struggle in terms of moral progress and spiritual visions.'[6]

The approach to reform which has long been known as 'Christian Socialism' or the 'social gospel' was shown in the Fifth Report of the Archbishops' Committees of Inquiry, published in 1918, and in a resolution (number 74) of the Lambeth Conference of Anglican bishops in 1920. This resolution stated:

> An outstanding and pressing duty of the Church is to convince its members of the necessity of nothing less than a fundamental change in the spirit and working of our economic life. This change can only be effected by accepting as the basis of industrial relations the principle of co-operation in service for the common good in place of unrestricted competition for private or sectional advantage. All Christian people ought to take an active part in bringing about this change, by which alone we can hope to remove class differences and resolve industrial discords.[7]

This message of restrained idealism was widely held among religious bodies concerned with social reform. Prominent among these was the Industrial Christian Fellowship (ICF), an Anglican society founded in 1919 on the basis of the former Navvy Mission. Its approach was one of evangelism combined with concern for wel-

[5] *LW* (Aug. 1921), 115.

[6] Quoted in P. P. Catterall, 'The Free Churches and the Labour Party in England and Wales, 1918–39', Ph.D. thesis (London, 1989), 509.

[7] Quoted in E. R. Norman, *Church and Society in England, 1770–1970* (Oxford, 1976), 245.

fare. Under the energetic direction of P. T. R. Kirk and with the effective aid of Geoffrey Studdert-Kennedy among others, the association worked through missionary districts, into which England was divided.[8] The ICF inaugurated the annual industrial Sunday in 1920 as a spiritual counterpart of the May Day Labour celebrations. 'Material well-being is a very desirable thing', said a publication of the ICF in 1938, but 'the primary need of man is not prosperity but Christ . . . We need some further criterion than the merely material. We need to take account also of man's spiritual welfare.'[9]

In the National Assembly of the Church of England, the Bishop of London (A. F. Winnington-Ingram) successfully proposed the appointment of a Standing Committee on Social and Industrial Questions; and Charles Gore, after relinquishing the bishopric of Oxford in 1919, inaugurated a Christian Social Crusade in the following year. Both of these bodies sought to put into effect the sentiments of the Lambeth resolution of 1920.[10] The continued need for voluntary service, however, was not forgotten amidst all the advocacy of collectivism: *The Church and Social Service*, a report commissioned by Archbishop Davidson, stressed the need for the maintenance of voluntary social service.[11]

In Scotland the developing movement for union between the Church of Scotland and the United Free Church helped to revive, under John White's leadership, the idea of a Christian Commonwealth which would be Scotland's version of the new post-war social order. But, while Church union succeeded in 1929, hopes of a united Christian Commonwealth (impossible to achieve in any case because of the religious plurality that was deeply entrenched) fell away in face of the bitter social disunity in the industrial strife

[8] R. Lloyd, *The Church of England, 1900–65* (London, 1966), 303–5; J. J. R. Armitage, *Labour: The Next Phase—the Industrial Christian Fellowship, its Aims and Operations* (London, n.d.); P. T. R. Kirk, *Industry and Class Warfare* (London, n.d.); *The Industrial Christian Fellowship: What It Stands For* (London, 1938); *Co-ordination: A Plea for Closer Co-operation between Diocese, Parish, and Church Societies* (London, 1939); *The Link* (quarterly journal of ICF), first issue (Oct. 1920).

[9] *The Industrial Christian Fellowship*, 12. Cf. address of Chairman, J. D. Jones, to assembly of Congregational Union, 12 May 1925, *CYB* (1926), 98.

[10] Norman, *Church and Society*, 246.

[11] J. Oliver, *The Church and Social Order: Social Thought in the Church of England, 1918–39* (London, 1968), 56.

of the 1920s; the Church took on the much more modest role of industrial conciliator.[12]

Social concern among many Evangelicals seems to have decreased after the early 1920s, and there was a more insistent stress on putting personal spiritual conviction before social action.[13] This always had to contend, however, with the conviction that 'what the world needs today is a great spiritual revival, whose immediate object is not the saving of souls in some future life, but the establishment here and now of a standard of life more creditable to human hearts and heads than that which obtains today'.[14] According to this view, spiritual revival must come through social action and not apart from it.

Church attempts to achieve more cooperation in industry naturally included efforts to end strikes by means of conciliation. Amid the strike-laden fractiousness of industrial relations in the post-war years up to 1926, some Church leaders tried to maintain the example, going back to the 1880s, of intervening in these disputes in order to obtain mutually agreed settlements. In October 1919 Archbishop Davidson joined Cardinal Bourne (Catholic Archbishop of Westminster) and Nonconformist leaders in order to urge the mutual conciliation of employers and trade unionists in a coal strike. In 1921 the Upper House of Canterbury Convocation declared that the recent Lambeth resolution number 74 should form the basis of a conciliatory end to another coal-mining dispute.[15] The speeches in this debate were notably favourable to the miners.[16]

Very soon after the war, and well before the collapse of the brief post-war boom, industrial disputes were clearly affecting the country, and Christian assemblies, associations, and individuals were ready with responses and advice. At the beginning of 1919 several short unofficial strikes for reduced working hours took place, in London and on Clydeside, where physical conflict developed. It was reported that on 2 February 'thousands of soldiers wearing

[12] S. J. Brown, 'The Campaign for the Christian Commonwealth in Scotland, 1919–39', in W. M. Jacob and N. Yates (eds.), *Crown and Mitre: Religion and Society in Northern Europe since the Reformation* (Woodbridge, 1993), 203 ff.

[13] D. W. Bebbington, *Evangelicalism in Modern Britain: A History from the 1730s to the 1980s* (London, 1989), 182, 194, 213–17.

[14] B. S. Rowntree, *Society and Human Relations* (London, 1924), 7.

[15] Lloyd, *The Church of England*, 258; *Year Book of National Assembly of the Church of England* (1922), 65; also p. 79.

[16] Oliver, *Church and Social Order*, 58–9.

steel helmets and full service kits were brought into Glasgow . . . One of the strike leaders, Emmanuel Shinwell, a Jewish tailor, was arrested at his home . . . and, along with (David) Kirkwood and (William) Gallagher, was kept under arrest in Duke street prison.'[17]

Debates on the industrial unrest took place at the February meetings of Convocation. In the Upper House of Canterbury Convocation, the Bishop of Peterborough (F. T. Woods) carried with unanimous agreement on 13 February a motion that the problem, whose roots were 'moral and spiritual', could be resolved only by 'a willingness for new adventures in comradeship on the part of employers (as, for example, in admitting the workers to a larger share in the management); and also a new readiness for conciliation and restraint on the part of the workers'.[18] A peace conference, he said, was necessary not only at Versailles to replan Europe, but at home to reorganize industry. The Church should insist 'that no reconstruction was worth the name that did not tend to development of personality and improvement of character, and that it was precisely because immortal souls were involved that these mere material reforms were so necessary'. He hoped to see interdenominational councils of social welfare established in every town and many villages, uniting 'all who in every place look for the coming of the Kingdom of God'.[19] Hensley Henson, Bishop of Hereford, warned against being too one-sidedly sympathetic towards the workers—he 'believed it to be a most pestilent fallacy that labour was the most important of all factors which went to the creation of wealth'—and was consequently involved in altercation with Bishop Gore.[20]

In the four years from early 1920 the attention of Christian social reformers was partly engaged in planning a large interdenominational Conference on Christian Politics, Economics, and Citizenship. The impetus to hold this conference came from the post-war desire for reconstruction, and was sustained by concern about the growth of unemployment and industrial strife, centred in the coal industry, from later 1920. Christian sympathy with the unemployed was displayed in all manner of situations and organizations. Some-

[17] *BW*, 6 Feb. 1919, p. 315.
[18] *CCC*, 13 Feb. 1919, iii. 1, p. 160 (pp. 134–60 for debate).
[19] Ibid. 142–3.
[20] Ibid. 146–57.

times, for example, clergy and ministers associated with Communists on local committees to aid unemployed workers—though a later organization, founded by a Catholic, was directed towards 'preventing those out of work from being exploited by the Communist Party'.[21]

The desire to reform the social order was stimulated by the spectacle of growing unemployment, not least among women who were discharged because they were no longer needed to form a wartime workforce. An international Quaker conference at Oxford in August 1920 was especially concerned with these problems, and an extension of the conference emphasized the need to continue the pre-war trend of building new towns in order to improve the environment.[22] A. E. Garvie, a Congregational minister with probably as great an interest in social reform as anyone in his denomination, said in his chairman's address to the assembly of the Congregational Union of England and Wales in September 1920: 'the present economic conditions offend the sense of right. Truth, justice, and mercy are violated in our industrial system'. While not advocating the espousal of any economic or social theory as a remedy (for he believed that none had 'permanent and universal applicability'), he thought that current tendencies were rightly leading towards 'an increasing control of industry by the community' without going so far as general nationalization. 'Service and partnership' were the ideals 'which should be made dominant in industry by the testimony and influence of the Christian Church'. Wealth should be more evenly distributed, for 'sounder is the economic condition of a country where a moderate standard of living is widely diffused than where there are extremes of great wealth and deep poverty'.[23]

In April 1921 Garvie urged in a letter to Archbishop Davidson that the Churches should speak out in the current industrial crisis. About this time Davidson issued his own statement. He reiterated the opinion of a committee of the 1920 Lambeth Conference (which itself reaffirmed an opinion in the report of the 1908 Lam-

[21] R. Croucher, *We Refuse to Starve in Silence: A History of the National Unemployed Workers' Movement, 1920–46* (London, 1987), 31; *U.*, 11 Dec. 1936, p. 23.

[22] *Towards a New Social Order, Being the Report of an International Conference Held at Oxford, August 20–24 1920* (London, 1920); and, on the continuation conference, *Towards a New Social Order: Report of the 'New Town' Conference Held at Oxford, August 24–27 1920* (London, 1920).

[23] *CYB* (1921), 74–89.

beth Conference) that 'the fundamental Christian principle of the remuneration of labour is that the first charge upon any industry must be the proper maintenance of the labourer'.[24] The Bishop of Lichfield (J. A. Kempthorne) gave his opinion in a Convocation debate on 27 and 28 April 1921 that the railway and coal industries should be nationalized, and condemned 'the wasteful, vulgar, and extravagant luxury shown by a considerable part of the community' at a time when many workers were being asked to accept lower wages. But the Bishop of Birmingham (Russell Wakefield) and the Bishop of Lincoln (W. S. Swayne) doubted the efficacy of nationalization and preferred cooperative agreements between the mine-owners and miners as a long-term solution to the current troubles.[25]

In 1922 the York social enquirer Seebohm Rowntree (reflecting a strong Quaker interest in reform of the industrial system at this time) published *Industrial Unrest: A Way Out?*, proposing that all employers should be under a statutory obligation to raise wages within a given time to a certain minimum level. The resources for this would have to come, if necessary, from increased output by the workers and from savings in administrative costs.[26] He also called for the general adoption of moderate working hours, increased old age pensions, cooperation between capital and labour in the direction of industry, and the sharing of profits with the workforce. In his capacity as managing director of the Rowntree cocoa works, he could state that 'we are giving an increasing share of responsibility to the workers . . . working conditions are fixed by mutual consent and (are) not dictated by the management'.[27] The desirability of cooperative arrangements between workers and management was also stressed by Richard Tawney in *The Acquisitive Society*, first published in 1921. Tawney was a leader among lay Anglican social reformers, similar to Temple among clerical reformers. But Tawney's message, like Rowntree's, was a moderate one:

> it is not private property, but private ownership divorced from work, which is corrupting to the principles of industry; and the idea of some Socialists

[24] DP 272, fos. 349–54.

[25] *CCC*, 27–8 Apr. 1921, iii. 7, pp. 245, 252, 289–92, Cf. W. C. Bridgeman to Archbishop Davidson, 30 Apr. 1921, and Davidson to Bridgeman, 2 May 1921, DP, 272, fos. 357–61.

[26] B. S. Rowntree, *Industrial Unrest: A Way Out?* (New York, 1922), 13–15.

[27] Ibid. 24.

that private property in land or capital is necessarily mischievous is a piece of scholastic pedantry as absurd as that of those Conservatives who would invest all property with some kind of mysterious sanctity. The fundamental issue is . . . not between the large farmer or master and the small, but between property which is used for work and property which yields income without it.[28]

Such ideas favoured the modification of the existing capitalist system rather than its abolition. But some Christian thinkers, and not only the few Communist sympathizers among them, believed that the existing industrial system was incompatible with Christianity. A minority view at the Anglo-Catholic Summer School in 1930, voiced particularly by A. J. Penty, urged the ultra-idealistic vision—impossible, of course, to realize—of a return to a peasant economy as being the only system which could be run according to Christian principles.[29]

Copec (the Conference on Christian Politics, Economics, and Citizenship) was held in 1924, appropriately during the brief period of the first Labour Government. It was the clearest public demonstration in the twentieth century of the predominant New Liberal or Fabian Socialist strain in social reform among British Christians. The Conference had been suggested in 1919 by Temple's Collegium group. Preparations began in 1920 with the appointment of a council of 350, Temple being chairman and the Quaker Lucy Gardner acting as secretary. The council seemed to be influenced in its methods by the example of the Archbishops of Canterbury and York in appointing their wartime committees of inquiry. The council appointed twelve commissions to investigate a broad variety of social questions, and each produced a voluminous report. The reports dealt with such matters as 'the nature of God and His purpose for the world'; education, housing, contraception, and crime; industry and property; and international relations. Some large preparatory meetings were held in order to stimulate public interest. A great many questionnaires were issued, and seventy-five study circles were formed with the responsibility of answering them.

When the Conference was due to meet, Davidson was in possibly strategic absence (on holiday in Italy), but he did send a message of

[28] R. H. Tawney, *The Acquisitive Society* (London, 1921; rev. edn., 1945), 188–91, 99–100.

[29] Oliver, *Church and Social Order*, 132–5.

commendation to be read at the gathering. Bishop Henson and other critics of collective social reform were thoroughly out of sympathy with the whole venture, and expressed their serious doubts about it. Cooperation between Churches was a leading feature of the venture, and the huge body of 1,500 delegates met in interdenominational conclave when the conference was held at Birmingham from 5 to 12 April 1924. Bishop Temple was chairman of the conference, A. E. Garvie vice-chairman, and the Wesleyan William Reason edited records of the proceedings for publication. The three Roman Catholic delegates (the Jesuit Fathers O'Hea and Walker and Miss Ada Streeter), who had taken part in the preliminary discussions, withdrew from the Conference on somewhat obscure grounds. Their reasons seem to have been connected with reluctance to join the other Churches in blaming themselves for laxity in social-reforming efforts hitherto. Nevertheless, some Catholics remained present to observe the proceedings.

The Copec reports and conference added a great deal of new flesh, but only to existing bones. Copec's conclusion regarding the industrial system, for example, echoed the Fifth Report of 1918 by saying that the system was 'radically unchristian'.[30] Copec was not an original movement, and was not intended to be one. It was intended to advertise and confirm an existing trend rather than launch a new one. Temple said at the conference that it was a continuation of the growth of social consciousness in the Church, as shown already by the encyclicals of Pope Leo XIII, the Fifth Report, and the Report of an American Interdenominational Committee on Christianity and Industrial Reconstruction.[31] Copec was itself only a national preparation for a wider, international conference on the Life and Work of the Church to be held at Stockholm in August 1925. Copec's significance lay mainly in its role as an unprecedentedly wide gathering combining Christian contributions (shown in the reports) to the well-established movement for social reform by collectivist means.

The long-term impact of Copec has been seriously questioned. One historian has stated that 'it is a little difficult to say what . . . Copec achieved, beyond unusually voluminous

[30] Ibid. 66ff.; Norman, *Church and Society*, 279–313; *The Pilgrim* (Oct. 1924), 72–85; *The Times*, 8 Apr. 1924, p. 9; 11 Apr., p. 8.

[31] Norman, *Church and Society*, 285.

reports'.[32] But in fact the mountain of Copec paperwork did a good deal more than merely labouring to produce a mouse. The effects of the Copec movement and its reports, certainly when set in the general context of collectivist discussion and planning which marked the inter-war years, were far from insubstantial. A historian who is critical of Copec and its message has said that the reports 'constituted a body of ideas and attitudes which, while not especially original or systematic, provided a whole generation with statements of social teaching'; and that—through the activities of such people as Malcolm Spencer (a Congregational minister and prolific writer on social questions) and Maurice Reckitt (a leading Anglo-Catholic social reformer, also a prolific writer)—'Copec became the stimulus for much of the so-called "Christian sociology" in the years between the wars'.[33]

A Continuation Committee of Copec was supported by a wider body, the Companions of Copec. Some regional conferences were held later in 1924 to follow up the main Copec gathering, and a number of regional committees were established. One of the latter, in north-east England, produced in 1928 the report *Industrial Tyneside*, which in turn gave rise to the Tyneside Christian Social Council. Through a similar Copec initiative, a Home Improvement Society was started in Birmingham, in order to buy and renovate slum properties before letting them to the poor. The Anglo-Catholic Summer Schools of Sociology beginning in 1925, and local efforts to construct house-building schemes by clergy, such as Basil Jellicoe in St Pancras, London, and Charles Jenkinson in Leeds, reflected the reforming spirit of Copec, if not perhaps the direct influence of the conference.[34] The report of the Council of the Congregational Union for 1924–5 emphasized the importance of Copec in strengthening interest in social questions: 'Evidence from every quarter shows that our Churches have been roused to a new interest in the social aspects of the Gospel.' The National Free Church Council urged all Nonconformist churches in England to observe Sunday, 5 April

[32] S. Mayor, *The Churches and the Labour Movement* (London, 1967), 370, Cf. J. Kent, *William Temple* (Cambridge, 1992), 134.

[33] Norman, *Church and Society*, 305, 306.

[34] R. Kenyon, *The Catholic Faith and the Industrial Order* (London, 1931), 1–3, 169–75; Lloyd, *The Church of England*, 313–33.

1925 (the anniversary of the beginning of the conference) as 'Copec Sunday'.[35]

From 1929 the aims and work of Copec were continued by a new interdenominational body, the Christian Social Council, which was inaugurated at a special service in Westminster Abbey on 21 January 1929. The formation of this body emerged from discussions between the Copec Continuation Committee and the Social Service Committee of the Lambeth Conference. The Roman Catholic Church was linked to the new Council by means of informal liaison arrangements.

Copec might have disappointed the more ardent social radicals, who ridiculed its initials as standing for 'Conventional Official Platitudes Expressing Caution'. But its achievements, apart from its size and bulk, were enough to ensure that it would not be forgotten.[36] The Copec movement was one of the contributions to the planning for social reconstruction which marked the inter-war years and the Second World War. It was with perhaps pardonable exaggeration that an enthusiast for Copec wrote that 'the Copec report could well be regarded as a blueprint for the Welfare State'.[37]

Christians who wanted social reform through collectivism had little hope of gaining what they wished in the inter-war years. The Governments of the time were probably less sympathetic to their point of view than they would have been if the economy had been healthier. On rare occasions there was friction between government ministers and Church leaders. One of these occasions was the General Strike of 1926, when Archbishop Davidson aroused the hostility of Ministers (and many others) through attempting to conciliate in the dispute.

The General Strike did not produce a clear confrontation between Church leaders and the Government, for no Church leader expressed support of the strike. In regard to Church involvement, the main difference lay between those clergy and organs of Church

[35] *CYB* (1926), 70–1, Cf. ibid. (1927), 80–2; and NFCC Minutes of Executive Committee, 9 Mar. 1924, bk. 5, p. 70.

[36] Oliver, *Church and Social Order*, 71–4; A. E. Garvie, *Memories and Meanings of my Life* (London, 1938), 241–2.

[37] Quoted in R. Davies, A. R. George, and G. Rupp (eds.), *A History of the Methodist Church in Great Britain*, iii (London, 1983), 361.

opinion who, while far from defending the General Strike, advocated conciliation, and those such as Bishop Henson who were thoroughly against the Strike (Henson described it as 'criminal'), and disapproved openly of Davidson's conciliatory actions.[38] Another difference arose over the opinion of some Christians that, as the Churches represented all social classes, their leaders should not make any pronouncement in a dispute which was one of intense class division.[39]

The long-running coal dispute over questions of reduced wages and extended working time, and over the broader question of nationalization, came to a new head when the report of the Samuel Commission was published in March 1926. This displeased the Miners' Federation by rejecting nationalization and recommending reduced pay in the case of some miners, though it also rejected the owners' wish for a longer working day. The opinions expressed by religious newspapers and organizations were varied. A manifesto addressed to the archbishops and bishops of the Church of England by the League of the Kingdom of God claimed that the principle of a living wage would be destroyed if miners' wages suffered any reduction, and this view was also held by the *Church Times*.[40] The *Baptist Times*, however, accused A. J. Cook, the miners' leader, of distorting the Samuel Commission's proposals: 'we hope that wiser counsels than Mr Cook's will prevail, and that other leaders will see that the case is one for negotiation' rather than summary rejection of the Commission's conclusions.[41] But it was not only intransigence on the miners' side that the *Baptist Times* deplored: 'by their high-handed methods the owners seem likely to convert a dispute in their own industry into a war between labour and capital in all industries.'[42]

The need for conciliatory negotiation was the predominant message of Christian opinion, which felt impelled to express itself positively in the dispute. Archbishop Davidson began to urge conciliation as the special contribution which the Churches should make. In mid-April Davidson sent a letter to each bishop in his

[38] Norman, *Church and Society*, 338–9.
[39] P. Catterall, 'Morality and Politics: The Free Churches and the Labour Party between the Wars', *Historical Journal*, 36 (1993), 674–5.
[40] Oliver, *Church and Social Order*, 80–1.
[41] *BT*, 8 Apr. 1926, p. 263.
[42] Ibid., 29 Apr. 1926, p. 323.

province urging that 'people should in all our churches be called to united prayer':

We pray that those with whom responsibility rests in our social and industrial life may be enabled, under the guidance of the Holy Spirit of God, to take a large and public-minded view of our difficulties, to consider general rather than sectional needs and advantages.[43]

Negotiations to resolve the mining dispute did not succeed. By the time the owners submitted their terms for a new national wage agreement to the Miners' Federation on 30 April (including an extension of the working day, which the Samuel Report had rejected), most of the miners were already locked out. The Trades Union Congress implemented its decision to order the general downing of tools in sympathy, and the only General Strike in British history to date commenced on 3 May. The more constructive Church expressions urged conciliatory negotiations in the coal dispute, but by no means commended the General Strike. In fact, the general stoppage was widely condemned by religious assemblies and newspapers, though some sermons were strongly in sympathy with the strikers.[44] R. F. Horton, a leading Congregationalist, found praise for the 'splendid mistake' of those who struck in sympathy with the miners.[45] But, in a declaration at High Mass in Westminster Cathedral on 9 May, Cardinal Bourne, who had condemned the prospect of a general stoppage in 1913,[46] denounced the strike as morally unjustified. It was 'a sin against the obedience which we owe to God . . . and against the charity and brotherly love which we owe to our brethren'. Strongly defended by the *Tablet* and pleasing to the Government, Bourne's declaration brought a trenchant riposte from Tawney and George Lansbury and annoyed some Catholic members of the Labour Party.[47]

When the strike ended inconclusively on 12 May, James Harvey, Moderator of the United Free Church of Scotland, declared this 'a victory for God',[48] and the Church of Scotland *Life and Work*

[43] DP 273, fo. 12.
[44] S. P. Mews, 'The Churches', in M. Morris (ed.), *The General Strike* (Harmondsworth, 1976), 322–5.
[45] *BW*, 20 May 1926, p. 125.
[46] E. Oldmeadow, *Francis, Cardinal Bourne*, ii (London, 1944), 216.
[47] Oliver, *Church and Social Order*, 86, 88; Oldmeadow, *Francis, Cardinal Bourne*, ii. 218–19; *T.*, 15 May 1926, p. 639; Mews, 'The Churches', 330–4.
[48] S. J. Brown, 'The Social Vision of Scottish Presbyterianism and the Union of 1929', *Records of the Scottish Church History Society*, 24/1 (1990), 91.

magazine said that the strike had 'proved its utter futility as an argument of any kind'.[49] The *British Weekly* said that the general stoppage had replaced reason with coercion and 'brute force'.[50]

On the day the strike began, a letter from Bishops Woods (Winchester) and Garbett (Southwark) appeared in *The Times* advocating a government subsidy for the mining industry rather than expecting sacrifices from the miners: 'There are moments in a nation's life when the sacrifice of strict economic principles to higher considerations of justice, mercy and humanity is at once worldly wisdom and spiritual duty.'[51] But this view was far from commanding general acceptance among clerics, some of whom objected to the alleged contradiction between morality and conventional economic practice.[52]

On 6 May the Continuation Committee of Copec wrote to all clergy and ministers urging them to use their spiritual influence in favour of conciliatory negotiations.[53] Davidson, in probably the most celebrated actions of his twenty-five years as Archbishop of Canterbury, first spoke in the Lords on 5 May, disapproving of the Strike but calling on the Government to act in order to end the industrial bitterness; then, two days later, met a group of leading Anglicans and Nonconformists to discuss making a conciliatory appeal for a settlement. The ensuing appeal called for the resumption of negotiations in a cooperative spirit, on the basis of three conditions to be simultaneously adopted—cancellation of the General Strike by the TUC; a government offer to subsidize the coal industry for a short period; and withdrawal by the mine-owners of the new wage terms.[54] These proposals were approved by the President of the Free Church Council, Cardinal Bourne, Ramsay MacDonald (leader of the Labour Party), and Stanley Baldwin, the Conservative Prime Minister. Some leading Conservatives, however, expressed strong disapproval of the conditions to Davidson.[55]

[49] *LW* (June 1926), 131. Cf. S. J. Brown, '"A Victory for God": The Scottish Presbyterian Churches and the General Strike of 1926', *Journal of Ecclesiastical History*, 42 (1991), 596–617; and Brown, 'Campaign', 208–9.

[50] *BW*, 20 May 1926, p. 122. Cf. *Methodist Times*, 20 May 1926, p. 11.

[51] Oliver, *Church and Social Order*, 83–4.

[52] Ibid. 84.

[53] Ibid. 86; *G.*, 14 May 1926, p. 381; DP 273, fos. 41 ff.

[54] Oliver, *Church and Social Order*, 84; *Industrial Christian Fellowship, Annual Report* (1926–7), 12–13; Davidson's memo., 23 May 1926, DP 15, fos. 70–87.

[55] Ibid., fos. 87–95; Davidson to Bishop E. S. Talbot, 25 May 1926, ibid. 6, fo. 107.

Davidson was refused permission to broadcast the appeal by John Reith, General Manager of the British Broadcasting Company, who was fearful of a possible takeover of his organization by Ministers; and the government *British Gazette* refused to print the appeal.[56] But it was published in *The Times* and other newspapers, and its general intentions were repeated in denominational resolutions, such as one which was adopted by the Baptist Union assembly (then meeting at Leeds) and telegraphed to the Prime Minister and the TUC.[57] Henson, among some other Anglican clerics, condemned the appeal, claiming that it substituted 'a declamatory, sentimental socialism' for proper religious teaching, and encouraged 'those who were carried into the wickedness and folly of the general strike to imagine themselves more or less released from the general condemnation'.[58]

The General Strike was called off on 12 May. The TUC leaders accepted Sir Herbert Samuel's plan for possible negotiations and Baldwin's offer of a further subsidy to the coal industry on a short-term basis. To this extent the appeal of Davidson and other Church leaders for conciliation could claim a share in success. The miners' leaders, however, denounced the TUC 'betrayal' and continued the coal strike for six months, after which the miners had to return to work on the owners' terms. Thus ultimately the success of the interdenominational attempt at conciliation was very limited. The general stoppage had ended, but the miners' strike continued unsuccessfully and left a legacy of industrial bitterness and undiminished class conflict.

The most positive development for the Churches in the crisis was probably the advance in cooperation between themselves. 'It draws us very close together,' wrote the Congregationalist R. F. Horton to Davidson about his intervention; and another Nonconformist minister, Herbert Gray, wrote to the Archbishop: 'for the first time in my life it has been possible to feel that the Christian forces in this

[56] G. K. A. Bell, *Randall Davidson, Archbishop of Canterbury*, ii (London, 1935), 1306–14; Reith to Davidson, 8 May 1926, DP 273, fos. 73–4; also memos. by Davidson, 8, 11, and 23 May 1926, ibid., fos. 77–9, and DP 15, fos. 65, 68, 84–5; Bishop of Ripon (E. A. Burroughs) to Davidson, 10 May 1926, ibid. 273, fos. 91–2.

[57] *BH* (1927), 203–9; *BT*, 20 May 1926, pp. 339–40; *BW*, 6 May 1926.

[58] Oliver, *Church and Social Order*, 85–6; Norman, *Church and Society*, 338–9; letter from Henson in *Newcastle Daily Journal*, 4 June 1926 (in DP 273, fo. 303); O. Chadwick, *Hensley Henson: A Study in the Friction between Church and State* (Oxford, 1983), 170; also pp. 165–6.

country were united and courageous, and for that we have to thank your leadership . . . A new sense of unity has been given to us.'[59] M. E. Aubrey, Secretary of the Baptist Union, regretted that at such times of 'national danger' there was no central body representing the different Churches which could attempt to express a common Christian opinion. He hoped that the Churches might not be found scattered and unprepared to face a future crisis.[60]

As the coal stoppage continued after the General Strike, there was another intervention by religious leaders, and this also aroused contrasting reactions. The Director of the ICF, P. T. R. Kirk, gathered together a 'Standing Conference of the Christian Churches on the Coal Dispute', consisting of nine Anglican bishops and eleven Nonconformists, to try and settle the conflict.[61] The Government could hardly be impressed by this development, as the Standing Conference supported the miners' claims, and Baldwin said that its efforts were like 'an attempt by the Federation of British Industry to bring about a revision of the Athanasian Creed'.[62]

After the miners' strike ended, the industrial tension continued and was heightened by the passage of the Trades Disputes and Trade Union Bill in 1927. Among the provisions of this measure, sympathetic stoppages such as the recent General Strike were declared illegal. The bill was opposed by the League of the Kingdom of God and the Copec Continuation Committee, but had some support in religious opinion, including that of Hensley Henson. He accused the League of the Kingdom of God of 'binding Christianity to the service of partisan politics' (he was unattached to a party himself), and attacked the power of the trade unions as 'a ubiquitous, cruel, and continuing tyranny'.[63]

In the year of the General Strike appeared Tawney's *Religion and the Rise of Capitalism*, advancing the firm though unoriginal thesis that economic individualism stemmed from the 'Protestant ethic'. The argument was too sweeping and one-sided to be historically convincing; but it gave Protestant social reformers further reason to be ashamed of their individualist heritage, and boosted

[59] Horton to Davidson, 12 May 1926, DP 6, fo. 108; Gray to Davidson, 13 May 1926, ibid. Cf. Temple to Davidson, 13 May 1926, ibid., fo. 106.

[60] *BT*, 20 May 1926, p. 340.

[61] Oliver, *Church and Social Order*, 89–92; Norman, *Church and Society*, 339–40.

[62] Ibid. 340.

[63] Oliver, *Church and Social Order*, 96–7.

the morale of Roman Catholics who advocated collectivism. Another important work appearing a few years later claimed that the collectivist approach to social policy was based on true Christian ideals, and that competitive acquisitiveness was not. This was Garvie's *The Christian Ideal for Human Society*, published in 1930. The same approach was evident in the annual Social Service Lectures, an interdenominational venture which began in 1926, the trustees being appointed by the Wesleyan Methodist Conference.[64] Thus the expressions of Christian social radicalism in their various (and disputed) forms of books, newspaper articles, conferences, and resolutions continued into the 1930s, when they had exceptionally high unemployment figures to feed on.

The industrial depression and very high unemployment of the 1930s were accompanied by unprecedentedly high living standards for the majority who held regular jobs. The cost of living dropped substantially on account of falling prices caused by contraction of markets. The unemployed could participate very little in this growing prosperity, the subsistence benefit which they obtained from the State yielding them little if anything to spend on luxuries.

Church leaders and members, whatever their political and social views, were constantly made aware of growing unemployment and its problems. A vicar in South Wales wrote in December 1930 to Cosmo Lang (Archbishop of Canterbury from 1928):

> never was South Wales—in a mining sense—so depressed as today. In my own parish of 6,000 people the only colliery which provided employment has closed since the end of August, and previous to that worked on an average four days a week for two or three years. The result is that poverty and suffering are very acute . . . I would dearly love placing the situation before some of our Churches by preaching our Lord's compassion to them—because probably thousands think that the unemployed are thriving on the dole . . .[65]

Lang also received a letter at this time from Alfred Sharp, President of the NFCC, expressing deep thanks 'for your courtesy and consideration in advising me of the action you are taking in

[64] Norman, *Church and Society*, 320; A. E. Garvie, *The Christian Ideal for Human Society* (London, 1930).
[65] E. Illtyd Jones (Pontypridd) to Lang, 16 Dec. 1930, LP 103, fos. 180–2.

requesting the Churches to offer special prayers for the guidance of the Government and the Nation in dealing with unemployment'.[66]

Church conferences and assemblies repeatedly expressed opinions on the industrial and social problems. Among numerous Anglican examples, P. T. R. Kirk (Director of the ICF) stated in a letter in *The Times* in October 1932 that he had just presided at a conference of clergy which had discussed for some days 'the world financial crisis with special reference to the unemployed'. The Church, he said, would not demand any extreme political cures, but only remedies which must be 'just to all classes of human society, and . . . free from every element of bitterness and retaliation'.[67] Concern was shown about the treatment of the unemployed, especially the amount of benefit they received. The *Church Times* in November 1932, when unemployment had reached its highest inter-war peak of nearly three millions, said that the country was bound to provide as generously as possible for 'those who are deprived of their livelihood by causes beyond their control', that 'the administration of the Means Test in some areas gave rise to justifiable discontent', and that every possible opportunity should be opened to the unemployed for 'recreation, occupation, and education'.[68] Nevertheless, said this paper, the Church as a body—whatever action its individual members might take—could not accept Lansbury's view that it should ally itself with one particular party, namely the Labour Party which he led.[69]

In 1933 the Upper and Lower Houses of Canterbury Convocation carried resolutions displaying, in addition to sympathy with the unemployed, a desire for remedies to be found for 'our present distress'. Cyril Garbett, Bishop of Winchester, in moving one of these resolutions, emphasized a common assumption that the Church's role was to arouse concern and alarm rather than to support specific solutions: 'where economists, statesmen, bankers, and financiers had all failed, it was not likely that they [the Church] would have the expert knowledge to solve that most difficult problem.'[70] Most speakers in the Upper House supported Garbett, but

[66] Sharp to Lang, 17 Dec. 1930, ibid., fo. 185.
[67] *The Times*, 17 Oct. 1932 (in LP 115, fo. 138).
[68] *CT*, Supplement, 'The Church and Unemployment', 4 Nov. 1932, pp. 1 ff.
[69] Ibid., 11 Nov. 1932, p. 567.
[70] *CCC*, 19 Jan. 1933, ix. 3, p. 123.

Bishop Headlam stated at length a minority objection to what was now almost the orthodoxy of advocating collectivist policies. What was needed to improve the economy, he insisted, was to encourage the natural operation of market forces, to lower taxation and abolish the dole so that industry would have more money to expand. 'If one were able to reduce the taxation of the country by one-half, and to do away with the unemployment dole, in a very few months he believed that the greater number of those who were at present unemployed would be employed.'[71] Headlam also complained of 'the enormous amount of harm' which the ICF was capable of doing. But a defence of the ICF came from Michael Furse, Bishop of St Albans, one of its members, who felt called on to deny that it was 'in the pay of the Bolshevists'.[72]

That the view of Temple (now Archbishop of York) on taxation was quite opposed to Headlam's was demonstrated in the columns of *The Times* in 1934. In that forum Temple clashed with Neville Chamberlain, Chancellor of the Exchequer, by suggesting that any budget surplus should go to relieve the unemployed rather than to cut taxes.[73] The Conference of the Methodist Church, recently established as a united body, welcomed the Unemployment Act of 1934 but called for more generous levels of benefit, such as prevailed before 1931.[74]

In February 1935 the National Assembly of the Church of England debated a report on unemployment from its Social and Industrial Commission. The report harked back to the language of the Fifth Report of 1918 by saying that the unemployment problem indicated 'some fundamental defect or disorder in the present social and economic system'. After Lord Hugh Cecil among others had criticized the report, a significantly softer resolution than originally intended was passed in vindication of the document.[75] A resolution to be placed before an Anglican meeting in the Albert Hall, London, in November 1935 originally referred to 'the unreason, injustice, and ruthlessness of our present social system'; but the word 'ruthlessness' was omitted on the advice

[71] Ibid. 128–30; Oliver, *Church and Social Order*, 155–6.
[72] *CCC*, 19 Jan. 1933, ix. 3, pp. 129, 139.
[73] Mayor, *Churches and the Labour Movement*, 371.
[74] Campbell, 'Methodism', 151.
[75] Oliver, *Church and Social Order*, 156–7.

of Temple, Lang, and Lord Halifax before the resolution was adopted.[76]

In November 1936 another debate in the National Church Assembly on unemployment and its effects was initiated by Kirk. He described the distressed areas as 'islands of depression and hopelessness amid the rising tide of prosperity', thereby alluding not inaccurately to the large and widening gap between the long-term unemployment of the minority and the growing prosperity of the regularly employed majority. The resolutions adopted urged the government to speed the economic revival of the distressed areas, where depressed industry was still much in evidence, by increasing its powers under the Special Areas Act of 1934.[77]

After retreating during the 1920s from prominent involvement in social criticism and giving emphasis for a while rather to anti-Catholicism and the desirability of restricting Irish immigration, the Church of Scotland began to revive its official social concerns in the early 1930s. After the union of the Church of Scotland and most of the United Free Church in 1929, the enlarged national establishment inaugurated a Forward Movement. But this was concerned mainly with evangelization and moral improvement through the strengthening of the parish system. Concern with social issues was nevertheless reviving, and the Church and Nation Committee submitted a report to the General Assembly of 1932 which pressed the Church to urge more government intervention. 'The principle of *laissez-faire*, that self-interest and free competition are sufficient guides in industry', had, claimed the report, 'disintegrated for the present, and the logical alternative is conscious direction, planning, and control'. But, in discussion of the report, it appeared that a majority in the Assembly was unhappy with this view. A motion criticizing the means test (assessment of the value of private means and possessions in order to decide eligibility for unemployment benefit) for its alleged harshness had to be replaced by a compromise motion urging the government to apply the means test 'with wisdom and Christian discernment'.[78]

[76] Halifax to Lang, 25 July 1935, LP 137, fos. 323–4; Temple to Lang, 26 July 1935, ibid., fo. 325; Lang to Temple, 3 Aug. 1935, ibid., fos. 333–5; Revd A. C. Don to S. H. Wood, 7 Oct. 1935, ibid., fos. 334–5.

[77] Oliver, *Church and Social Order*, 158; *Year Book of the National Assembly of the Church of England* (1938), 150–1; *G.*, 20 Nov. 1936, pp. 794, 800; 27 Nov. 1936, p. 807; *CT*, 27 Nov. 1936, p. 633.

[78] Brown, 'Campaign', 211–14; *LW* (May 1933), 102–4.

The Church and Nation Committee returned to the attack at the next annual General Assembly in May 1933, noting that unemployment had risen still higher in the intervening period and that more people were falling into the category of long-term unemployed:

we keep silence at the peril of our country and our Christian cause. There is much capital lying idle, raw material is cheap, schemes of national and municipal importance cry out for action, our unemployed are maintained at an annual cost of a hundred and twenty-two million pounds, and are now subjected to influences which, unless countered, lead to physical deterioration and moral degeneration. To say that the present effort is the best that can be done is to acknowledge a degree of failure that will bring speedy and dangerous repercussions . . . In a day of abundance, when the standard of living ought to be rising, it is, for great numbers, being definitely lowered.[79]

On submitting its annual report to the 1937 General Assembly, the Church and Nation Committee could take satisfaction in mentioning a substantial drop in unemployment, and found encouragement in new government plans for the distressed areas. But the Committee urged the need for further action. The General Assembly of that year noted alleviations which had taken place in the operation of the means test, but said that further reform was needed in that respect.[80] A campaign for building more churches and halls was launched in 1932 and headed by John White; its somewhat disappointing financial returns might have been partly owing to objections that money should go to help the unemployed rather than to church extension.[81]

The means test was also the object of some Roman Catholic clerical opprobrium. Bishop Mageean of Down and Connor denounced it as 'an invasion of the homes of the poor' at the annual meeting of the St Vincent de Paul Society (a Catholic association for social action) at Belfast in December 1936. He also found hard words for the inadequacy of unemployment relief.[82] The *Tablet* believed, as it stated in 1938, that in contemporary Britain the main contribution of Catholics lay in trying to alter moral values in order

[79] *RGACS* (1933), 460; cf. ibid. (1934), 468–76, (1936), 419–25.
[80] Ibid. (1937), 517–19, (1938), 525, 536.
[81] Brown, 'Campaign', 215–16.
[82] *U.*, 18 Dec. 1936, p. 17.

to dethrone 'false dogmas', such as the assumption that the creation of wealth was among the primary responsibilities of human beings. It was important for Catholics to be well represented in the main political groups, despite the fact that politicians were likely to 'reproach Catholics for keeping their main effort in the field of general moral principles, which do not lead inevitably to any one political programme'.[83]

Among Nonconformists, concern over rising unemployment was as pronounced as elsewhere in the religious spectrum. The increase in the number of coal miners without work caused the executive committee of the NFCC to call in 1929 for training schemes to encourage entry into the new, growing industries, and for more public works; and in 1931 for public money to be spent on objects that would 'increase national efficiency, offer permanent employment so far as possible to the unemployed, and reduce the possibilities of demoralization owing to unemployment'.[84] The Congregational Union noted with gratitude that the Christian Social Council was making a special study of unemployment in cooperation with similar councils in other countries through the Christian Social Research Institute at Geneva; and the unemployment question was repeatedly discussed at assemblies of this Union throughout the 1930s.[85] At the autumn assembly of the Union in October 1935 the Chairman, Angus Watson, called for a 'national prosperity loan' of a billion pounds to be raised in order to finance public works to reduce unemployment. He pointed out that a large amount of this sum could be provided from savings in unemployment benefit payments:

> The Prosperity Loan should almost certainly cost the nation nothing, but at most it would cost it a hundred and fifty millions by way of interest at the end of five years, or less than half of the annual expenditure incurred by our present Social Services. At the end of that time I believe that the expenditure would be so justified as to enable us to continue it, and the great bulk of our employable citizens would be at work . . . What is the alternative? To let two millions of our fellow-citizens rot in idleness; to watch the continuance of the creeping paralysis of national stagnation and decay.[86]

[83] *T.*, 30 July 1938, p. 132.
[84] NFCC Minutes of Executive Committee, 11 Mar. 1929, bk. 6, p. 73; 9 Mar. 1931, bk. 6, p. 142.
[85] *CYB* (1932), 161, (1934), 64–5, (1936), 66–7, 116–17.
[86] Ibid. (1936), 117–19.

A number of religious conferences were held on social questions in the 1930s. An international and interdenominational conference at Oxford in July 1937, on 'Church, Community, and State', repeated the Copec message about the marked shortcomings of the existing economic and social system, emphasizing as an example of this the continuing unemployment problem. A pamphlet entitled *The Call of Oxford*, one of the numerous publications issued by the Christian Social Council, publicized this message.[87] Roman Catholics did not participate officially in this conference; but in the same year a new body, Catholic Action, commenced under the presidency of the Archbishop of Westminster. Its aims were to renew the call for greater social equality in the papal encyclical *Rerum novarum* of 1891, with the additional object of repelling the revolutionary aims of Communism.[88] However, despite the pressure of the unemployment question in the 1930s, there was no further Copec in this decade. It might have seemed that 1934, ten years after the conference and the height of the unemployment crisis, was the time to hold a repeat performance. The absence of such an effort might lend some support to the view that Church pressure for social change was losing momentum in the 1930s.

Whether or not this opinion is correct, Church organizations and leaders not only continued to make broad calls for social reform, but gave much practical aid to the large numbers of poverty-stricken members of society in the 1930s. One aspect of this activity was the production of the results of a detailed investigation, *Men without Work*, on the condition of the unemployed. The investigation was initiated by Temple in 1933 and financed by the Pilgrim Trust from 1936. The very thorough and highly praised report did not appear until 1938, when the unemployment figures had gone down considerably, though there were still persistent pockets of unemployed in the 'special areas'.[89] The General Assembly of the Church of Scotland was informed in 1939 that

> the problem of unemployment in Scotland remains as disquieting as ever. With 250,000 names on the unemployed lists at the Labour Exchanges, the situation is worse than it was a year ago. Nor are the prospects for the

[87] Oliver, *Church and Social Order*, 191–7; *CYB* (1939), 130–1, (1940), 187.

[88] *U.*, 18 Dec. 1936, p. 10.

[89] F. A. Iremonger, *William Temple, Archbishop of Canterbury, his Life and Letters* (London, 1948; new impression 1949), 441–2; letter from Temple in *The Times*, 23 Jan. 1934 (repr. in LP 130, fos. 219–20).

immediate future particularly bright . . . It is encouraging, however, to know that legislation is proposed to facilitate the provision of loans for new industrial undertakings in certain areas of heavy unemployment.[90]

The alleviation of the distress caused by unemployment was seen as far inferior to its cure. But if members of the Churches could only preach the need for a cure, hoping that politicians would hear their message and produce technical schemes to implement it, they could act more directly over alleviation. Churches were responsible for a great deal of material aid to the unemployed and their families, distributing vast amounts of food, clothing, and toys. For example, the distress fund of the Congregational Union of England and Wales, commencing operations in 1920 and continuing active for many years under the capable direction of Mrs Dorothy Mellor, received donations and goods from their more prosperous members for distribution to the needy.[91] The Society of Friends (Quakers) ran a scheme to provide allotments for the unemployed, among other special philanthropic activities.[92] A scheme was evolved for selling tickets to pilgrims who visited cathedrals in July 1934, the proceeds going to aid relief work in distressed areas.[93] Individual churches ran meetings, concerts, and recreation rooms for the out of work. The Church of Scotland opened three halls for the unemployed in Glasgow in 1931–2, and three in Aberdeen and four more in Glasgow in 1932–3. An instructional centre in manual skills was also opened in Glasgow and visited by the Prince of Wales, instructors giving their services free.[94] The Bishop of London, Winnington-Ingram, remarked in Convocation that 'some of the richest churches in London' had donated clothes to poorer areas, and that 'there had been a great feeling of gratitude on the part of the poorest part of the population at the fact of these rich churches coming down and taking their own presents'.[95] Among Methodists on Tyneside, Maldwyn Edwards, Superintendant of the

[90] Report of Church and Nation Committee, in *RGACS* (1939), 515–16.
[91] *CYB* (1932), 158, (1933), 148–53, (1934), 152–4, (1935), 163–4, (1937), 210–16, (1940), 187. Cf. letters from Revds Roger Lloyd (Great Harwood Vicarage, Blackburn) and E. Illtyd Jones (Dowlais Rectory, Glamorgan), in *G.*, 1 May 1936, p. 304.
[92] G. Finlayson, *Citizen, State, and Social Welfare in Britain, 1830–1990* (Oxford, 1994), 224–5.
[93] Letter from Hewlett Johnson, Dean of Canterbury, in *The Times*, 15 May 1934 (repr. in LP 124, fos. 129–30).
[94] *RGACS* (1933), 453–4, (1934), 474, Cf. *LW* (1933), 104.
[95] *CCC*, 19 Jan. 1933, ix. 3, pp. 134–5.

Gateshead Mission, organized debates, concerts, and classes in useful work for the unemployed.[96]

The former chapel of a Baptist congregation which had obtained a new church (Queen's Road, Coventry) was used as a centre for the unemployed. A new institute with the same use was run by this congregation from late 1933. Two years later this institute was catering for fifty (mostly elderly) unemployed men: 'it offered a reading room, a billiards room, handicraft rooms and a library, with a wireless, a good fire, and dance music from a loudspeaker, all for a penny a week.' Moreover, 'with dinner at twopence (and pudding a penny more) and tea at twopence . . . a dozen workless ate daily at the Institute'.[97] Other examples of practical initiatives against poverty were campaigns against malnutrition conducted by the ICF and, on a joint basis, by Congregationalists and Presbyterians.[98]

A committee of the Congregational Union took steps 'to offer friendship and a welcome' to migrants who came from the distressed areas to work in districts where industry was expanding.[99] Much attention was also given to aiding the distressed areas themselves. Voluntary 'adoption schemes', whereby a more prosperous area or an organization 'adopted' a distressed district in order to help it, had much religious support. In 1936, ninety-six of these schemes were in operation, including those between Surrey and Jarrow (Co. Durham), Bath and Redruth (Cornwall), and the BBC and a club in Gateshead.[100] George Bell, Bishop of Chichester, undertook in 1932 to provide money from his diocese for at least a year to a 'Sussex Salford Fund'. This fund financed the successful efforts of five young Sussex ladies, led by the Hon. Ruth Buckley, to open and run social centres in the Salford area, where the adult unemployment rate was one in three in the early 1930s. Bell also encouraged the collection of goods in Sussex for distribution in distressed areas. In 1937 the aims of the Sussex Salford Fund were taken over by the National Council of Social Service.[101]

[96] Campbell, 'Methodism', 147–8.

[97] C. Binfield, *Pastors and People: The Biography of a Baptist Church* (Coventry, 1984), 215–16.

[98] Oliver, *Church and Social Order*, 159–60; *CYB* (1940), 185.

[99] *CYB* (1940), 186–7.

[100] Finlayson, *Citizen*, 222.

[101] R. C. D. Jasper, *George Bell, Bishop of Chichester* (London, 1967), 78–9; printed letter from Bell 'to the clergy and laity of Sussex' on 'Unemployment and

Another way in which Churches linked their desire to improve social conditions with their intimate knowledge of particular areas was in their consistent advocacy of extensions in housing provision. As already noted, individual clergy such as Basil Jellicoe and Charles Jenkinson became celebrated for their successful efforts in house-building in their localities.[102] Housing concerned not only governments and local councils but Church leaders and organizations in this period of intensive house construction, which succeeded in reducing but not eradicating nineteenth-century slums. There were debates and resolutions on the housing situation in the Convocations, General Assemblies, and Union assemblies.[103] Bishop Garbett told Convocation in 1933 that for a prosperous landlord to let insanitary and decrepit premises to tenants was as bad as running a brothel.[104] Garbett, an indefatigable denouncer of slum conditions as 'contrary to the will of God', also spoke strongly in favour of housing improvements. In 1933 he published a pamphlet, *The Challenge of the Slums*, which stated that, 'if there is created a strong and informed Christian conscience on bad housing, the demand for changes in the conditions under which the poor live will eventually be irresistible'.[105]

The differing wider views on social reform continued to be expressed in the 1930s. The same leading Church figures as in the previous decade, with a few exceptions, continued to participate in the contest between desire for collectivism and desire to sanction no further encroachments on individualism. In 1933 there appeared a volume entitled *Christianity and the Crisis*, edited by Percy Dearmer (a well-known Anglo-Catholic clergyman), advocating the former approach as a solution to the critical economic and social situation. The book contained essays by, among others, P. T.

the Church', Nov. 1933, BP 164, fos. 55–6; Dame Alice Godman to Bell, 26 July, 2 Aug. 1933, ibid., fos. 1–2, 12–13; Hon. Ruth Buckley to Bell, 28 July 1933, ibid., fos. 3–4; Bell to Buckley, 31 July 1933, ibid., fos. 5–6; Buckley to Bell, 2 Aug. 1933, ibid., fos. 7–8; Bell to Godman, 4 Aug. 1933, ibid., fos. 14–15; *G.*, 4 Dec. 1936, p. 864.

[102] Oliver, *Church and Social Order*, 140–51.

[103] e.g. *BH* (1935), 189; *CCC*, 13 Feb. 1930, viii. 2, pp. 70–86; *PAGAFCS* (1927), 636.

[104] *CCC*, 1 June 1933, ix. 4, p. 348. Cf. his speech in Convocation, ibid., 13 Feb. 1930, viii. 2, pp. 71–6.

[105] C. Garbett, *The Challenge of the Slums* (London, 1933), 25. Cf. B. S. Rowntree, *The Human Needs of Labour* (London, 1937), 86–91; Norman, *Church and Society*, 349–50.

R. Kirk, Hewlett Johnson, and Maude Royden (Anglicans), A. E. Garvie (Congregationalist), and S. E. Keeble and C. Unwin (Methodists).[106]

In 1931, to commemorate the fortieth anniversary of *Rerum Novarum*, Pope Pius XI issued an encyclical, *Quadragesimo anno*, on 'the social order'. In this a *via media* was firmly maintained. The dangers of individualism and collectivism, of excessive advantages enjoyed by capital and exaggerated claims sometimes made by labour organizations, were alike stressed. 'The uplifting of the proletariat' and 'a just distribution' of wealth for the common good of all were urged.[107]

After Alfred Blunt became Bishop of Bradford in 1931 he fully agreed with a statement made at his diocesan conference in December 1932 by W. D. L. Greer (later Bishop of Manchester): 'I would rather see the unemployed rot on the streets than that we should put up centres to amuse and interest them and leave the root causes untouched.'[108] At a meeting of the National Assembly of the Church of England in February 1935, Blunt, says his biographer, was 'bubbling with fury and stunned with depression at the "unmitigated imbecilities" of the Bishop of London [Winnington-Ingram], the "disguised prejudice" of the Bishop of Durham [Hensley Henson], and the "sentimental rhetoric" of the Archbishop of Canterbury [Lang]'. Of this meeting Blunt wrote in the *Church Messenger* of May 1935:

> The debate in the Church Assembly, through much of which I sat with intense feelings of shame and indignation, made certain inferences very clear to me . . . It was mostly from the laymen present that one heard repeated or applauded the view that the Church has no business to concern itself with any attempt to find possible ways of solution for the unemployment problem, on the ground that it is a problem of economics; which means in effect that the Church is only to try and minister to those whom a bad economic system injures, without concerning itself with the character of the system itself.[109]

[106] P. C. Dearmer (ed.), *Christianity and the Crisis* (London, 1933).

[107] V. M. Crawford, *Catholic Social Doctrine, 1891–1931* (Catholic Social Guild Year Book, Oxford 1931), 92–3 ff. Cf. C. C. Clump, *A Catholic's Guide to Social and Political Action* (Catholic Social Guild Year Book, Oxford, 1939), 26–30.

[108] J. S. Peart-Binns, *Blunt* (Queensbury, Yorks., 1969), 170.

[109] Ibid. 172.

The very opinion which Blunt so deplored was endorsed by Dean Inge, and by Bishop Headlam in his book of 1933, *What It Means To Be a Christian*:

Christianity . . . does not teach us the divine right of Kings, nor the holiness of democracy. It is neither Republican, nor Monarchical. It is indifferent to socialism, or individualism, or communism. It gives us certain principles of conduct which bid us . . . care for the well-being of our fellow-men. How that well-being may be attained is a matter for the economist, the politician or the legislator.[110]

Even Temple wrote in 1933 that the Church should concern itself, as a body, only with general moral principles and should not try and judge between one theory of improvement and another, 'the rights and wrongs of bi-metallism, or social credit, or "technocracy"'.[111]

In the inter-war years, it was largely a matter of hopes unrealized for the many Christians who wanted a more collectivist approach by Government to deal with economic and social questions. After the flurry of curtailed legislation in the first two years after the First World War, individualism generally held sway in the regulation of the intense and much-disputed issues which arose from the beginning of the 1920s. It was only in the more concentrated atmosphere of social thought which developed during the Second World War, when collectivism appeared to a widening number of people to be a desirable approach to the future, that the hopes of the social radicals in the Churches began to receive official acceptance.

[110] A. C. Headlam, *What It Means To Be a Christian* (London, 1933), 148–9; Norman, *Church and Society*, 332–4.
[111] Quoted in ibid. 325.

3
Churches and Personal Morals and Behaviour, 1918–1939

There were many opportunities for innovation and development in personal behaviour in the inter-war years. Activities such as drinking and watching football and cricket matches, cycling and rambling, and reading books and newspapers were inherited from pre-war decades and did not change radically in the 1920s and 1930s, though some of them showed a marked increase. But there was a particularly large growth in gambling opportunities, cinema-going developed enormously, and broadcasting originated and rapidly spread. There was wider acceptance and use of artificial contraceptive methods, and an increase in divorce and in the legal facilities for it.

In some ways the growth of unemployment probably contributed to the increased time spent on leisure, as more people had perforce a larger amount of time in which to engage in such pursuits. But they had less money to do so, and leisure usually required the expenditure of money. Leisure spread mainly because of the increasing prosperity of the majority who obtained rising real wages from regular employment. There were also additional incentives to participate in leisure opportunities, notably private agreements reached for holidays with pay during the 1920s and 1930s, culminating after a struggle in an Act of 1938 making this mandatory among employed workers.

Personal behaviour embraces a vast range of actual or potential activities, and the Churches would claim to have a natural interest in every one of them. But this chapter will concentrate mainly on drinking, gambling, cinema, broadcasting, birth control, and divorce.

The core of the Churches' interest in social questions was an attempt to instil and preserve morality in both public policy and personal behaviour. This approach could not be homogeneous, as there were differing views about morality among Christians. Nor was it an approach that tried to prevent change; indeed the virtues of change were sometimes clearly seen. 'Morality that is merely traditional becomes archaic, artificial, unreal, and finally repugnant to the developing moral sense of mankind,' wrote Bishop Hensley Henson in his significant book, *Christian Morality*, in 1936; 'the Christian ethic . . . is always in process of becoming, never something finished and complete'.[1] But change had to be tempered by moral consciousness in its reception and adoption. Since there was a substantial degree of consensus about Christian morality, there was a good deal of similarity in the official attitudes and responses of the different Churches. But there was also much scope for disagreement, and during the twentieth century this has shown itself not least in a widening divergence between the Roman Catholic Church and Protestant Churches. Artificial birth control has been the chief point at issue in this respect, especially after the cautious but tolerant declaration of the 1930 Lambeth Conference of Anglican bishops; but there has also tended to be a more tolerant attitude to gambling in the Catholic Church than in other Churches.

A central part of the Churches' social attitudes concerned the use of Sunday, the Christian day of rest. Some of the Churches' social concerns were given particular emphasis when applied to activities on a Sunday. The high Victorian Sunday with its rather rigid insistence on little secular activity had been crumbling for decades, at least since the 1880s. By the 1920s there was a very wide range of attitudes among Christians about work and leisure activities which might be deemed permissible on a Sunday. But it is likely that in the inter-war years the majority of Christians still wished to keep Sunday 'special' by preventing on that day certain social activities which took place on weekdays.

The preservation of this stand, however, became increasingly difficult as leisure opportunities spread and multiplied. The Bishop of Kingston (Frederick Hawkes) lamented in a Convocation debate in 1933 that, 'owing to the commercialisation and secularisation of society, religion was being crowded out'.[2] The Lord's Day Observance Society, the Imperial Alliance for the Defence of Sunday, and the Scottish Sabbath Protection Association felt strongly about the need to discourage Sunday pursuits which were thought

[1] H. H. Henson, *Christian Morality: Natural, Developing, Final* (Oxford, 1936), 296, 169.

[2] *CCC*, 19 Jan. 1933, ix. 3, p. 189.

frivolous, commercial, or dangerous; and this view was often echoed in Church assemblies and committees. The annual conference of the Primitive Methodist Church in 1919 resolved that:

we view with concern the growing disregard of the Lord's Day as a day for rest and worship, as is evidenced in the cries for Sunday theatre and cinema performances, Sunday sport, and Sunday newspapers. We deplore the tendency to adopt the Continental idea of the Sunday in preference to the English idea.[3]

Similar resolutions came from the Lord's Day Committee of the Church of Scotland General Assembly, the NFCC, and other Church bodies.[4]

There were often disputes between Christians over games-playing and cinema attendance on Sundays. To many, allowing cinemas to function on Sundays was practically a backward step towards paganism, whereas the Bishop of Croydon, E. S. Woods (a liberal Evangelical), spoke for many Christians in arguing to the contrary:

The Church should say plainly that Sunday is not an unsuitable day for some forms of recreation . . . There were masses of young people in the streets of all big urban centres on Sunday evenings who literally had nowhere [to go] and nothing to do . . . for a very large majority of these young people it simply did not enter their heads to come to church. Was there anything that could be done for them? . . . he would say: open the cinemas and give them healthy films.[5]

A liberal, if perplexed, view was also taken by the *Church Times* in 1938:

The natural reaction against the Puritan gloomy Sunday has had the inevitable result of going too far . . . The day of rest has become the day of rush and hustle . . . Sunday was the family day. Now on the Lord's Day the family is distributed over golf courses and tennis courts, and is dashing about the country in Baby Austins . . . What can be done about it? We are entirely opposed to the banning of games in the park on Sunday afternoon.

[3] *Primitive Methodist Year Book* (1919), 213.

[4] *RGACS* (1921), 728–30; also (1931), 541–6, (1935), 473–6; *Year Book of the National Assembly of the Church of England* (1933), 153; NFCC Minutes of Executive Committee, 13 Mar. 1933, bk. 6, p. 205.

[5] *CCC*, 19 Jan. 1933, ix. 3, pp. 167–8; S. G. Jones, *Workers at Play: A Social and Economic History of Leisure, 1918–39* (London, 1986), 176. Cf. D. W. Bebbington, *Evangelicalism in Modern Britain: A History from the 1730s to the 1980s* (London, 1989), 211.

We continue our traditional opposition to all Puritan restrictions. We do not believe that to shut the cinemas would mean filling the churches.[6]

Cyril Garbett, Bishop of Winchester, advised in a Convocation debate in 1934 that a median approach to the use of Sunday should be adopted, avoiding old-fashioned puritanical views but also trying to prevent undue laxity in observance.[7] *The Tradition of Sunday*, a pamphlet issued in 1930 by Anglican, Methodist, Baptist, Congregational, and Presbyterian representatives, stated that the Sunday duties of Christians included attending public worship, practising private devotions, and engaging in 'Christian service' if the opportunity offered.[8]

The question of allowing Sunday opening of cinemas, the most popular form of entertainment outside the home in this period, was the central issue concerning Sabbath observance at this time. In spite of the continuing existence of the Sunday Observance Act of 1780, some cinema shows were already taking place on Sundays before 1914, and during the 1920s this practice spread. But there was a great deal of objection to the practice, and a decision in the High Court of Appeal in January 1931 made clear that such shows were illegal.[9] In April of that year a bill was introduced into the House of Commons to allow cinema shows, concerts, lectures, and debates on Sundays, but this was defeated. Further bills followed, and in July 1932 the National Government easily passed its Sunday Entertainments Bill allowing cinemas (but not theatres) to open on Sundays. Clear opposition, however, was voiced in the debates on the measure. It was said, for example, that Wales, where strong protests were being made against the bill, should be excluded from the measure; and that such a bill would lead to the introduction of the dreaded 'continental Sunday'.[10]

The new Act legalized Sunday cinema shows in areas where they were already taking place, and said that this permission would be extended to other places if local polls were in favour of Sunday opening.[11] Cinema-opening on Sundays spread after the Act, but

[6] *CT*, 2 Dec. 1938, p. 607.
[7] *CCC*, 24 Jan. 1934, ix. 5, pp. 16–19ff.
[8] Ibid. 26–7. Cf. *BH* (1932), 193.
[9] S. G. Jones, *The British Labour Movement and Film, 1918–39* (London, 1987), 115ff.
[10] HC Deb. 266, 715–99; 267, 1821–1983.
[11] Jones, *The British Labour Movement and Film*, 118.

there were marked regional differences in the extent of the practice. By 1934 nearly all cinemas in London were opening on Sundays, and over a quarter of cinemas in England as a whole; but in Scotland and Wales, where sabbatarianism was stronger, only 7 per cent of cinemas were opening on a Sunday.[12] Strong popular objection to Sunday cinema shows was indicated in some areas, resulting in the banning of these shows in local polls, while in other districts opinion as recorded in the polls was clearly in favour. Clerical opinion continued to be divided. Bishop E. S. Woods might have been reasonably happy with the Act of 1932, but the Communist sympathizer Hewlett Johnson, the 'red Dean' of Canterbury and previously Dean of Manchester, believed after a public poll that Sunday cinemas were not wanted by the workers of Manchester: 'they knew that the opening of cinemas was just another step in robbing them or attempting to rob them of their leisure upon Sunday . . . in bulk they voted against it, and the cinema interests in Manchester from that time until he left sang very low.'[13]

A number of other matters sometimes considered to be desecrations of the Sabbath aroused the attention and concern of Church assemblies in the inter-war years. Pleasure-seeking on Sundays through going on trips, dancing, playing games, listening to brass bands in parks, and going up in aeroplanes was among these issues. In 1922 a committee of the Free Church of Scotland General Assembly lamented in its annual report that in quiet country parishes 'the peace of the Sabbath is broken in summer by groups of noisy trippers who arrive in charabancs and make the sweetest spots of earth hideous with their caterwaulings'.[14] In 1930 the same body protested against 'the deliberate attempt on the part of the English-controlled railway companies to thrust the Continental Sabbath upon the Highlands of Scotland'.[15] The Church of Scotland presbytery of Dundee agreed in 1932 to send a deputation to the town council deploring the opening of the Palais de Danse on Sunday

[12] Ibid.; G. I. T. Machin, 'British Churches and the Cinema in the 1930s', in D. Wood (ed.), *The Church and the Arts* (Studies in Church History, 28; Oxford, 1992), 483.

[13] *CCC*, 19 Jan. 1933, ix. 3, pp. 195–6.

[14] *PAGAFCS* (1922), 899. Cf. memorial sent to town council by Church of Scotland presbytery in Aberdeen; Church of Scotland Aberdeen Presbytery Minutes, 22 Feb. 1921, CH2/1/28, pp. 49–50.

[15] *PAGAFCS* (1930), 339.

evenings.[16] The Baptist annual assembly in 1923 resolved unanimously to protest against the permitted use of municipal parks for the playing of games on Sundays;[17] and complaints were frequently made about the Sunday opening of shops.[18] The executive committee of the NFCC appealed to the Air Minister in 1931 'to use his influence to prevent all unnecessary flying on the Lord's Day', and the Edinburgh presbytery of the Church of Scotland was so concerned about Sunday flying that it appointed a special committee to help organize protests on the subject.[19]

The question of the use of Sunday was already in a transitional stage in the inter-war years. Sunday observance was by no means in complete retreat, as there were many occasions—for example, over Sunday cinema-opening and Sunday golf—where the attempts at 'encroachment' for leisure purposes were defeated. Nevertheless, the trend was for secular activities on Sundays to grow in these years, and the trend continued. That continental Sunday could not be kept out.

The consumption of alcohol was one of the personal social activities which had been of concern to the Churches for nearly a century before 1918, and continued to be so in the inter-war years. Opinions on temperance often showed signs of division within Churches. This was the case among Roman Catholics;[20] and it was said of temperance opinion in the Church of Scotland that 'divergent views are widely held within its borders'.[21] It was by no means always clear whether temperance in alcohol consumption meant only moderate drinking, or whether complete abstinence was aimed at; but a wide area of temperance campaigning was undisguisedly directed at promoting the latter.

[16] Church of Scotland Dundee Presbytery Minutes, 7 Sept. 1932, CH2/103/41, p. 184.

[17] *BH* (1924), 193. Cf. *PAGAFCS* (1924), 1331.

[18] e.g. *RGACS* (1934), 483–4.

[19] NFCC Minutes of Executive Committee, 25 Sept. 1931, bk. 6, p. 158 (also ibid., 13 May 1933, bk. 6, p. 215); Church of Scotland Edinburgh Presbytery Minutes, 6 Oct. 1931, CH2/121/51, p. 308; 4 Oct. 1932, ibid., pp. 474–5; 7 Nov. 1933, CH2/121/52, p. 27; 3 Apr. 1934, ibid., p. 99; etc.

[20] S. G. Jones, *Workers at Play: A Social and Economic History of Leisure, 1918–39* (London, 1986), 170–1. See the religious divisions in voting on temperance questions in Glasgow town council, in J. C. Gordon, 'The Temperance Movement and the Labour Party in Glasgow, 1920–76', MA thesis (Newcastle upon Tyne, 1982), 10–20.

[21] *LW* (Oct. 1923), 258.

Temperance advocates had considerable hopes of making permanent gains at the end of the First World War, but these hopes were slowly dashed. The Central Liquor Control Board was abolished by a Licensing Act of 1921, and only two of the nine points of the Temperance Council of the Christian Churches of England and Wales were realized. As early as December 1918, disappointment with the Government's lack of interest in permanent drink reform was being shown by Church bodies.[22] In 1920, however, the Temperance (Scotland) Act of 1913 came into operation, establishing local option on the basis of polls whether to accept drink sales; this brought some successes for its supporters. Such successes were few for the temperance cause as a whole in the 1920s, but drink consumption did continue to go down.

Disappointment with government action did not prevent a renewal of zeal in the temperance cause in the post-war years. The Wesleyans, whose leadership concentrated especially on temperance and gambling in their social reforming aims at this time, commenced in 1919 a Forward Movement for total abstinence through the seven-year-old Abstainers' League. The Conferences of the Wesleyan, Primitive Methodist, and United Methodist Churches all showed in that year a determination to advance total abstinence, and these three denominations later commenced campaigns for this purpose.[23] But this approach had its critics within those denominations. At the Wesleyan Conference of 1919 a motion by Walter Runciman, a leading Liberal politician, to make it a recognized duty of Christians to set an example of personal abstinence, met with considerable opposition. This was partly on the ground that it might some time be used as a test of Wesleyan membership, threatening non-teetotal members with compulsory resignation. The motion passed only in diluted form.[24]

Wesleyans also acted interdenominationally to advance the temperance cause. Henry Carter, a Wesleyan minister who exerted himself for the advancement of temperance to probably a greater extent than any other minister or clergyman in the early twentieth

[22] e.g. Dundee United Free Church Presbytery Minutes, 11 Dec. 1918, CH3/9/18, pp. 31–2; retrospective account in *New Campaigner: Being the Official Organ of the Temperance Council of the Christian Churches of England and Wales* (2nd and 3rd quarters, 1927), 29–30.

[23] D. P. Campbell, 'Methodism and Social Problems in the Inter-War Period, 1918–39', M.Litt. thesis (Oxford, 1987), 49–50.

[24] Ibid. 51–2.

century, was one of the secretaries of the Temperance Council of the Christian Churches in 1920. The other secretaries at this time were C. J. Irwin (Secretary of the Catholic Total Abstinence League of the Cross), E. H. Joy (a Salvation Army colonel), and C. F. Tonks (Secretary of the Church of England Temperance Society). The presidents of this body in 1920 had an equally interdenominational complexion: they comprised Archbishop Davidson, Cardinal Bourne, the Baptist John Clifford, and General Bramwell Booth of the Salvation Army. The council of this organization consisted of representatives of Baptist, Roman Catholic, Anglican, Congregational, Quaker, Primitive Methodist, United Methodist, and Wesleyan Methodist societies.[25] Similar interdenominational cooperation was sometimes shown in local temperance gatherings and initiatives.

Davidson, in sending an encouraging address to a United National Campaign for Temperance launched in 1923, stressed that the Churches were united in their support, though their temperance aims did not include prohibition or public ownership of the drink trade. 'We are soldiers of Christ fighting a great evil, and the splendid thing is that we are one army,' echoed Kenneth Gibbs, Archdeacon of St Albans. 'All the divided forces of Christ have come together to fight in perfect union under His leadership.' The specific objectives of this campaign were local option, Sunday closing, no sale of alcohol to persons under 18 years of age, and annual licensing of drink sales in private clubs.[26] Of a parallel Scottish Churches' Temperance Campaign it was noted that 'the Churches are at last proving to the community that if doctrinal and ecclesiastical divisions still separate them they are able to move together in matters of great social value to the country'.[27]

In Scotland the temperance message of the Churches in the early 1920s was largely concerned with supporting the 'no-licence' option of the Temperance (Scotland) Act, which was put into operation in 1920. The first public polls under the Act's local-option provisions, with voting on one of three choices ('no change', 'restricted licence', or 'no licence') for each local-government area, took place in November 1920.[28] A total of 447,311 votes was given for 'no

[25] H. Carter, *Local Option: Shall We Support It?* (London, n.d. [1920]), 1 ff.
[26] *New Campaigner*, 1 (Sept. 1923), 4, 9, 27.
[27] *LW* (Dec. 1922), 270.
[28] e.g. Church of Scotland Dingwall Presbytery Minutes, 5 May 1920, CH2/92/15, p. 143, and Aberdeen Presbytery Minutes, 28 Sept. 1920, CH2/1/28, p. 16.

licence', but in only forty districts was there a majority for this course, whereas 493 districts returned majorities for 'no change' (i.e. maintenance of the current licensing arrangements).[29] The outcome of the first polls was thus disappointing for temperance advocates, and later results were no better for them. Although in the polls of November 1926 most of the areas which had previously adopted 'no licence' reaffirmed their decision, there was no extension of these areas.[30] The Free Church of Scotland's Committee on Religion, Morals, and Temperance noted in 1922 that, 'so long as Scotland spends more than five times on strong drink than she spends on education, no one can claim that the country is in a sound condition'.[31] There was little further reduction of spending on drink, and the system of local polling did not survive the Second World War.

Elsewhere in Great Britain local option remained an aim of many bodies, but it was never obtained. Some of the objects of temperance concern displayed aspects of the changing social scene. The executive committee of the NFCC condemned a trend among publicans to install the new wireless receivers on their premises, as these might attract more customers and spread the habit of public-house attendance.[32] The same committee deprecated the building of public houses on the new post-war housing estates, calling for the inhabitants of these areas to be allowed to decide whether to have these premises in their midst. The committee also declared that 'the present enormous and ill-advised expenditure upon intoxicating drink greatly aggravates the grave national and social evil of unemployment'.[33] The need to educate the young in the dangers of alcohol was constantly emphasized, and for this purpose it was suggested that the Bands of Hope should be revived.[34]

Unity between the temperance advocates in different Churches was rightly emphasized, but there was also continuing diversity on

[29] Church of Scotland Aberdeen Presbytery Minutes, 25 Jan. 1921, CH1/1/28, pp. 39–40.

[30] *New Campaigner* (1st quarter, 1927), 4; *RGACS* (1927), 926; Campbell, 'Methodism', 55; C. Brown, *The Social History of Religion in Scotland since 1730* (London, 1987), 205–6.

[31] *PAGAFCS* (1922), 900.

[32] NFCC Minutes of Executive Committee, 4 May 1923, bk. 5, pp. 25–6.

[33] Ibid., 26 Mar. 1928, bk. 6, p. 44; 10 Mar. 1930, bk. 6, p. 113.

[34] e.g. *Primitive Methodist Year Book* (1919), 212, (1920), 205–6, (1921), 204; *CYB* (1923), 31–2.

the drink question within practically every Church. It was alleged in 1926 that the Church of England Temperance Society and the Catholic Total Abstinence League of the Cross had little support in their respective Churches.[35] There was a large amount of Anglican episcopal support for temperance, but Hensley Henson was known as 'the liquor bishop' because of his refusal to condemn 'the trade', disliking State intervention against drink as much as State intervention for social security.[36] It was noted that Lord Salvesen, a representative of the Church of Scotland at the Life and Work Conference at Stockholm in August 1925, held views on the drink question which reflected those of the licensed trade rather than those officially endorsed by the General Assembly.[37] In November 1923 the Church of Scotland's Edinburgh presbytery voted by a majority to accept a motion that church members within its bounds be advised to vote for 'no licence' or 'limitation of licences' in the forthcoming triennial polls under the 1913 Act. A counter-motion had been put, recommending that the presbytery take no action; but this was defeated as it obtained only fifteen votes against thirty-one for the other motion.[38] A clash over the 'no-licence' policy occurred also in the Aberdeen presbytery of the Church of Scotland in March 1926, when a motion disapproving of this policy was defeated.[39] Despite the existence of a Catholic Total Abstinence League, the *Tablet* in December 1936 berated the BBC for presenting wine 'not as one of the great marks of civilization but as "alcohol", a dangerous and discreditable drink'.[40]

Success in obtaining legislative restrictions on drink after the First World War was not very great. The Temperance Council of the Christian Churches in England and Wales (TCCC) had a programme of nine points—Sunday closing in England (it had existed in Wales since 1881); shorter opening hours on weekdays; reduction of the number of licensed premises; increased powers for the

[35] Letter from C. W. Fryers in *Newcastle Daily Journal*, 3 June 1926 (extract in DP 273, fo. 303).
[36] O. Chadwick, *Hensley Henson: A Study in the Friction between Church and State* (Oxford, 1983), 164–5.
[37] *New Campaigner*, 9 (4th quarter, 1925), 5.
[38] Church of Scotland Edinburgh Presbytery Minutes, 14 Nov. 1923, CH2/121/37, p. 39.
[39] Church of Scotland Aberdeen Presbytery Minutes, 31 Mar. 1926, CH2/1/28, pp. 441–2.
[40] *T.*, 12 Dec. 1936, p. 823.

local licensing authorities; control of drink sales in private clubs; abolition of grocers' licences; banning of the sale of liquor to persons under 18; local option throughout the UK; and the provision of alternatives to the tavern for non-alcoholic refreshment and recreation.[41] The only points actually gained were shorter opening hours than those of pre-war days (by means of a Licensing Act of 1921), and the banning of sales of drink to young persons under 18 (with some exceptions) by a bill introduced by Viscountess Astor and passed in 1923.[42] Bills to establish local option in England and Wales were introduced in the Lords by the Bishop of Oxford (Hubert Burge) in 1921 and 1922, but were not successful, despite having the support of most of the bishops.[43] A bill to introduce local option in Wales was talked out of the Commons in February 1924.[44]

The extent of Parliament's willingness to pass temperance legislation in the 1920s was thus disappointing to the anti-drink movement. Even the hope placed in local option faded when the Scottish polls produced only a small 'no-licence' vote. By 1925 the temperance campaign among the Methodist denominations showed signs of flagging.[45] In 1929, when Edwin Scrymgeour (Prohibitionist MP for Dundee and President of the Scottish Prohibition Party) introduced his Liquor Traffic Prohibition Bill into the Commons (of course to no avail), the *Methodist Recorder* condemned it as 'almost draconian'.[46] The Church of England Temperance Society seemed to have trouble in surviving by the late 1920s. Its independent existence came into question, and in 1929 it was absorbed into the new Board of Social Responsibility established by the National Church Assembly.[47]

Nevertheless temperance advocates were heartened by continuing falls in drink sales and convictions for drunkenness. The view was not infrequently expressed that the country was quite rapidly

[41] *CCC*, 14 Feb. 1919, iii. 1, p. 239; 7 May 1919, iii. 2, pp. 339–40; NFCC Minutes of Executive Committee, 26 Sept. 1919, bk. 4, p. 235; 15 Mar. 1920, bk. 4, p. 251.

[42] *New Campaigner* (2nd and 3rd quarters, 1927), 31–2; *CCC*, 2 May 1923, v. 2, pp. 221–2.

[43] *CCC*, 3 May 1922, iv. 3, pp. 371–82; 6 July 1922, ibid. 601–5; *New Campaigner*, (3rd quarter, 1924), 4–5, (2nd quarter, 1925), 1–3; *The Times*, 11 Apr. 1924, p. 15.

[44] *New Campaigner* (2nd quarter, 1924), 1 ff.

[45] Campbell, 'Methodism', 65–9.

[46] Ibid. 69.

[47] *CCC*, 28 Mar. 1928, vii. 7, pp. 6–18.

sobering up, but there were also warnings of the need to continue acting in order to 'defend the position we have won'.[48] Temperance continued in quite a buoyant mood, seizing opportunities of different kinds in order to spread its message. As the coal strike of 1926 ended, the TCCC distributed 400,000 handbills and 16,000 posters through clergy and ministers, warning the miners not to spend all their restored wages in the public house.

Already by this time the TCCC was proposing to plan 'a worthy national celebration' in 1932 for the centenary of the pioneering temperance actions of Joseph Livesey and his Preston companions. These had signed the first total abstinence pledge and commenced the first English teetotal movement.[49] At a conference representing all the Churches in Wales, held in December 1926, it was unanimously agreed that a TCCC for Wales should be set up, separately organized from the existing council but working in cooperation with it.[50] The united forces of Scottish temperance, denominational and other, were represented in a large National Convention held in Glasgow in March 1926.[51] The Temperance Council of the Church of Scotland General Assembly reported in 1927 its hope to build up a temperance organization 'as wide as the Church'.[52] In January 1932 a Royal Commission on the licensing system in England and Wales published its report. This did not go so far as to propose local option or Sunday closing in England, but it did recommend reduced opening hours, tighter control of clubs, reduction of licences, and separate treatment for Wales. It was hailed as 'a victory for the temperance movement' by the Council of the Congregational Union. The *New Campaigner*, the official publication of the TCCC, said that 'claim after claim that we have advanced throughout the past decade has been endorsed by the Commission'.[53] The only fly in the ointment for the moment was hostile reaction to the Commission's recommendations by the United Kingdom Alliance, which firmly advocated local veto as a means to prohibition.

[48] *BT*, 8 Apr. 1926, p. 263; *CYB* (1930), 114.

[49] *New Campaigner* (3rd quarter, 1925), 2, (1st quarter, 1927), 1, 3; *CYB* (1932), 147.

[50] *New Campaigner* (1st quarter, 1927), 5.

[51] *PAGAFCS* (1927), 636.

[52] *RGACS* (1927), 904.

[53] *New Campaigner* (1st quarter, 1932), 3–26, (2nd quarter, 1932), 4–7; NFCC Minutes of Executive Committee, 12 Feb. 1932, bk. 6, pp. 168–9; *CYB* (1933), 74, 156; *BH* (1933), 191–2; Campbell, 'Methodism', 69–72.

The year 1932 proved in fact to be one of considerable triumph for advocates of temperance. They were encouraged by conferences held to promote the Royal Commission's recommendations, and by services and pilgrimages to commemorate the Livesey centenary. The centenary, noted the temperance committee of the Congregational Union, provided new ground for a determined effort to achieve 'the removal from our midst of the curse of drink and the power of "the trade"'.[54] Shadows, however, were being cast over the movement by signs of reaction from an alarmed and shrinking drink trade. The temperance committee of the Church of Scotland General Assembly reported in 1931 that, while 'year by year intemperance becomes less and less obvious' and 'our streets are becoming freer and freer of the degrading sights due to indulgence in liquor', temperance propaganda was now being confronted 'by the frantic efforts of the liquor trade to popularize their beverages and, by means of attractive advertisements, to create a desire for intoxicating drink'. Nevertheless this committee remained confident: 'the fact that such efforts are now made affords the most gratifying testimony to the success of Temperance work'. The committee went on to indicate the large volume of this continuing work by stating that, for example, 1,659 meetings had been addressed by its agents in the past year.[55]

But, as the 1930s proceeded, the temperance movement was thrust on to the defensive. The price of beer was reduced in the 1933 Budget. From that year a large advertising campaign by brewers took effect, assisted by the emblazoning of their products on roadside hoardings to attract the attention of the increasing number of motorists. This was condemned by the NFCC's executive committee as 'a deliberate and systematic attempt to extend the beer-drinking habit amongst the young people of the nation'.[56] That this was no groundless fear was indicated by a public statement by Sir Edgar Sanders, Director of the Brewers' Society, that 'we want to get the beer-drinking habit instilled into thousands, almost millions, of young men who do not at present know the taste of beer'.[57]

[54] *CYB* (1932), 148.

[55] *RGACS* (1931), 603–4.

[56] NFCC Minutes of Executive Committee, 21 Sept. 1933, bk. 6, p. 223. Cf. *BH* (1934), p. 190.

[57] Quoted in *CYB* (1935), 183.

Clearly, in face of this threat, there was no room for complacency. Temperance advocates had to bestir themselves anew. Opposition to the brewers' initiative was shown, for example, by the recommendations of the Social and Industrial Commission of the National Church Assembly. These were summarized by the Bishop of London (Winnington-Ingram) at his diocesan conference in 1934 as 'the regulation of all registered clubs, the maintenance of the present restriction of the opening hours for public houses, the policy of "fewer and better" public houses, and the teaching of temperance and hygiene in the (State-aided) schools'.[58] Winnington-Ingram moved successfully in the Church Assembly that these recommendations be agreed to.[59] The Church of England *Guardian* newspaper singled out 'the rise of the clubs' as the main current problem for temperance reformers:

> It is most undesirable that public houses, which have been proved by experience to be indispensable and which might be made to serve a much more useful and respectable part in the social scheme, should be to any extent superseded by clubs. For public houses are subject to the strictest supervision; the clubs are subject to hardly any. The proprietor of a club has only to pay a registration fee of five shillings and liquor can then be 'supplied' to all the members without any necessity for a licence for the 'sale' of drink . . . What is happening now is extraordinarily unfair. The brewer and the publican are heavily taxed and stringently regulated, and if custom is regularly taken away from them by the unbridled clubs there will be no funds available for the improvement of public houses.[60]

The Baptist Annual Assembly similarly deplored that 'the Government is not prepared to take action in the immediate future to secure stricter control of Registered Clubs in spite of widespread dissatisfaction with the present state of the law'.[61] A bill to regulate the supply of alcohol in clubs was in fact rejected by the Lords in March 1939, with government approval though with the vocal opposition of Archbishop Lang and some other bishops.[62] Opposition was also voiced by denominational bodies to attempts to reduce the duties on spirits, and to the growth of the 'cocktail habit'

58 *G.*, 8 June 1934, p. 371.
59 Ibid., 29 June 1934, p. 424.
60 Ibid.
61 *BH* (1936), 219.
62 *New Campaigner* (Spring 1939), 3, 13–30.

as a fashionable pastime.[63] Along with such expressions came repeated calls to counter the menace of increased drinking and of growing convictions for drunkenness. These rises, it was assumed, were being encouraged by the brewers' campaign and by increased prosperity coming from the economic recovery of the mid-1930s.[64] The *Guardian* held in December 1935 that the brewers' campaign was threatening to undermine the good work of the TCCC during the twenty years of its existence—a period in which 'alcohol consumption has been reduced to less than half, and the convictions for drunkenness have been reduced to less than a quarter of the pre-war figures'.[65] The Church of Scotland temperance committee noted in 1936 that the consumption of beer was increasing (from 19,194,000 barrels in 1932 to 22,710,000 in 1935), as was that of spirits. This was 'a reversal of healthy progress'.[66] It was in fact the first turning of the tide in alcohol since the 1870s.

Thirty years later, in the 1960s, the non-medicinal use of alcohol was to be replaced by the non-medicinal use of drugs—with their potentially more dangerous effects—as the big social concern related to personal consumption. Already in the inter-war years a drugs problem was by no means overlooked in the discussions and resolutions of Church bodies. In 1924 the autumn assembly of the Congregational Union unanimously expressed the hope that forthcoming League of Nations conferences would 'save the world from the debauching conditions attending an over-production of opium and cocaine, estimated to be between ten and twenty times its legitimate needs'.[67] A report to the General Assembly of the Church of Scotland on the international drugs trade in 1931 said that it was now recognized as hopeless 'to stop the transit from country to country of morphine, cocaine, heroin, and similar drugs so long as their production is unrestricted'.[68] Even in the inter-war

[63] e.g. Church of Scotland Dundee Presbytery Minutes, 11 Mar. 1936, CH2/103/42, pp. 57–8, and Edinburgh Presbytery Minutes, 7 Apr. 1936, CH2/121/52, pp. 422–3; *RGACS* (1936), 509.

[64] NFCC Minutes of Executive Committee, 19 Sept. 1935, bk. 6, pp. 289–90.

[65] *G.*, 13 Dec. 1935, p. 854. Cf. ibid., 14 Feb. 1936, p. 104; *CYB* (1937), 226–7.

[66] *RGACS* (1936), 515. Cf. ibid. (1937), 626–7; *CYB* (1938), 192, (1939), 228–35; NFCC Minutes of Executive Committee, 23 Mar. 1936, bk. 6, p. 299; *BH* (1938), 261, (1939), 216; *New Campaigner* (Midsummer 1937), 8–9.

[67] *CYB* (1925), 57. Cf. Church of Scotland Dingwall Presbytery Minutes, 5 May 1920, CH2/92/15, p. 143.

[68] *RGACS* (1931), 569–70.

years drink was beginning to be rivalled by drugs as a matter of religious, and other, concern.

Cosmo Gordon Lang, Archbishop of York, said at a session of the Canterbury Convocation in 1928 (whither he and other bishops of the province of York had been invited) that intemperance was rapidly diminishing but that 'other things, notably and particularly gambling, were everywhere providing the excitement which people used to resort to drink to obtain'.[69] The suggestion that gambling was replacing drink as a popular (and potentially dangerous) pastime was commonly made in the 1920s—for example, by Bishop Winnington-Ingram in the Church Assembly in 1926. By the 1930s the danger was compounded when the continued spread of gambling was joined by an increase in drinking.

The Churches' message, as shown in resolutions of different denominations, was usually firmly against gambling, even of the petty variety which accounted for a good deal of such activity. The raffles which took place at many churches as a means of fund-raising were an embarrassment to the Churches' anti-gambling campaigns and preaching. Religious opinion was divided on the irritating matter of church raffles. While the *Church Times*, in a leading article against gambling, said that 'it is foolish to wax morally indignant over raffles at church bazaars', the Church and Nation Committee of the Church of Scotland called on churches to purge themselves of raffles; and Archbishop Temple said in 1932 that he urged his clergy to have no lotteries or raffles at their bazaars.[70]

But the Churches were concerned far less with small amateur instances of gambling than with the commercial kind which brought large profits to its promoters. Of larger-scale gambling of this kind the assemblies and newspapers of the British Churches were usually united in voicing disapprobation in this period; though the Roman Catholic Church, which invested regularly in lotteries in order to raise funds for its work, took a rather more lenient view.

An Anglican rector, in a letter to the press, gave three reasons for regarding betting as 'not only foolish but immoral'. It tended 'to

[69] *CCC*, 28 Mar. 1928, vii. 7, p. 16.

[70] *CT*, 11 Nov. 1932, p. 573; *RGACS* (1930), 445–6; F. A. Iremonger, *William Temple, Archbishop of Canterbury, his Life and Letters* (London, 1948; new impression, 1949), 445. Cf. *LW* (June 1925), 148–9.

make chance the rule of life, whereas the law of God is based upon order and design'; it encouraged the desire 'to get rich without effort, to make money without work'; and 'it teaches men to get their neighbour's goods without giving him any return'.[71] These arguments were similar to those put forward by Temple in an article of November 1927,[72] and were often advanced by clerical opponents of gambling. The sheer speed of the extension of gambling in the inter-war years was a matter of great concern, as were the spreading ramifications of the gambling industry because of its profitability—for example, the publication of betting information and tips in newspapers in order to sell more copies.[73] The Church and Nation Committee of the Church of Scotland reported to the General Assembly in May 1939 that:

> The Committee has had under consideration the inclusion of betting news in public libraries and is of opinion that all such news should be blacked out. Public libraries are intended to provide information, instruction and recreation for such as cannot afford to buy all the newspapers and periodicals they may wish to read. Their purpose is not to provide at the public expense facilities for those who wish to gamble. Experience shows that where betting news is not obliterated respectable citizens, in search of news or desirous of consulting advertisements, are hindered and prevented by others who crowd the files and loiter over them.[74]

In a social survey he published in 1931, *In the Heart of South London*, Bishop Garbett said that gambling had 'become a mania. In every street there is a bookmaker's tout who thrusts slips into the hands of passers-by and calls at every house.'[75] Canon Peter Green of Manchester wrote what was probably the most widely read denunciation of gambling in this period—*Betting and Gambling*, first published in 1925.[76] Another Anglican clergyman, R. C. Mortimer, later Bishop of Exeter, wrote *Gambling* in 1933, in which he took a more lenient view than Green, holding that gambling was a legitimate indulgence but that the State should restrict the opportunites for it in order to prevent dangerous

[71] Letter of Harold Bucke, *BW*, 3 June 1926, p. 178.
[72] Extract in TP 67, fo. 95.
[73] NFCC Minutes of Executive Committee, 26 Feb. 1923, bk. 5, p. 20.
[74] *RGACS* (1939), 522–3.
[75] Quoted in E. R. Norman, *Church and Society in England, 1770–1970* (Oxford, 1976), 348.
[76] Cf. H. E. Sheen, *Canon Peter Green: A Biography of a Great Parish Priest* (London, 1965), 89–90, 110–12.

excess.[77] Competing with Green for the place of best-known clerical opponent of gambling in this period was the Wesleyan Methodist Benson Perkins, author of *The Problem of Gambling* (1919) and Chairman of the Christian Social Council for twenty years from 1932. But the publications of individual clerics and ministers on gambling were only the more public reflection of numerous debates and resolutions in different Church assemblies.

Gambling spread so widely in the inter-war years mainly because of three developments—the rapid expansion of the football-pool business; the introduction and instant popularity of greyhound racing; and the appearance on racecourses of the Totalizator (or 'Tote') machine, which greatly speeded up the process of placing bets. Football pools were already flourishing by 1907, and began to spread much more widely in the early 1920s when the commercial entrepreneurship of John Moores (founder of Littlewoods at Liverpool) was applied to them. By the mid-1930s as many as ten million people did the football pools, spending £40 million annually on this by 1938.[78] The pools had become easily the biggest example of mass commercial betting in the country, and remained so until a National Lottery (abolished in 1823) was revived in 1994. So many people made their small contributions to the pools every week that, like giving something to a church raffle, the practice came to be regarded as above or beyond gambling. It was found in a survey published in 1951 that 'Mr F—was opposed to gambling on religious grounds, but did a football coupon every week because he did not regard it as gambling'.[79] Many members of Churches would have agreed with this attitude, but Church committees and assemblies sometimes strongly objected to football pools.[80]

Greyhound racing was by no means entirely new in the post-war world, but in the 1920s a new American variant which involved racing the dogs round a circuit rather than running them in a straight line proved much more popular than the latter system. In 1926 the first British circuit opened at Belle Vue pleasure park, Manchester, and in the following year the White City in London

[77] Norman, *Church and Society*, 349.

[78] R. Holt, *Sport and the British: A Modern History* (Oxford, 1989), 182–3; M. Clapson, *A Bit of a Flutter: Popular Gambling and English Society, c.1823–1961* (Manchester, 1992), 162 ff.

[79] Clapson, 175.

[80] e.g. Church of Scotland Dundee Presbytery Minutes, 8 Jan. 1936, CH2/103/42, pp. 29–30.

began to hold greyhound races. The new tracks mushroomed in the late 1920s, 'offering cheap gambling and a night out for ordinary working people who found it difficult to go to horse-racing'.[81] In 1927 a regulating body, the National Greyhound Association, was founded to promote the sport and prevent corrupt activities such as giving drugs to dogs and bribes to trainers. Annual attendances at licensed dog tracks throughout Great Britain reached thirty-eight millions in 1936, though the annual number of attenders (as opposed to attendances) was probably only a million.[82] In Scotland greyhound racing had become the second most popular spectator sport, after football, by the late 1930s.[83]

If dog racing was the poor man's horse racing, it also brought more gambling temptations for the poor man; and the Churches' anti-gambling forces reacted swiftly. A large interdenominational protest gathering in the Guildhall, London, in December 1927 gave rise, within a few days, to an interdenominational National Emergency Committee of Christian Citizens, formed in response to revelations of the 'moral peril associated with greyhound racing'.[84] Henry Carter, a leading Wesleyan temperance campaigner, turned his attention to gambling in *Facts about Greyhound Racing*, which he produced in 1928. This booklet publicized the aims of the new committee, including the adoption of local option to decide on whether tracks should be opened.[85] As early as September 1926, the General Secretary of the NFCC's executive committee drew attention to 'the new gambling menace' of the dog track, and in March 1928 this committee declared itself 'deeply impressed by the evils attendant upon greyhound and other similar racing'.[86] The Baptist Assembly in May 1928 voted unanimously to condemn 'the establishment of greyhound racing tracks with their open and continuous facilities for betting'.[87] Local action was sometimes taken in protest against dog racing. The Church and City Committee of the Church of Scotland presbytery of Edinburgh organized a

[81] Holt, *Sport*, 186.
[82] Clapson, *A Bit of a Flutter*, 146; P. Green, *Betting and Gambling* (2nd edn., London, 1935), 111.
[83] Clapson, *A Bit of a Flutter*, 146; Campbell, 'Methodism', 114.
[84] Campbell, 114.
[85] Ibid. 115–17.
[86] NFCC Minutes of Executive Committee, 23 Sept. 1926, bk. 5, p. 118; 26 Mar. 1928, bk. 6, p. 44.
[87] *BH* (1928), 200.

public meeting in January 1932 against 'the great civic and national menace' of gambling on dog races, and the Dundee presbytery agreed in 1937 to 'take all possible steps . . . to prevent the establishment of dog racing tracks within the bounds of the presbytery'.[88]

Anti-gambling opinion was opposed to the introduction of mechanical Totalizators on racetracks. They speeded the reception of bets, though they also threatened the livelihoods of bookmakers. Betting was expanding so quickly, however, that bookies seemed to survive in undiminished numbers in spite of the 'Tote'. 'Tote clubs' were another growing menace in the eyes of anti-gambling opinion. The NFCC executive committee resolved in 1932 that it regarded

> with the utmost gravity and concern the establishment in alarmingly increasing numbers of Tote and similar clubs throughout the country. These so-called clubs exist for the encouragement of betting and drinking and constitute a serious menace to the best interests of the community.[89]

Church assemblies which adopted anti-gambling resolutions naturally hoped to influence Governments to pass anti-gambling legislation. The Congregational Union assembly resolved in May 1925 to 'urge upon His Majesty's Government the necessity for such legislative and administrative reforms as would reduce this growing menace to national well-being'.[90] The Aberdeen presbytery of the Church of Scotland, fearful that children used as messengers to carry betting slips would be taught to bet through this practice, asked the General Assembly 'to take steps to promote legislation to prohibit children from carrying betting slips to bookmakers or to do what seemeth in their wisdom best'.[91]

But in their quest for legislation Church bodies had mixed fortunes, receiving some encouragement from government action but also some disappointment. In the early post-war years anti-gambling opinion was successful in objecting to the proposed sale of premium bonds to boost national revenue, but unsuccessful in objecting to a tax on betting. This tax, which was adopted in Winston Churchill's Budget of 1926, was seen as lending sanction

[88] Church of Scotland Edinburgh Presbytery Minutes, 6 Dec. 1932, CH2/121/51, p. 497; Dundee Presbytery Minutes, 7 Apr. 1937, CH/103/42, p. 200.

[89] NFCC Minutes of Executive Committee, 9 Dec. 1932, bk. 6, p. 196.

[90] *CYB* (1926), 6.

[91] Church of Scotland Aberdeen Presbytery Minutes, 31 Mar. 1925, CH2/1/28, p. 372.

and indeed dignity to a dubious pursuit.[92] In order to raise still more money from racing the Government passed a Racecourse Betting Bill in 1928, which was also condemned by anti-gambling opinion. The Wesleyan Conference said that the bill represented 'a strengthening of the vested interest in gambling' created by the State when it introduced the betting tax.[93] The betting tax was repealed in the Budget of 1929, but was replaced by higher licence duties on bookmakers and a tax on the profits gained through Totalizators.

In 1931 a Royal Commission on Lotteries and Betting, including ten representatives of the Christian Social Council (such as Temple and Benson Perkins), commenced its investigations. The Commission's report of June 1933 was followed by the introduction of a Betting and Lotteries Bill, passed in 1934. Opponents of gambling had stated, perhaps without a great deal of hope, what they wanted such a measure to achieve. The Church and Nation Committee of the Church of Scotland proposed in 1933 that Totalizators be prohibited except at horse races, and that Tote clubs should be made illegal.[94] Both of these reforms were recommended by the Royal Commission, together with severe restrictions on bookmakers' advertisements and other inducements to gambling. But the Church and Nation Committee well realized that legal provisions, although welcome, were not enough: 'Although legal enactments may control and regulate organized forms of gambling, the gambling instinct cannot be eradicated by legislation. Education and quickening of conscience in the Christian use of money are the only sure means of effecting improvement.'[95]

In any case, the Betting and Lotteries Act did not adopt the Commission's recommendation to ban Totalizators on dog tracks. Also—in what provided a clear loophole for the church raffle—small lotteries for charitable purposes were legalized. The

[92] e.g. Church of Scotland Edinburgh Presbytery Minutes, 26 Nov. 1919, CH2/121/36, p. 165; Dundee United Free Church Presbytery Minutes, 11 Apr. 1923, (CH3/91/18, p. 245); *BH* (1924), 189, (1927), 219–20; *CYB* (1924), 5; NFCC Minutes, 3 Mar. 1924, bk. 5, p. 48; 5 Feb. 1926, ibid. 89; 30 Apr. 1926, ibid. 100–1; *MR*, 22 Apr. 1926, p. 12; 29 Apr. 1926, p. 3; *BW*, 29 Apr. 1926, p. 94; 20 May 1926, p. 126; Campbell, 'Methodism', 99–110.

[93] Ibid. 113.

[94] *RGACS* (1933), 468–9.

[95] Ibid. 469.

Congregational Union assembly declared in May 1934 its regret 'that the Bill proposes to legalize such small lotteries as Bazaar Raffles'.[96] On the other hand, the Act pleased anti-gamblers by, for example, limiting both horse and dog betting to 104 days in the year and making it illegal for people under 18 to bet.[97] On account of these provisions, the Church and Nation Committee concluded that, while the Act included regrettable features, 'nevertheless it contains provisions that indicate a real advance in the curtailment of betting facilities and in the reduction of betting inducements'.[98] Church raffles continued to be firmly discouraged by some ecclesiastical authorities, despite the permission for them now clearly given by law.[99]

The Betting and Lotteries Act, through its even-handed distribution of stipulations, brought a certain equilibrium to the gambling scene. But it did not stop campaigns against gambling. Methodist opponents of gambling concentrated on attacking football pools for the rest of the 1930s, and fruitlessly called on the Government to prohibit them. In April 1936 A. J. Russell, a Liberal MP who was a Methodist, introduced a bill to ban football pools, but failed abysmally when the second reading was defeated by 311 votes to 24.[100] 'The vote was emphatic and must be accepted as such,' ruefully noted the Church of Scotland's Church and Nation Committee:

> Pool gambling is now a recognized business, splendidly organized, covering the entire country and employing hundreds of thousands of people . . . It is estimated that twenty million coupons are distributed by the leading firms each week, half of which are filled in and returned . . . (probably) one million pounds is 'invested' in Pools alone every week during the football season . . . This, of course, is but one aspect of the betting craze . . . Although there are now less than two hundred dog-racing tracks in the country, compared with over three hundred in 1932, some of these tracks are very prosperous, and the totalisator receipts are very considerable . . . On the whole, it cannot be maintained that much progress, if any, has been made in the effort to combat gambling.[101]

[96] *CYB* (1935), 68.
[97] *RGACS* (1935), 472–3, 512–15.
[98] Ibid. 472.
[99] Ibid. 473.
[100] Campbell, 'Methodism', 123–4.
[101] *RGACS* (1937), 513–14.

Other Church comment bore the same message. 'Gambling in England has gone merrily on its way during 1937,' said the Church of England *Guardian* in January 1938.

Horse-racing, greyhound-racing, football pools, and gaming machines draw their followers in ever-swelling crowds, and it is estimated that the total annual betting turnover in Great Britain is anything between three and five million pounds . . . the gambling spirit persists, and if it is checked by law at one point it finds its expression elsewhere: *sic ne perdiderit non cessat perdere lusor.*[102]

On this note it is appropriate to end an inquiry into the Churches and gambling in the inter-war years. 'The Church', said the Church of Scotland's Church and Nation Committee in 1939, 'must ever live a higher ethic than any Government can enforce or any public endorse . . . The attitude of the Church is that gambling is not only a coarse and uncultured practice, indicative of ethical insensitiveness, but also a direct denial of the spirit and example of Christ.'[103] Nevertheless, the more the Churches had preached against gambling, the wider had gambling spread. New opportunities, sporting and mechanical, had opened up for gambling, and had been exploited with rigorous commercial acumen. There was a poignant contrast, moreover, between the Churches' declining membership and attendance figures and the growing numbers betting at race courses and completing pools coupons. Such facts helped to make it appear, as Archbishop Lang said in 1936, that God was being crowded out.

Drinking and gambling, like reading and open-air pursuits, were time-honoured and regular contributors to the leisure which was increasing in the inter-war years, especially in the 1930s. Newer contributors to the leisure boom were the cinema and the radio (then more commonly called the 'wireless'). The cinema was the older of these, having become well established before 1914 and spreading further during the war. Its attractions were greatly increased by the introduction of sound films by 1929. Consequently the 1930s were marked by the formation and growth of large rival cinema-owning businesses, which built huge 'picture palaces' perhaps more distinguished for their comfort than for many of the

[102] *G.*, 7 Jan. 1938, p. 3. Cf. *RGACS* (1939), 523.
[103] *RGACS* (1939), 523–4.

films they showed. By 1939 annual cinema attendances reached 1,500 million. This represented attendance at least once a week by 40 per cent of the population—a figure which left the shrinking church attendance very far behind.

The cinema had attained its apogee, rivalled only by the radio as a popular diversion. Television was slowly developing as a broadcasting medium from 1936, when transmissions from Alexandra Palace in north London began. But the Second World War temporarily ended televised broadcasting, while the position of the cinema held firm during the conflict. Cinema attendances in fact reached their highest level in the later 1940s.[104] The revival and rapid expansion of television in the 1950s were to place cinema attendances on a declining curve, causing the frequent closure of cinemas. But in the 1930s the boast of Mark Ostrer, head of the British Gaumont organization, seemed quite believable: 'the cinema today is . . . so universal in its appeal that I doubt if television can stand up to it for a long time to come.'[105]

The Churches were deeply interested in the cinema and its moral and cultural effects, for reasons which comprised the question of Sunday opening (as has already been described); the treatment of sacred subjects on film; the use of film for spreading a religious message; and the impact of film on the general moral health of society.

The growth of film naturally came to involve the question of whether God and Christ could be represented in this medium, and if so in what form. Their representation in public plays performed in theatres was prohibited by the censoring powers of the Lord Chamberlain—though this did not, of course, extend to nativity and other religious plays performed in churches.[106] In regard to films, there was more uncertainty in this matter, as the censoring powers were in the hands of the British Board of Film Censors (a body appointed by the film industry, but conventional enough in its approach in the inter-war years) and the local councils, which could

[104] B. S. Rowntree and G. R. Lavers, *English Life and Leisure, a Social Study* (London, 1951), 228; J. Curran and V. Porter (eds.), *British Cinema History* (London, 1983), 375; J. Richards, *The Age of the Dream Palace: Cinema and Society in Britain, 1930–9* (London, 1984).

[105] Quoted in A. Briggs, *The History of Broadcasting in the United Kingdom*, i (London, 1961), 599.

[106] John Masefield to G. K. A. Bell, Dean of Canterbury, 5 Oct. 1927, BP 153, fo. 69.

decide whether or not to show films which had been passed for exhibition by the Board. The Public Morality Council, an interdenominational body whose president was the Bishop of London, Winnington-Ingram, sent a deputation in 1930 to Edward Shortt, President of the British Board of Film Censors, urging the 'reverential treatment of the presentation of Sacred Rites' on film.[107]

In the 1930s one film in particular caused anxiety in regard to these matters. This was *Green Pastures*, a film about the religious attitudes of black people in the USA, which included the representation of God as an old negro pastor. The play on which the film was based was banned by the Lord Chamberlain in 1930, but the film was publicly shown in 1936 after being endorsed by the Board of Film Censors. The showing aroused considerable religious dispute, widely differing reactions occurring. The executive committee of the NFCC decided in December 1936 that 'grave exception must be taken to such representation of the Deity upon the stage or in films, especially when such exhibitions are removed from the devotional atmosphere which may provide some justification for them, and are treated as an ordinary means of entertainment'.[108] In the same month three Congregational ministers at Preston declared that the film was 'sheer blasphemy' in a letter to the *Christian World*, their denominational newspaper. But another letter in reply, published in the same paper, said that the film was 'fundamentally reverent' and gave no dishonouring picture of God such as would justify an accusation of blasphemy.[109] The Moderator of the Free Presbyterian Church of Scotland asked Archbishop Lang to try and persuade the Board of Film Censors to withdraw its approval of the film. But Lang, though he had originally disapproved of the play, had now decided to accept both the play and the film. His chaplain told the Moderator that Lang had been impressed with the fact that 'many clergy of all denominations have spoken warmly of the good that the film may do'.[110]

Lang was naturally intolerant, however, of any film which deliberately mocked a religious ceremony, and in May 1937 he had to

[107] PMC, 31st Annual Report (1930), 11. See Machin, 'British Churches and the Cinema,' 477–80.

[108] NFCC Minutes of Executive Committee, 4 Dec. 1936, bk. 6, p. 317.

[109] *Christian World*, 3 Dec. 1936, p. 7 (letter from P. H. Goodwin *et al.*); 10 Dec. 1936, p. 8 (letter from C. F. Garden).

[110] A. C. Don to James McLeod (Moderator of the Free Presbyterian Church), 26 Jan. 1937, LP 16, fo. 11.

condemn a film which ridiculed the coronation service of King George VI. His chaplain wrote to the President of the Board of Film Censors:

It would be, in the Archbishop's opinion, deplorable if the deep impression made by the Coronation Service as broadcast over the wireless and as represented in the Coronation films should be impaired by the fact that sometimes on the very same evening this travesty of the Coronation Ceremony is thrown upon the screen.[111]

In 1938 Lang agreed with a decision by the London County Council not to permit the showing of a film on the life of Christ, *From the Manger to the Cross*. Altogether, by the end of the inter-war years the question of sacred portrayals on screen and stage had been by no means resolved, and it produced further controversy.

It was a common interdenominational opinion that film should be used to spread the Christian message. George Bell, Bishop of Chichester, who appointed the first diocesan Director of Religious Drama, authorized the first film service in an English cathedral in January 1938. Bell believed that 'through religious drama religious truth may be brought home afresh'.[112] The *Methodist Times and Leader* advocated that film be used for the purposes of religion. A Roman Catholic special committee was formed to consider the use of film in religion as well as the social effects of the cinema. A Baptist minister in Coventry said at the annual meeting of his congregation in 1933 that the cinema was 'that great gift of God which we in our blindness have allowed to get into the devil's hands. We must capture it for Christ's kingdom.'[113]

In March 1933 took place the inaugural meeting of the Cinema Christian Council. This was originally an Anglican body authorized by the Archbishops of Canterbury and York, and was presided over by the Bishop of Croydon (Edward Woods). Members included a wide spectrum of figures, such as Hewlett Johnson (the 'Red' Dean of Canterbury), the President of the Mothers' Union (Mrs Theodore Woods), and the rising Conservative Harold Mac-

[111] A. C. Don to Lord Tyrell, 26 May 1937, ibid., fo. 81.

[112] R. C. D. Jasper, *George Bell, Bishop of Chichester* (London, 1967), p. 121; *G.*, 7 Jan. 1938, pp. 3, 11; 14 Jan. 1938, p. 19; G. K. A. Bell, 'The Church and Religious Drama', in *Chichester Diocesan Gazette* (1938) (BP 155, fos. 9–10).

[113] *Methodist Times and Leader*, 14 Mar. 1935; Sir James Marchant to Archbishop Lang, 3 Feb. 1933, LP 14, fos. 22–5; C. Binfield, *Pastor and People: The Biography of a Baptist Church* (Coventry, 1984), 213.

millan. The Council aimed to promote 'the practical use and the development of the Cinema in the cause of religion, education, recreation, and social welfare at home and in our Dominions and Colonies', and to 'raise the moral and aesthetic standard of the cinema'.[114] The original Council did not last as long as a year, but it was revived in 1935 as an interdenominational organization. It now had some forty members, including representative Nonconformists such as Scott Lidgett (Methodist), Sidney Berry (Congregationalist), and M. E. Aubrey (Baptist). There were no Roman Catholic members, but Catholics began to take an interest in the Council's work and some of them attended its third summer school in 1938. But factionalism also developed. A breakaway Anglican group, the Church of England Film Society, was launched by Brian Hession, an Aylesbury clergyman, in 1937, and an Anglo-Catholic film group (the Seven Years' Association) also preferred to work on its own.[115]

In 1939 the Cinema Christian Council united with the Guilds of Light (a body with similar aims) and the Religious Film Society, whose main supporter was J. Arthur Rank, Methodist owner of the Rank Organization. The combined association was known as the Christian Cinema and Religious Film Society, and worked closely with a production company, Religious Films Limited.[116] The society encouraged the use of films by church organizations such as Mothers' Meetings, Girls' Friendly Societies, Scouts, and Guides. By 1942 the society could state that it had helped 700 churches to install film projectors and had gathered together a large film library. During the year 1941/2 it received 9,000 bookings for films.[117]

A wider concern about the moral quality of films shown in cinemas was central to the churches' social considerations. The nature of the worry was indicated by a report of the Church and Nation Committee to the Church of Scotland General Assembly in 1931, stating that the cinema could be a welcome counter-attraction to the public house, but could also be a bad influence on the young on account of the suggestiveness and the emphasis on materialistic

[114] Draft statement of Bishop of Croydon, Mar. 1933, LP 14, fos. 72–8; leaflet on Cinema Christian Council, 'private and confidential', ibid., fos. 82–3.

[115] *CT*, Jan. 1938, p. 3; 21 Jan. 1938, p. 55. See Machin, 'British Churches and the Cinema', 480–2.

[116] *The Christian Cinema and Religious Film Society*, undated leaflet, TP 24, fos. 20–1.

[117] Ibid.

values found in some films.[118] The same fears existed over plays and other stage productions: for example, a deputation saw the Lord Chamberlain in 1935 about the occurrence of semi-nudity on the stage.[119] The debates in the House of Commons on the Sunday Entertainments Bill in 1932 exemplified the expression of different views on the innocuousness or otherwise of the cinema film. John Buchan the novelist, who was Conservative MP for the Scottish Universities, said: 'The really vicious film is not very common . . . What we have to complain of much more is silliness and vulgarity . . . which may be a real danger if it results in a general degradation of the public taste and a communal softening of the brain.'[120] Sir Charles Oman, Conservative MP for Oxford University, said that 'the picture palace industry at present is very wickedly conducted', and the cinema trade's own British Board of Film Censors licensed a lot of empty, rotten, and deleterious material. He noted that an investigating committee in Birmingham had surveyed 285 films and found seventy-nine of them thoroughly objectionable. Over half of these 'objectionable' films had been licensed for showing to children as well as adults, including titles such as *One Mad Kiss*, *His Other Wife*, and *Too Hot for Paris*. But George Lansbury, leader of the Labour Party and former President of the Church Socialist League, said that Oman had 'read out a lot of silly nonsense' and that the cinemas should rather be commended for elevating the moral tone of the country:

> When I was a boy the things to go to were . . . sinks of iniquity, in the East End of London, where you could go for twopence and see and hear the foulest things possible. No cinema comes within a thousand miles of them, and to talk as people talk today, as if we were living in an age of downright vice and crime is an insult to the intelligence of the people.[121]

Lansbury thought that the cinema was silly but harmless, Buchan that it was silly and possibly harmful, and Oman that it was definitely harmful. Debate on whether films shown in the cinema (and on television) were damaging or not was even livelier in the 1960s and later, when the licence given to films was a great deal freer than in the relatively strait-laced 1930s. Even in the 1930s, however, a

[118] *RGACS* (1931), 552–5.
[119] NFCC Minutes of Executive Committee, 22 Feb. 1935, bk. 6, p. 270.
[120] Quoted in Machin, 'British Churches and the Cinema', 484.
[121] Quoted in ibid. 485.

considerable amount of concern was expressed by Church bodies about films which were 'debasing or immorally suggestive'.[122] The NFCC wanted a new censorship authority to be established, answerable to Parliament.[123] It seems fairly clear, however, that films which could definitely be regarded as immoral were few in number.

The Public Morality Council had both a stage-plays committee and a cinema committee. These were respectively responsible for examining the plays and the films shown in London. Complaints were made by the Council to the Lord Chamberlain about plays which were thought to be of a harmful tendency.[124] The Council employed critics to inspect 617 films in 1929, and was pleased to note that a great many of these films could be regarded as free from objection; though a number had been found to be morally dubious, 'treating marital infidelity as a matter of course' or being 'based on low life without any very strong tendency of an uplift character'.[125] In 1930, 599 films were seen, fifty-one of which were 'most unsatisfactory'. In that year, the cinema committee was glad to note that American producers (whose films formed a large majority of those shown on British screens) had issued a code which aimed to uphold the sanctity of marriage; to ban obscenity, undue exposure of the flesh, pointed profanity of language, and any reference to 'sex perversion'; and to ensure that 'ministers of religion . . . should not be used as comic characters or as villains'.[126] The Council found that it had less and less ground to complain about films as the 1930s went on. In 1937, portions of only twenty-six films, out of a total of 756 seen, were thought to demand protest.[127] By the end of the inter-war years the Churches—or bodies such as the Public Morality Council which were largely representative of the Churches—had little reason to think that the British cinema was a menace to morality and domestic stability.

Whereas the cinema was over twenty years old in 1918, public broadcasting was an innovation in the years following the war. The British Broadcasting Company was formed in 1922, and was

[122] *BH* (1933), 192, (1934), 195.
[123] NFCC Minutes of Executive Committee, 4 Apr. 1932, bk. 6, p. 173.
[124] PMC, 30th Annual Report (1929), 19–22.
[125] Ibid. 18.
[126] PMC, 31st Annual Report (1930), 11–18; Machin, 'British Churches and the Cinema', 487.
[127] PMC, 38th Annual Report (1937), 21–2.

replaced by the British Broadcasting Corporation in 1927. The new medium was as popular as the cinema in the inter-war years and later, though by the 1950s television was encroaching rapidly on the popularity of both. The number of wireless (radio) licences grew rapidly. On 1 January 1923 there were 25,744 licence holders, on 1 January 1927 there were 2,178,259, and on 1 September 1939 there were 9,082,666.[128]

In these early years of broadcasting there were few complaints from the Churches about the standard of programmes or the amount of time given to religion. In 1927, 2.25 hours of broadcasting per week were given to religious services, talks, and discussions, compared with 16.43 hours per week given to dance music. In 1930, 5.32 hours were given to religious broadcasts compared with 11.48 given to dance music.[129] Sir John Reith, General Manager of the British Broadcasting Company from December 1922 and Director-General of the British Broadcasting Corporation from 1927 to 1938, wished to spread not only good taste by means of the radio but the Christian message as well. 'I must take Christ with me from the very beginning and all through this difficult work . . . I can do all things through Christ,' he wrote on 28 December 1922, just after assuming his leading role in the new organization.[130] Reith told Archbishop Temple in a letter of 20 June 1930 that he was 'more anxious about the general religious policy of the BBC in matters great and small than about anything else'.[131] The first Advisory Committee of the BBC was concerned with religious broadcasts. This was the Central Religious Advisory Committee (CRAC). After a meeting in March between Reith and Archbishop Davidson, the Committee was formed and first met in May 1923. Bishop Garbett had been appointed by Davidson as chairman. By 1931 the Committee had fourteen members representing the main denominations—seven Anglicans, five Nonconformists, and two Roman Catholics. Each regional broadcasting station also had its religious advisory committee. In 1933 F. A. Iremonger, later Dean of Lichfield, became the first Religious Director of the BBC and held that office successfully for six

[128] A. Briggs, *The History of Broadcasting in the United Kingdom*, ii (London, 1965), 6, 450.

[129] Ibid. 35.

[130] C. Stuart (ed.), *The Reith Diaries* (London, 1975), 128–9.

[131] Briggs, *History*, ii. 227.

years.[132] The early favour won by religious broadcasting owed a great deal to the vigorous preaching style of H. R. L. (Dick) Sheppard, who from January 1924 conducted an undenominational broadcast service from St Martin's-in-the-Fields parish church in central London every second Sunday in the month. Reith much appreciated his efforts because his Christianity was centred on 'the application of the teaching of Christ to everyday life'.[133] 'We have tried', Reith said in a speech in January 1927 when the Corporation commenced, 'to reflect that spirit of common-sense Christian ethics which we believe to be a necessary component of citizenship and culture'.[134]

In January 1931 the two Houses of Canterbury Convocation passed resolutions recording 'grateful appreciation of the service rendered to the cause of religion by the BBC'.[135] 'The British Broadcasting Corporation deserves our gratitude for the admirable manner in which it attunes itself to the Church's seasons,' said the *Guardian*. 'The Christmas programmes are always happily and reverently devised and the same may be said for those at Easter.'[136] But there was a desire by some for more dogmatic religious broadcasts than came, for example, from the St Martin's-in-the-Fields services. The Roman Catholic Archbishop of Liverpool (Richard Downey) called in 1931 for a less 'emasculated Christianity' on the radio, and for the broadcast of 'very definite doctrines so long as this is done without denunciation of other creeds'.[137] A Roman Catholic Radio Guild was founded in 1935 to try and obtain more Catholic services, and some supporters of the Guild wanted a separate Catholic radio station. On the other hand, ultra-Protestants felt that Roman Catholics had too much time on the air already.[138] The Bishop of Southampton, Arthur Karney, expressed the view in 1935 that 'wireless services give inoculation of the mildest form of Christianity yet discovered'.[139]

[132] K. M. Wolfe, 'Christianity and the BBC, 1922–51: The Politics of Sacred Utterance', Ph.D. thesis (London, 1982), 12.

[133] Ibid. 70–81.

[134] Briggs, *History*, ii. 228, 237; J. C. W. Reith, *Into the Wind* (London, 1949), 116.

[135] Briggs, *History*, ii. 239; *CCC*, 21 Jan. 1931, viii. 4, pp. 52–62 (cf. ibid., 19 Jan. 1933, ix. 3, pp. 208–9).

[136] *G.*, 17 Apr. 1936, p. 267.

[137] Briggs, *History*, ii. 238.

[138] Ibid. 240.

[139] Ibid.

Apart from what some thought the excessive blandness of religious broadcasting, there was the contradictory complaint that some programmes permitted too free an expression of personal religious views.[140] A complaint was made by the Aberystwyth Free Church Council about Sabbath-breaking on the radio by the broadcasting of a talk on gardening at 2 p.m. every Sunday (a predecessor of the present *Gardeners' Question Time*). On this incident the *Church Times* commented that very good men could be very silly men, and thought it deplorable to 'make a public and entirely ridiculous criticism of the engagement of an expert to explain on Sunday afternoons how best the amateur gardener can prune his mulberry bushes'.[141] The Baptist Annual Assembly felt impelled to object, by unanimous resolution in 1938, to 'some needless vulgarisms in speech' in some of the radio programmes, 'and a tendency to fall back on drink as a staple theme of merriment'.[142]

There were other complaints of a similar kind—for example, in the correspondence of Archbishop Lang.[143] But such complaints were few, and in general there was a harmony between the Churches and broadcasting in the Reith era which was in sharp contrast to the argument which developed in the Greene era thirty years later. The *Universe* aptly summarized the situation in the 1930s:

Catholic listeners have various complaints to make, but so, probably, has every other section of the public. Considering the enormous diversity of interests in a country like this and the enormous complexity of the BBC's work, we should think that the Corporation on the whole does very well. It is doubtful if any country in the world has so good a service, taken all round.[144]

While there were expressions of gratitude for the BBC's aid to the cause of religion, there was also concern that the new broadcast services should not become a substitute for traditional churchgoing. The necessity of maintaining corporate public worship was emphasized in the same resolution of the Canterbury Convocation

140 *CCC*, 21 Jan. 1931, viii. 4, p. 60.

141 *CT*, 27 Nov. 1936, p. 611.

142 *BH* (1939), 215.

143 Miss Janet Algar to Lang, 1 Mar. 1939, LP 168, fo. 1; Sir Stephen Tallents to A. C. Don, 16 Mar. 1939, ibid., fos. 3–5; Don to Sir John Tallents, 18 Mar. 1939, ibid., fo. 7.

144 *U.*, 24 Dec. 1936, p. 12. Cf. A. Peel, *Thirty-Five to Fifty* (London, 1938), 145, 165–7.

which thanked the BBC for its religious efforts.[145] It was difficult to say whether broadcast services kept people away from church, for it was not known how many of the listeners were (or had been) churchgoers. A survey conducted by Seebohm Rowntree indicated that half of the respondents listened to a religious broadcast each week and that they believed that radio was taking religion to many people who seldom, if ever, attended public worship.[146] Similarly Donald Soper, a young Methodist religious broadcaster and Superintendent of the West London Mission, believed that radio preaching was very valuable as a means of spreading the Gospel to the millions who were outside the Churches.[147] 'There was no question of competition between the BBC and the Church,' stated Canon E. G. Selwyn.[148] It also seemed clear, however, that broadcast services were doing hardly anything to revive churchgoing. Canon Selwyn believed they were in danger of creating 'a kind of passive worshipper, who obviously gave only a small part of what worship meant'.[149]

Cinema and broadcasting may have represented *par excellence* the notable leisure wave of the inter-war years, but so to some degree did increasing car ownership. There were 139,000 private cars on British roads in 1915, and 2,034,000 in 1939.[150] Between 1945 and 1995—a period twice as long—there has been about the same rate of increase in motor traffic as in the inter-war years. Britons in the 1920s and 1930s were very conscious of an enormous increase in the volume of motorized vehicles. They, and not least Church bodies, were also very conscious of the increase in motor accidents, which often occurred because of excessive drinking.[151] The Temperance Committee of the Congregational Union noted that many accidents would be avoided if drivers abstained from

[145] *Year Book of the National Assembly of the Church of England* (1932), 180; *CCC*, 21 Jan. 1931, viii. 4, p. 57.

[146] M. Pegg, *Broadcasting and Society, 1918–39* (London, 1983), 162–3.

[147] *CT*, 27 May 1938, p. 631.

[148] Speech in Lower House of Convocation of Canterbury, 13 Feb. 1930, *CCC*, viii. 2, p. 112.

[149] Ibid. 113.

[150] *The Longman Handbook of Modern British History, 1714–1987*, ed. C. Cook and J. Stevenson (2nd edn., London, 1988), 222–3.

[151] For the growing importance of traffic accidents from the beginning of the century to 1939, see C. Emsley, '"Mother, what *did* policemen do when there weren't any motors?" The Law, the Police, and the Regulation of Motor Traffic in England, 1900–39', *Historical Journal*, 36 (1993), 357–81.

drinking.[152] In 1934, nearly a quarter of a million people were killed or injured on the roads of Great Britain.[153]

A report on road safety by the Church of Scotland's Church and Nation Committee to the 1937 General Assembly gave a fairly typical summary of Christian concern over this matter:

> There are many indications that the Government is awake to road dangers and anxious for their diminution, by encouraging the widening and straightening of roads, by the establishment of the speed limit in built-up areas, by the multiplication of lights and sign-posts, by the institution of pedestrian crossings, and the circulation of the Highway Code, it has taken the readiest means at its disposal to make the roads safer for all ... [But] the problem of road safety will not be solved until the selfish spirit, which is responsible for so many accidents, is eliminated. It is the concern of the Church through all her agencies to do what she can to effect this purpose ... the best service can be rendered by ministers and office-bearers striving to foster this spirit of unselfishness.[154]

Two years before this, the Church and Nation Committee had suggested that ministers of the Church be requested to refer to this matter in public worship.[155] A motion of 1938 in Canterbury Convocation by Cyril Garbett (now Bishop of Winchester), carried unanimously, called on all Christian citizens to strive to arouse the national conscience to the loss of life and the suffering caused by road accidents.[156]

Aspects of leisure, both old and new, were thus of continuous concern to the Churches in the inter-war years. So, too, were other matterns which affected personal behaviour, notably the expansion of birth control and the extension of the grounds for divorce.

In regard to birth control there was, as we have already seen, some diversity in the attitudes of different Churches by 1918. Although there had been no papal declaration on the subject,[157] authoritative statements against the use of artificial methods of contraception had been made by the Roman Catholic Church. It had been made clear, however, in evidence to the National Birth

[152] *CYB* (1937), 189.
[153] *RGACS* (1935), 471.
[154] Ibid. (1937), 528–9. Cf. *BH* (1939), 216; *PAGAFCS* (1935), 194.
[155] *RGACS* (1935), 471.
[156] *CCC*, 20 Jan. 1938, i. 3, p. 135.
[157] Father Henry Davis, SJ, to Marie Stopes, 6 and 21 July 1928, SP BL Add. MS 58553 (unfoliated when seen).

Rate Commission in 1913, that the Roman Catholic Church did not object to use of the 'safe period'.[158] Nonconformist Churches, on the other hand, had not attempted to restrict individual freedom of conscience on the matter of using artificial methods. The Church of Scotland did not make a specific authoritative declaration on birth control until 1960, when it confirmed the support of freedom of conscience which its members had long believed its position to represent. The clear declaration against using artificial birthcontrol methods—but not against using the 'safe period'—made by the Anglican bishops at the Lambeth Conference of 1908 was repeated at the next Lambeth Conference in 1920. But at the subsequent Conference in 1930 a resolution was carried by 193 votes to 67 giving a cautious permission to the use of artificial methods in special circumstances related to the personal needs of married couples. It was made clear that abstinence from such methods was still preferred, but the barrier for Anglicans had been officially broken—freedom of conscience could now be employed. This signified the beginning of division between the Roman and Anglican Churches over the issue, adding to the division already existing between the Roman and Nonconformist Churches. Until that point, Rome and Canterbury had appeared united on the question, opposing artificial methods but permitting use of the 'safe period'. But thenceforth they were divided, and the Roman Catholic Church became isolated over the matter among ecclesiastical organizations in Great Britain. Hensley Henson described the 1930 resolution as a decisive breach with ecclesiastical tradition.

Marie Stopes, founder of the Society for Constructive Birth Control and editor of the *Birth Control News*, was the leading campaigner for artificial contraception in inter-war Britain. She based her efforts not merely on 'neo-Malthusian' anxiety about population growth (within inter-war Britain there was rather a concern about population decline) but mainly on the glories of human love generated by the intense physical oneness obtained by the intercourse of a married couple in an atmosphere of freedom.[159] Her

[158] R. A. Soloway, *Birth Control and the Population Question in England, 1877–1930* (Chapel Hill, NC, 1982), 237–8.

[159] M. Stopes, *A New Gospel to All Peoples: A Revelation of God Uniting Physiology and the Religions of Man* (London, 1920), 16–17; Soloway, *Birth Control*, 236–7.

seminal book *Married Love*, published in 1918 (and followed by *Wise Parenthood* in the same year), justified her approach to the subject and showed her regard for convention by stressing that she wished to spread the contraceptive message only among the married. Such exclusiveness was, of course, impossible to uphold in practice, and not the least of the weapons of her critics was the accusation that her message would undermine marriage.

Stopes's first birth-control (or 'family-planning') clinic was opened in 1921. By 1939 there were sixty-five such clinics run by the Family Planning Association (formerly the National Birth Control Council).[160] It appeared in 1918 that Stopes might win the support even of Roman Catholics, as she received some praise for *Married Love* from this quarter. But her hopes in this direction were soon dashed as it became clear that she would meet only opposition from the Roman Catholic Church. In March 1919 Stopes wrote that she found that Church's attitude to her campaign 'deplorable'—a description that she was also inclined to extend to the Anglican response at this time.[161] She had some Anglican supporters immediately after the war, however, including Dean Inge and Hewlett Johnson. Temple later gave a cautious approval to her aims, and by the early 1930s perhaps her clearest Anglican champion was Canon Percy Dearmer, an Anglo-Catholic who harboured deep suspicions of the Roman Catholic Church.[162] But other leading Anglicans such as Davidson, Gore, and Winnington-Ingram were against her, and the pronouncement of the Lambeth Conference in 1920 was clearly negative.[163]

The attitude of Roman Catholic priests among Stopes's correspondents was also, it was now being shown, clearly averse to her efforts. 'A friend has lent me *Wise Parenthood* and *Married Love*,' wrote a Jesuit, F. M. de Zulueta, in October 1919. 'I had hoped that no woman would write such books . . . It appears to me that a

[160] M. Abendstern, 'Expression and Control: A Study of Working Class Leisure and Gender, 1918–39—a Case Study of Rochdale Using Oral History Methods', Ph.D. thesis (Essex, 1986), 78.

[161] Stopes to F. M. de Zulueta, SJ, 18 Mar, 1919, SP BL Add. MS 58553, unfoliated when seen; Soloway, *Birth Control*, 244–6.

[162] Johnson to Stopes, 14 Sept. 1919, SP BL Add. MS 58551, unfoliated when seen; Temple to Stopes, 30 Nov. 1929, ibid.; Dearmer to Stopes, 3 Mar. 1933, ibid., BL Add. MS 58549, fo. 82. For Inge's opinions, see Norman, *Church and Society*, 336.

[163] Davidson to Stopes, 23 Oct. and 11 Dec. 1922, SP BL Add. MS 58551; Stopes to Gore, 9 Feb. 1927, ibid.

pagan might have written as you do, though he would probably not have quoted the Word of God.'[164] Stopes replied that she was a Quaker, and that her books in no way conflicted with Christ's teaching. But her correspondent rejoined that she was in 'grave and unnatural sin', and in clear conflict with what, as a Catholic, he believed to be 'the only genuine Church'.[165] De Zulueta's opinion of Stopes's writings did not improve. He told her in 1920 that a pamphlet she had written and sent to him was 'a most profane compound of imaginary mysticism and pornography'.[166] In 1922 Stopes sued Halliday Sutherland, a medical practitioner and recent convert to Catholicism, for libel on account of allegations he had published that she was exploiting the position of the poor in order to spread her methods. She initially lost the case, then won on appeal, but lost again when Sutherland appealed to the House of Lords. Cardinal Bourne, Archbishop of Westminster, gave £400 to aid Sutherland's case. The case advertised Stopes's conflict with the Roman Catholic Church as well as winning abundant publicity for her birth-control campaign.[167] Sutherland formed the League of National Life in 1926 as an interdenominational association against artificial contraception. Stopes's contest with Rome continued, but it was not always acerbic. In 1928 she wrote to the Jesuit Henry Davis about his book entitled *Birth Control, the Fallacies of Dr Marie Stopes*: 'it is a great improvement compared with the usual attack upon me by your co-religionists, and I am glad to be the object of serious thought by Roman Catholics.'[168] But Stopes and Rome remained diametrically opposed in their standpoints. A code of social principles published by the Catholic Social Guild in 1929 stated that 'birth prevention, the cause of depopulation, is essentially immoral, and moreover makes for the certain ruin of nations'.[169]

[164] De Zulueta to Stopes, 7 Oct. 1919, SP BL Add. MS 58553.

[165] Stopes to de Zulueta, 11 Oct. 1919, ibid.; de Zulueta to Stopes, 15 Oct. 1919, ibid.

[166] De Zulueta to Stopes, 9 July 1920, ibid.

[167] Soloway, *Birth Control*, 246–8. Cf. H. G. Sutherland, *Birth Control: A Statement of Christian doctrine against the Neo-Malthusians* (London, 1922); R. Hall, *Marie Stopes, a Biography* (London, 1977), 213–41, 256ff.

[168] *T.*, 22 May 1926, pp. 645–6; Stopes to Davis, 7 June 1928, SP BL Add. MS 58553; also 30 June and 18 July 1928, ibid.; Davis to Stopes, 8 June, 6 and 21 July 1928, ibid.

[169] *A Code of Social Principles* (Catholic Social Guild Year Book, Oxford, 1929), 35.

Stopes eventually received more encouragement from the Church of England as it became willing to tolerate artificial contraception. She deliberately engaged in correspondence with Anglican clergy and Nonconformist ministers, seeking their approval and frequently gaining it, though also meeting a good deal of hostility.[170] Her more favourable clerical correspondents sometimes emphasized their desire to help the poor by making contraceptive devices more readily available and distributing pamphlets advocating their use.[171] 'I have several parishioners, poor but with large families, whom I am desirous to help with advice about contraceptive methods,' wrote a vicar at Ashton-under-Lyne to the Secretary of the Society for Constructive Birth Control and Racial Progress. 'I should like to give each of them a medium sized Pro-Race rubber cap as recommended by M. Stopes, and directions for using it.'[172] Another clerical correspondent assured Stopes that she had 'lots of supporters and friends' among Anglo-Catholic clergy and laity.[173]

Some Nonconformist ministers were enthusiastic supporters of Stopes's mission.[174] But the Free Church of Scotland took up a position on the issue which, paradoxically, linked it more clearly to the Roman Catholics than to any other Christian body, condemning books which advocated birth control as 'pernicious and impure literature'.[175] Some leading Congregationalists were grudging in their acceptance of artificial contraception. A. E. Garvie said he had a strong repugnance to the practice though he could not condemn it, and R. F. Horton told Stopes that he preferred moral restraint to artificial methods.[176] James Barr, a Scottish United Free Church minister who was Labour MP for Motherwell, said in the

[170] Soloway, *Birth Control*, 240–1; SP BL Add. MSS 58550, 58551.

[171] e.g. Herbert Bindley to Stopes, 11 Apr. 1922, ibid. 58551 (unfoliated when seen).

[172] R. W. Cummings to Secretary of CBC Society, 21 May 1923, ibid. Cf. P. Youlden Johnson to Stopes, 2 Apr. 1924, ibid. 58549, fos. 26–7; W. Owen to Stopes, 17 June 1926, ibid. 58551; J. Lask to Stopes, 23 Aug. 1926, ibid.; G. C. Hutt to Stopes, 5 Feb. 1938, ibid. 58554, fo. 194.

[173] R. Godfrey to Stopes, 24 Feb. 1933, ibid. 58552.

[174] Soloway, *Birth Control*, 240.

[175] *PAGAFCS* (1926), 251; also ibid. (1927), 635–6. Cf. D. Maclean, *The Counter-Reformation in Scotland, 1560–1930* (London, 1931), 282.

[176] A. E. Garvie, *Memories and Meanings of my Life* (London, 1938), 245; R. F. Horton to Stopes, 20 June 1929, SP BL Add. MS 58554, fo. 154; Principal W. B. Selbie to Stopes, 18 Feb. 1922, ibid. 58551.

Commons in 1926 that the deliberate thwarting of conception was an immoral affront to God.[177]

During the 1920s the argument over birth control emerged in many different places. These included Copec and the counsels of the Labour Party. A frank discussion took place in the proceedings of Copec, on 8 April 1924, when Miss M. E. Roach, representing the Winchester diocesan conference, asked: 'how, if the Church is going to approve the use of contraceptives within the bond of marriage, can it forbid and condemn their use outside marriage?'[178] The Labour Party was, perhaps, particularly susceptible to divisions over contraception because it had a large Catholic element as well as a vocal liberationist one. The latter included the Workers' Birth Control Group and the National Conference of Labour Women. The Labour Government of 1924 refused to agree that the rate-aided dispensation of contraceptives could be given at government welfare centres. But in 1925 the National Conference of Labour Women voted in favour of this subsidized assistance by the huge majority of 876 to 6. Some Catholic delegates supported the resolution, though Catholic opinion at the Conference was clearly divided.[179] The Labour Party Conference in 1927 took a contrary view, by defeating, by over two million votes, a resolution in favour of rate-aided birth-control assistance at welfare centres. At the Conference a veteran defender of Catholic principles, James Sexton (a former Liverpool docker who was now an MP), hinted at damaging defections from the party by saying that Catholic electors, most of whom usually voted Labour, would not agree with Labour support of artificial birth control. In the following year even the National Conference of Labour Women was persuaded to reverse its stand and support the party leadership, by the very narrow margin of 257 votes to 254.[180] By 1930, however, about fifty local authorities were demanding the right to decide for themselves whether birth-control assistance could be given in government centres. This met strong Catholic resistance, and there were threats of political action against these authorities.[181] At a by-election at North Lanark in 1929, it was alleged that Catholics had been

[177] Soloway, *Birth Control*, 290.
[178] *The Times*, 9 Apr. 1924, p. 9.
[179] Soloway, *Birth Control*, 288.
[180] Ibid. 295–6.
[181] Ibid. 309.

advised to vote Liberal because the Labour candidate, Jennie Lee (the future wife of Aneurin Bevan), was not clearly opposed to birth control. Miss Lee, however, won the contest by a substantial margin.[182]

Resolution 15 of the Lambeth Conference of 1930 gave a tentative approval to individual decision in the use of artificial contraception, provided the decision to use such methods came from a sense of 'moral obligation' and 'Christian principles'.[183] Resolution 18 of the same conference, however, urged the need for legislation to forbid the display of contraceptives for purposes of sale, and to restrict the ways in which contraceptives could be advertised and the extent to which they could be sold to the public. This resolution reflected recent expressions of concern by religious bodies,[184] and was clearly intended to soften the blow of 'betrayal'—as many Anglicans would regard the substance of resolution 15. After the conference, Lang told the Lower House of Canterbury Convocation that the bishops had acted 'in the presence of a great and growing change, almost revolution, in the customs of married life throughout the whole world'.[185] This acknowledged the importance of changes in social behaviour in guiding the episcopal decision; and this attitude was also shown by Lang and other bishops over the matter of extending divorce provisions a few years later. But it was an attitude that was firmly rebutted by the Roman Catholic Church. Cardinal Bourne said that the bishops at the Lambeth Conference had 'abdicated any claim which they might have been thought to possess to be authorized exponents of Christian morality'. Pope Pius XI's encyclical of December 1930, *Casti Conubii*, endorsed this statement by confirming the Catholic Church's revulsion from the 'grave sin' of using artificial contraception.[186]

Anglican and Nonconformist opinion continued to be divided internally on the use of contraceptive methods. Some Anglican bishops, including Henson and Winnington-Ingram, remained firmly opposed to artificial birth control. Lord Hugh Cecil, an An-

[182] *Scotsman*, 23 Nov. 1929 (quoted in C. Burness, 'The Long Slow March: Scottish Women MPs, 1918–45', in E. Breitenbach and E. Gordon (eds.), *Out of Bounds: Women in Scottish Society, 1800–1945* (Edinburgh, 1992), 167.

[183] Norman, *Church and Society*, 347; Soloway, *Birth Control*, 251–2.

[184] Ibid. 251.

[185] Quoted in ibid. 253. Cf. *T.*, 11 Oct. 1930, p. 1.

[186] Soloway, *Birth Control*, 254; M. Stopes, *Roman Catholic Methods of Birth Control* (London, 1933), 85–7.

glo-Catholic and a leading Conservative politician, wrote memoranda denouncing resolution 15 of the Lambeth Conference for encouraging moral relativism. The decision seemed to imply, he said, that sexual intercourse using contraceptive methods was 'chaste or unchaste according to the circumstances and motives':

> to make the chastity of sexual intercourse depend not on its own character but on circumstances and motives is, I believe, unknown to Christian moral teaching. If consideration of circumstances and motives be allowed to determine the chastity of contraceptive intercourse, why not also fornication and adultery? I suggest the conclusion that contraceptive intercourse is always, in all circumstances and prompted by whatever motive, unchaste. Circumstances and motives may sometimes immensely mitigate the guilt of the unchastity, they may almost completely excuse it. But however venial its guilt may sometimes be, contraceptive intercourse is always unchaste.[187]

The view of some non-Christians, such as Bertrand and Dora Russell, that the morality of sexual intercourse depended on circumstance was, Cecil held, fundamentally opposed to the traditional Christian view that there is 'a distinct virtue of chastity'. The Lambeth bishops themselves had greatly weakened this traditional view by means of their declaration. They were to some extent 'agreeing with the anti-Christian propaganda of our time'.[188] Cecil's opinion elicited replies which defended the bishops' resolution. An anonymous respondent stated that 'the whole development of humanity depends upon the use and progressive adaptation of "natural" discoveries for men's highest ends', and that these beneficial discoveries included artificial contraceptive methods—'it cannot seriously be argued that any "artificial" or "external" interference with men's bodily functions is immoral'.[189] The Bishop of Blackburn (P. M. Herbert) argued that a physical act, such as sexual intercourse, could not have a moral or 'chaste' character in itself: 'clearly no act has a moral character . . . *in vacuo*: it gains its moral character from its setting, which includes motives and circumstances.'[190] Thus there was developing among Christians an argument over moral relativism which was to become much more intense in the 1960s, particularly on account of the development of

[187] Memos. by Lord Hugh Cecil, 30 Sept. 1930, LP 104, fos. 370–1.
[188] Ibid., fos. 376–7, 380.
[189] Ibid., fo. 386.
[190] Ibid. fo. 388.

the contraceptive pill and a considerable growth of scepticism about marriage.

Moral traditionalists may have been depressed by the Lambeth resolution, but those who favoured the use of artificial contraception were naturally encouraged by it. Anglican clergy among the latter became more confident in their requests for information from Marie Stopes. The Church of Scotland magazine *Life and Work* praised the Lambeth decision:

> for the first time the Anglican Church has declared that under certain conditions the use of scientific methods is permissible. The burden of decision is left on the individual conscience, and it may well rest there. An enlightened Christian conscience is the strongest protection of morality, and will find the true line of conduct where a hard-and-fast rule may be thoroughly misleading.[191]

Medical opinion was becoming more favourable to Stopes's campaign during the 1930s. Some leading doctors, such as Lord Dawson of Penn and Sir Thomas Horder, had been firmly on her side for a considerable time. In 1936 Dundee became the first branch of the British Medical Association to link itself formally with a family-planning clinic.[192] Advocates of artificial contraception who gave evidence to a Convocation committee on marriage in May 1932 were only sorry that the bishops had not given more decisive support to the spread of contraceptive methods.[193]

The other Lambeth resolution on contraception, number 18, which urged the desirability of restricting the advertisement and sale of contraceptive devices, also obtained much support, not least from the PMC. That body's Birth Prevention Accessories Committee had already recommended in 1929 that steps be taken (including attempts to obtain parliamentary legislation) to prohibit the display of these accessories in shop windows and public places, lest they endanger public morals.[194] Following the Lambeth resolution, a member of the Council, Frederick Hawkes, Bishop of Kingston, agreed to become chairman of this Committee in order to strengthen liaison with the relevant committee of the Lambeth Conference.[195]

[191] *LW* (1930), 449–50.
[192] Soloway, *Birth Control*, 316.
[193] Ibid.
[194] PMC, 30th Annual Report (1929), 25.
[195] PMC, 31st Annual Report (1930), 24.

The increasing display and advertisement of contraceptives continued to be a matter of concern. This is shown by a resolution of the Lower House of York Convocation in January 1932 that the Home Office and the Post Office should be urged to act in the direction of prevention or restriction. This resolution in turn brought a protest from Marie Stopes against 'repressive action' which could do 'nothing but harm'; though she also said that she had long been an active and effective opponent of 'the abominable behaviour of commercial firms' in urging purchase of their contraceptive products.[196] During 1933 the PMC planned a parliamentary bill to restrict the sale, display, and advertisement of contraceptives, and this was amended after discussion with the Church of England Advisory Board. In December the bill was introduced by Lord Devon in the House of Lords and it passed that House in March 1934, but failed to make progress in the Commons and was eventually withdrawn.[197] Several other bills with this aim were drawn up by the PMC in the remainder of the decade, receiving support from Roman Catholic, Anglican, and Nonconformist leaders. One of these was brought into Parliament, being introduced by Richard Russell in 1938, but, although it received a second reading, it was unsuccessful.[198]

The question of dispensing contraceptives by automatic machines was the subject of correspondence involving the Archbishop of Canterbury, the Bishops of Ripon and Kingston, and Lord Dawson of Penn. In January 1933 the Bishop of Kingston said that automatic slot machines had been deleted from the PMC's proposed bill, because only one instance of the use of such a machine for dispensing contraceptives had been discovered and this had been stopped by the police. But the Bishop of Ripon (E. A.

[196] *Year Book of the National Assembly of the Church of England* (1933), 185; Stopes to Revd E. T. Kerby 4 and 13 Feb. 1932 (copies in SP BL Add. MS 58552, unfoliated when seen).

[197] PMC, 34th Annual Report (1933), 7–8, and 35th Annual Report (1934), 7–8; Howard Tyrer (Secretary of PMC) to A. C. Don (chaplain to Lang), 27 Nov. 1933, LP 116, fos. 186–7; Lang to Lord Dawson (memo. of meeting between them), 13 Dec. 1933, ibid., fo. 203; Lang to Bishop Winnington-Ingram, 22 Dec. 1933, ibid., fo. 214; Dawson to Lang, 22 Dec. 1933 (enclosing draft of bill), ibid., fos. 215–16; Lang to Dawson, 23 Dec. 1933, ibid., fos. 220–1.

[198] PMC, 37th Annual Report (1936), 6–8; 38th Annual Report (1937), 6–7; 39th Annual Report (1938), 6–7; 40th Annual Report (1939), 7; Lang to Dawson, 24 Mar. 1938, LP 159, fos. 85–6; HC Deb., 30 Mar. 1938, 333, 2007–11; Richard Russell to Howard Tyrer, 24 Jan. 1939 (copy), LP 159, fo. 117.

Burroughs) soon informed Lang that 'the evil is very much alive', photographs of a new and enlarged machine outside a chemist's shop in Leeds having been sent to him by the Chief Constable of that city. The bishop was 'amazed at the suggestion from the Public Morality Council' that no action was required: such machines should be quashed before they proliferated all over the country. Lang wrote to the bishop on 16 February that he had just interviewed the Bishop of Kingston and Lord Dawson about the matter, and that 'in the few instances in which it [the machine] has appeared it seems to have been speedily withdrawn'. The Bishop of Ripon, however, insisted again in May that 'the evil' was spreading, and sent Lang a copy of a confidential report by the Chief Constable of Leeds. Despite this, slot machines were not specifically mentioned in the bills prepared by the PMC, though, according to statements made later in the 1930s, the machines were a growing method of selling contraceptives.[199]

Another means of advertising contraception, through the medium of radio programmes, also caused alarm. After the subject had been referred to in radio talks, Cardinal Hinsley, Archbishop of Westminster, objected in April 1937 to any mention of the subject on the wireless. Opposition on this score also came from Mrs Bramwell Booth of the Salvation Army: 'The widespread sale of contraceptives is a great evil, and the depraved youngster can hear little of truth and honour except via the radio.'[200]

The advocates of contraception saw its propagation as a means of lessening the temptation to seek illegal abortion: if unwanted conceptions were avoided, abortion would be avoided as well. It was alleged that illegal operations for abortion were a frequent cause of death to mothers. Viscountess Astor gave this as one of her reasons for calling for more birth-control centres, in a speech in the Commons in 1935: 'A high percentage of maternal mortality is due to attempted abortion . . . The report of . . . [a] Commission on Maternal Mortality stated that, out of 3,085 maternal deaths inves-

[199] Bishop of Ripon to Lang, 18 Jan., 3 Feb., 11 May 1933, LP, 116, fos. 163, 172, 180; Bishop of Kingston to A. C. Don, 23 Jan. 1933, ibid., fo. 166; Lang to Lord Dawson, 6, 23, and 25 Feb. 1933 (copies), ibid., fos. 174, 177, 179; Lang to Bishop of Ripon, 16 Feb. 1933, ibid., fo. 175; Dawson to Lang, 23 Feb. 1933, ibid., fo. 178; *The Times*, 5 Feb. 1937; HC Deb., 30 Mar. 1938, 333, 2008; Lang to Sir Samuel Hoare (Home Secretary), 26 Mar. 1938, LP 159, fo. 90; Hoare to Lang, 1 Apr. 1938; ibid., fos. 91–2; Lang to Hoare, 21 Jan. 1939, ibid., fo. 115.

[200] Wolfe, 'Christianity', 126–7.

tigated by the Commission, 407, or nearly one in eight, were due to abortion.' In some cases, said Lady Astor, the only way of giving a woman a chance of 'not having to suffer a criminal abortion' was by informing her of 'a proper method of birth control'. She quoted the following statement from a letter of Marie Stopes published in *The Times* in 1929: 'in a given number of days, one of our travelling clinics received only thirteen applications for scientific instruction in the control of contraception, but eighty demands for criminal abortion.' The letter claimed that the fall then occurring in the birth rate owed more to abortion than to contraception.[201] Indeed it was accepted by experts that abortions were increasing in the inter-war years, a state of affairs perhaps owing a good deal to the high rates of unemployment. It was also revealed that the anti-abortion law was very ineffectual. There were thirty-three convictions for abortion in 1934, but in the following year 68,000 abortions were estimated to have taken place.[202] Thus the detection rate lagged very far behind the rate of crime, and the law was very widely flouted.

The growing practice naturally appalled those who were against abortion. A Cambridge clergyman had written to Stopes in 1922: 'I think the control of conception is a very wise and beneficent step towards national health, prosperity and happiness; but the practice of abortion is abhorrent and, I am convinced, utter folly.'[203] Against such views, however, the legalization of abortion was recommended for the sake of maternal health. Demands for legalization were frequently heard by 1930, and in 1936 the Abortion Law Reform Association was formed. It was argued by the feminist founders of this Association that both birth control and abortion were necessary contributors to the full emancipation of women. In Parliament legalization was advocated by Robert Boothby, Ernest Thurtle, and others.[204]

Thus by the later 1930s another demand for social reform and change in moral attitude had edged itself onto the agenda. But in this position it remained precarious for about twenty years. The

[201] HC Deb., 17 July 1935, 304, 1135–7; B. Brookes, *Abortion in England, 1900–67* (London, 1988), 6, 9.

[202] Ibid. 29, 56.

[203] P. W. Vale to 'Dear Sir or Madam', 14 July 1922, SP BL Add. MS 58551, fos. 138–9.

[204] Brookes, *Abortion*, 80, 90–1, 95–6, 108–12.

Birkett Committee on Abortion of 1937, which reported two years later, heard evidence from some religious groups, including the League of Catholic Women. This group argued that abortion would not be necessary if people would only practise natural birth-control methods and did not rely on the hazards of artificial means. Archbishops Lang (Canterbury) and Hinsley (Westminster) sent comments to the Committee which shared a vein of vehement denunciation of abortion; but the Modern Churchmen's Union wanted abortion to take place in some circumstances and urged legalization.[205] The Birkett Committee did not recommend legalization, as it accepted the view of the British Medical Association that 'any abortion may entail danger to life and health'.[206] The abortion issue did not become a major one until the 1960s, and Church leaders and councils only rarely felt called on to express an opinion on it before that time. When such a pronouncement was made over the next decade or so (for example, a Methodist statement in 1939), it was opposed to abortion. But in 1952 the Church of Scotland's Church and Nation Committee stated that, when circumstances dictated a choice, the life of the mother should be given priority over that of the foetus, and an Anglican statement of 1959 veered in the same direction.[207]

As for the decriminalization of homosexual acts, this was a matter which, unlike abortion, was as yet virtually never aired in public. The question never entered the publicly voiced concerns of Church leaders, though they had to take account of private manifestations of this sexual orientation among clergy and others. Letters would be received by them such as that written by a homosexual, Dr R. D. Reid (Headmaster of King's College, Taunton, until conviction at the Old Bailey in 1927), who wrote to Archbishop Lang in May 1938 that he hoped to obtain 'some relief for the unfortunate class of people to which I belong': 'Your Grace has little conception of all the misery and crime consequent upon the brutal attitude of the law and society, an attitude in which the Church by its silence acquiesces.'[208] Lang replied that, having much experience of the

[205] L. J. F. Smith, 'The Abortion Controversy, 1936–77: A Case Study in the Emergence of Law', Ph.D. thesis (Edinburgh, 1979), 49–50.

[206] Brookes, *Abortion*, 125–8.

[207] Smith, 'The Abortion Controversy', 97–9; *CT*, 29 July 1938, p. 111 (letter from Revd T. M. Parker, Pusey House, Oxford).

[208] Reid to Lang, 27 May 1938, LP 164, fo. 266.

problem from dealing with clerical cases, he could not believe that the position of homosexuals was as tragic as Reid represented: 'I am not at present prepared to suggest that offences of this kind should be put in the same position as indulgence of sexual instincts with the other sex.'[209]

Abortion and homosexual acts were matters which were far from coming to a head, in the sense of requiring legislative policy by a Government and the passage of resolutions by Church bodies. It was otherwise with divorce in the mid- and later 1930s. The prospect of passing important parliamentary bills to widen the facilities for divorce then coincided with a royal crisis over the same marital question. This was because the abdication of King Edward VIII took place over the divorce question.[210] Thereafter occurred the enhancement of facilities for divorce through the passage of a bill for England and Wales in 1937 and a bill for Scotland in 1938. The matter concerned the position of the Churches in relation to society, moreover, through an important archiepiscopal declaration which gave full recognition to the widening gap between Church opposition to divorce and the increasing number of divorces actually taking place. Only 910 petitions for divorce were entered in England and Wales in 1910 and 1,369 in 1914. On account of the effect of wartime disruption on family stability, however, the number rose to 5,789 in 1919.[211] There was then a diminution, and the average annual number for 1921–5 was 3,208. In 1921 4,401 divorces were granted in the law courts of Great Britain, and in 1929 3,396 were granted.[212] These figures were remarkably small when compared with later developments, especially from the 1960s, but in the inter-war years their slow upward trend was a cause of concern.

All Churches disliked divorce, since they shared the Christian view that marriage was ideally for life and should last until one of the partners died. They held to the sanctity and permanence

[209] Lang to Reid, 9 June 1938, ibid., fo. 270.

[210] For the abdication crisis, divorce reform, and Church opinion, see G. I. T. Machin, 'Marriage and the Churches in the 1930s: Royal Abdication and Divorce Reform, 1936–7', *Journal of Ecclesiastical History*, 42 (1991), 71–7.

[211] G. H. Morrell to Archbishop Davidson, 5 Mar. 1920, DP 417, fos. 104–5.

[212] A. M. Carr-Saunders and D. C. Jones, *A Survey of the Social Structure of England and Wales* (second edn., Oxford, 1937), 201; HC Deb., 20 Nov. 1936, 317, 2094; *LW* (Oct. 1922), 221; *CCC*, 4 June 1931, viii. 5, p. 219.

of marriage at a time when the institution of marriage was being challenged by some thinkers such as Bertrand Russell. Some Christians themselves, however, were coming to share the view that marriage should be a deeper emotional and sexual partnership than the conventional attitude to marriage perhaps allowed for, and this greater expectation from a marriage placed a greater strain on its continuance.[213] Permanence of marriage was often urged as the scriptural teaching of Christ, as it was, for example, in a resolution of the Lambeth Conference of 1930. But there was room for doubt as to whether the ideal could be broken, as it was argued by some that Christ's words permitted a marriage to be dissolved on account of adultery.[214]

Divorce was permitted under civil law for certain 'matrimonial offences', more of these being allowed under Scottish law than English. The Matrimonial Causes Act of 1857 for England and Wales allowed divorce for adultery (when committed by a wife) and for adultery together with cruelty (when committed by a husband). A Royal Commission on Divorce recommended in 1912 that these provisions be extended to include cruelty, desertion for at least three years, incurable insanity after five years' confinement, habitual drunkenness over a long period, and imprisonment under a commuted death sentence. But the only divorce reform between 1912 and 1937 was a Matrimonial Causes Bill—introduced by Lord Buckmaster and passed in 1923—which realized another recommendation of the Divorce Commission by allowing a wife to divorce her husband for adultery alone.[215] The Roman Catholic Church took the strongest stand by not recognizing divorce under civil law and excommunicating those who availed themselves of it; annulment of a marriage was, however, obtainable by papal dispensation. Under the Act of 1857 clergy of the Church of England could refuse to remarry the guilty party in a divorce case. Church of Scotland and Nonconformist ministers could also choose to act in this way. While there were thus differences of emphasis between Churches over divorce, there was underlying unity between them

[213] See J. Lewis, 'Public Institution and Private Relationship: Marriage and Marriage Guidance, 1920–68' *Twentieth Century British History*, 1/3 (1990), 233–5.

[214] Henson, *Christian Morality*, 200–2; *Yorkshire Post*, 7 Jan. 1932 (extract in LP 212, fo. 238).

[215] L. Stone, *Road to Divorce: England, 1530–1987* (Oxford, 1992), 390–6; *Year Book of the National Assembly of the Church of England* (1922), 32, 88–94; DP 417, fos. 109–12, 123–4, 141, 155, 172.

in the sense that all saw marriage as a lifelong union and all sought to discourage divorce. The increasing divorce rate could therefore be taken to mean that more people were disregarding or undervaluing Christian teaching.[216] If the Churches agreed that the civil law should widen the scope for divorce as reforming opinion wanted, this might be seen as a humane response but would also amount to recognition that the Churches and their teaching were becoming increasingly separated from society at large.[217] If Churches also confirmed their disapproval of divorce by refusing to remarry a divorced person or debarring him or her from communion, this would only accentuate the growing separation between Church and society.

The recognition that Church ideals of marriage were increasingly separate from social developments and expectations was quite frequently shown in debates and resolutions of Anglican bodies in the 1930s.[218] A resolution moved by Bishop Bell and adopted in the Upper House of Canterbury Convocation in May 1936 accepted the idea of some extension of divorce facilities on account of changes in social attitudes and behaviour:

> This House, recognizing that the full enactment of the Christian standard of marriage may not always be possible in a State which comprises all sorts and kinds of people, including many who do not accept the Christian way of life . . . is of opinion that some amendment of the State law relating to grounds of divorce may be demanded by the circumstances of the day.[219]

In carrying another resolution moved by Bell in this debate, Convocation also decided that additional grounds for acquiescing in divorce should be seriously considered—namely, the concealment of venereal disease or pregnancy by another man at the time of the wedding, or wilful refusal to consummate the marriage.[220] The same debate also showed that many leading Anglicans were prepared to alter their Church's discipline on marriage. It was resolved that 'it is a sacred responsibility laid upon the Church of

[216] A. R. Vidler, *Sex, Marriage, and Religion: A Discussion of Some Modern Problems* (London, 1932), 43–66, 146–7.

[217] *Western Mail*, 6 Jan. 1932 (extract in LP 112, fo. 237).

[218] See BP 146, fos. 122–97; 147, fos. 257–71; Bishop of Salisbury (Donaldson) to Lang, 4 May 1934, LP 128, fos. 86–7.

[219] *CCC*, 27 May 1936, i. 2, pp. 243, 246–7. Cf. open letter from Bell to his fellow-bishops, 30 July 1931, BP 148, fos. 19–22. See also *CCC*, 4 June 1931, viii. 5, pp. 217–42, and 5 June 1935, ix. 8, pp. 286–326; and Norman, *Church and Society*, 345–6.

[220] *Year Book of the National Assembly of the Church of England* (1937), 242–3.

England to enact such a discipline of its own in regard to marriage (as in other cases) as may from time to time appear most salutary and efficacious'.[221] Richard Parsons, Bishop of Southwark, said in support of this resolution:

> They were all agreed that marriage could not be dissolved without previous moral wrong, that it ought not to be dissolved, and that it was regrettable that it should be . . . (but) there were circumstances in which its dissolution might be recognised by the Church at any rate to the extent of admitting, if the church thought fit, to its Communion people who had contracted a second union during the lifetime of the former partner.[222]

On 27 October 1936 Mrs Wallis Simpson, whom King Edward VIII wished to marry, was divorced for the second time. The Government made clear to the king that, if he persisted in his intention to marry Mrs Simpson, abdication would be necessary. Stanley Baldwin, the Prime Minister, informed the Commons of this situation on 4 December 1936. On 10 December King Edward signed an Instrument of Abdication, and on the following day an Abdication Bill passed both Houses (the Commons voted 403 to 5 in favour, the five opponents voting for an amendment which called for a republic).

As the general Christian view in the country was that divorce should not be encouraged, there was unanimous interdenominational agreement in welcoming the outcome of the royal crisis. This was displayed by the reactions of different Church assemblies and newspapers.[223] But there was not a mutual exchange of compliments between Churches. The Roman Catholic Church tended to blame Protestant laxity as the cause of Edward's predicament. The *Universe* said that Edward had lacked 'the sure guidance and support on such matters that the Catholic Church gives her children—indeed he could not become a Catholic, should be want to, without losing his throne'; and asked how much weight could be given 'to the ponderous rebukes of Anglican prelates who falter and palter whenever any moral issue comes up for public discussion'.[224] The *Tablet* stated on 5 December that the King was being asked 'to forgo rights which the law of England, straying from the law of the

[221] Quoted Machin, 'Marriage and the Churches', 69–7. Cf. Lord Hugh Cecil to Lang, 20 Apr. 1934, LP 128, fo. 79.

[222] Quoted in Machin, 'Marriage and the Churches', 70.

[223] Ibid. 72–5.

[224] *U.*, 11 Dec. 1936, p. 14; 18 Dec. 1936, p. 14.

Catholic Church, extends to the ordinary people': 'it is his misfortune that he should be expected to live by a severer code than that exacted in modern English society, which has moved so far from the Catholic tradition, and that he is not allowed to avail himself of permissions which both Church and State in England extend to those over whom they legislate.'[225] After the adbication, the *Tablet* regretted that Edward had not abandoned his intention to marry Mrs Simpson and thus avoided 'a blow to the sanctity of marriage ties'. But it praised him for not simply having arranged to keep his throne by pursuing an unmarried relationship with her: 'it is an irony that he is in effect abdicating because of his high sense of propriety, at once too high and not high enough.'[226]

On 13 December Archbishop Lang made a controversial broadcast to the nation which attracted both support and condemnation. Lang's broadcast was perhaps influenced by a letter he received from A. C. Bouquet, a Cambridge theologian, suggesting that in his address Lang might 'in the name of Christian public opinion express his austere disapproval of influences which have in recent times polluted our Court life, and have misled a most promising ruler'. Lang said in the broadcast that Edward—whom he described as generous, active, and sympathetic—had 'sought his happiness in a manner inconsistent with the Christian principles of marriage, and within a social circle whose standards and ways of life are alien to all the best instincts and traditions of his people'.[227] In another broadcast two weeks later, inaugurating a 'Recall to Religion', Lang called for more emphasis on spiritual values in society and made his famous protest that God was being 'crowded out', with the consequence that there was 'a slackening, sometimes even a scorning, of the old standards of Christian morality'.[228]

Lang had always emphasized the ideal of indissoluble marriage, and his broadcasts demonstrated his conviction on this matter. Soon afterwards, however, he showed his willingness to accept divorce reform for the sake of the growing number in society who were little guided by Christian standards. A. P. Herbert, a novelist

[225] *T.*, 5 Dec. 1936, p. 768.

[226] Ibid., 12 Dec. 1936, p. 824.

[227] Revd Dr A. C. Bouquet to Lang, 11 Dec. 1936, LP 22, fos. 416–17 (quoted in Machin, 'Marriage and the Churches', 75); J. G. Lockhart, *Cosmo Gordon Lang* (London, 1949), 405.

[228] Quoted in ibid. 409–10.

and an Anglican who was Independent MP for Oxford University, had introduced a Matrimonial Causes Bill for England and Wales. This proposed to extend the grounds of divorce to include cruelty, desertion, and insanity, on the lines of the Royal Commission recommendations in 1912. Herbert argued that his bill would strengthen both morality and the Church, by facing more honestly the real state of matrimonial relations and reducing misery and deception.[229] The bill was given a second reading by seventy-eight votes to twelve in November 1936, both support and opposition coming from MPs of the same party and the same religious affiliation. Most of the twenty-three Roman Catholic MPs did not vote on the bill; still less did they attempt to form an organized Roman Catholic opposition. For these reasons they were rebuked by the *Universe*.[230] After a long delay the third reading was carried in May 1937 by 190 votes to 37.

In the House of Lords, where the bill was debated on 24 June and 19 July 1937, the measure was passed after an amendment was carried to reduce the minimum period of a marriage from five years to three before it could be dissolved. A few bishops spoke in favour of the bill, including Henson and Ernest Barnes (Bishop of Birmingham), and one (Michael Furse of St Albans) spoke against. A Roman Catholic peer, Lord Russell of Killowen, opposed on the ground that divorce was 'contrary to the teachings of Christ'. Most bishops abstained from the final division, when the bill was passed by seventy-nine to twenty-eight, and Furse was the only bishop to vote against. Those abstaining included Lang and Temple, both of whom had found praise for the bill but also had reservations about it.[231] Lang wrote: 'rightly or wrongly I came to the conclusion that it was no longer possible to impose the full Christian standard by law on a largely non-Christian population, but that the witness to that standard, and consequent disciplinary action towards its own members or persons who sought to be married by its rites, must be left to the Church.'[232] The day before the bill passed the Lords, the Methodist Conference had approved the bill by a large majority. The bill became law on 30 July. Before this a measure was intro-

[229] HC Deb., 20 Nov. 1936, 317, 2081–93.

[230] *U.*, 24 Dec. 1936, p. 12; 23 Apr. 1937, p. 14.

[231] HL Deb., 24 June 1937, 105, 730–86, 812–48; 19 July 1937, 106, 566–94; A. P. Herbert, *The Ayes Have It: The Story of the Marriage Bill* (London, 1937), 178–90.

[232] Lockhart, *Cosmo Gordon Lang*, 235.

duced into the Lords to widen the divorce provisions in Scotland by adding cruelty, insanity, and habitual drunkenness to the existing conditions embracing adultery and desertion. Having been agreed to by the Lords, this bill passed the Commons in 1938.[233]

Lang's view of the Matrimonial Causes Act of 1937 was officially adopted by the Convocations of the Church of England. In confirmation of Convocation resolutions in January 1938, the Upper Houses of the Canterbury and York Convocations resolved in June:

That while convinced that Christ's principle of a lifelong and exclusive personal union provides the only sure ground on which to base the relations of man and woman in marriage, and that the Church should therefore commend that principle as the true foundation for legislation by the State, this House nevertheless recognizes that its full legal enactment may not always be possible in a State which comprises all sorts and kinds of people, including many who do not accept the Christian way of life or the means of grace which the Church offers to its members.[234]

Anglican church members, and Roman Catholics for that matter, could not be segregated from the legal provisions affecting the rest of society. The 1937 Act opened up more 'matrimonial offences' to divorce proceedings for anyone in society, however much divorce might be disapproved by their Church. The parliamentary debates on the measure had shown the different opinions held by Anglicans about divorce. Nevertheless the Act made a concession to disapproval of divorce by removing the obligation under the 1857 Act for Church of England clergy to remarry the innocent party in a divorce suit. Henceforth the individual clergyman could grant or refuse a request for such remarriage. The Convocations, however, went beyond this by passing resolutions that the remarriage of neither the guilty nor the innocent party should take place in church. The bishops of the Church in Wales directed their clergy that 'in no case should the marriage of any person whose marriage

[233] Lang to Revd Daniel Lamont, Moderator of the Church of Scotland, 20 Mar. 1937 (copy), LP 152, fos. 319–20; Lamont to Lang, 1 Apr. 1937, ibid. 152, fo. 330; Lang to Revd A. Chisholm, 8 Apr. 1937 (copy), ibid., fo. 335; *PAGAFCS* (1937), 697; Church of Scotland Dundee Presbytery Minutes, 1 Dec. 1937, CH2/103/42, pp. 260–2.

[234] *Year Book of the National Assembly of the Church of England* (1938), 250–1, 259–61.

has been dissolved, and whose former partner is still living, be solemnized in church'.[235]

These resolutions, which are still in force, were generally accepted by the clergy but were not legally binding on them. By law, clergy could remarry parties to a divorce suit, and this could cause friction between a clergyman and his bishop. In February 1938 Archbishop Lang strongly advised one of his clergy not to remarry the innocent party to a divorce. 'I cannot compel you not to celebrate this marriage, which you have a legal right to do,' he wrote. 'I can only put before you what is expressed by the Resolutions of Convocation.'[236] Bishop Garbett was annoyed by members of his clergy who performed services of blessing in church after registry office weddings which involved parties to a divorce.[237] On the other hand, the controversial resolutions of Convocation caused Sir Francis Acland, a Liberal MP, to secede from the Church of England and become a Quaker. He protested to Lang that the Church, by adopting these resolutions, had shown that it 'has no intention whatever of bringing itself into line with the modern spirit which is visible in Protestant Churches all over the world'.[238]

The inter-war years, and especially the 1930s, had seen the Churches subjected to an unprecedented wave of social challenges and changes—an increase in gambling and later in drinking; a sharp growth in cinema attendance and in the consequent concerns over the moral quality of films; the wide spread of the use of artificial contraception; and extension of the opportunities for divorce. The broadcasting of religious services was taking place, but the Churches would have liked to receive evidence that this was stimulating people to attend church rather than stay at home. These were all cases of new moral and social challenges which could not simply be dealt with rapidly and put away. They were likely to last and to have long and powerful ramifications in social behaviour. Moreover, fundamental intellectual challenges were being posed to

[235] Resolution of Upper House of York Convocation, 21 Jan. 1937, ibid. 238, and of Upper House of Canterbury Convocation, 2 June 1938, *CCC* (1938), i. 4, p. xii; Letter from the Bishops of the Church in Wales, 'to be read from the pulpits of all churches in the province of Wales', 29 Jan. 1938, FP 17, fo. 50.

[236] Revd C. B. Deane to Lang, 25 Feb. 1938, LP 159, fos. 211–12; Lang to Deane, 26 Feb. 1938, ibid., fo. 213.

[237] C. Smyth, *Cyril Foster Garbett, Archbishop of York* (London, 1959), 391–3.

[238] Acland to Lang, 26 Nov. 1937, LP 148, fos. 9–11.

the Churches' doctrines by some of the same figures who were prominent in challenging the Churches' moral teaching. A. J. Ayer's somewhat inflammatory *Language, Truth and Logic*, published in 1936, challenged religious doctrines (and consequently the Churches) on the grounds that the doctrines—for example, the existence of God—were not empirically verifiable.[239]

Some of the changes and challenges aroused new differences between Churches over social matters, as was the case with the Lambeth declaration on contraception in 1930 in relation to the Church of England and the Church of Rome. Other changes accentuated differences which already existed between Churches, as occurred in the case of the responses of the Church of Rome and the Church of England to the Matrimonial Causes Act of 1937. The scale of social change and of challenge to traditional Church assumptions and behaviour was greater than at any time before the 1960s; and, as occurred again in that decade, the Churches, taken as a whole, were not doing well in their efforts to maintain membership and attendance levels. The Churches in the 1930s appeared, with some notable exceptions (particularly the Roman Catholic Church and the Church of Scotland), to be in a beleaguered state, challenged by falling statistics. The Churches in general were also challenged by falling (or at least changing) morals, and by intellectual challenges to their doctrines. Three decades later they were to be confronted again by the same formidable combination of forces.

[239] A. J. Ayer, *Language, Truth and Logic* (London, 1936); M. Warnock, *Ethics since 1900* (London, 1960), 85–90.

4
Churches and Social Matters in the Second World War

The social challenges which had arisen to affect the Churches in the 1930s and earlier continued to confront them during and after the Second World War. At the same time, the war provided more impetus for social planning and renewal which might be put into operation should victory in the armed conflict be secured; and this affected the position of the Churches as well as other aspects of society. War and the hoped-for victory—a distinctly evanescent mirage until 1943—also gave the inspiration to try and recover and advance the influence of religion. For example, the Methodist Conference agreed on a plan for a Forward Movement in 1940, and this led to the beginning of a Christian Commando Campaign in 1943, aiming at conversions in factories, mines, schools, cinemas, and public houses: 'the objective was to establish bridge-heads in territory which was increasingly foreign to the Church.'[1] Organization was under the superintendence of the Revd Colin Roberts, and the campaign commenced with missions to Nottingham and Reading in the summer of 1943; each involved numerous ministers, reached vast numbers of people, and obtained a promising number of conversions and rededications. About forty other campaigns were held at different places until the 'commando' effort culminated in a vast Greater London campaign in April 1947.[2] In some of the local campaigns there was a notable ecumenical element, in the form of cooperation from other Churches, but this was not a consistently prominent feature of the initiative.[3]

Ecumenical hopes, however, were encouraged by the war situation. Important moves took place towards serious discussion on

[1] D. Gowland and S. Roebuck, *Never Call Retreat: A Biography of Bill Gowland* (London, 1990), 55–8.
[2] Ibid. 58–67.
[3] Ibid. 63.

union between the Congregational and Presbyterian Churches in England, a joint conference being formed on the subject by 1945.[4] On a wider front, the British Council of Churches was boldly formed at a most uncertain stage of the war, out of several preceding bodies, including the Christian Social Council and the Commission of the Churches for International Friendship and Social Responsibility (created after the Oxford Conference in 1937). The new Council, intended as a branch of a World Council of Churches, was inaugurated on 23 September 1942 at a service in St Paul's cathedral in London.[5] It was not at all surprising that Archbishop Temple, who succeeded Lang at Canterbury in 1942, should have attained his apogee of conference involvement by acting as president of the British Council of Churches until his unexpected death in 1944.

Some progress was also made in Protestant–Catholic cooperation. On 1 August 1940 the Archbishop of Westminster, Cardinal Hinsley, founded the Sword of the Spirit, a movement for the establishment of a Christian world order of justice and peace. Hinsley was president, Christopher Dawson vice-president, and Barbara Ward the energetic and influential secretary. Strongly supported from the Anglican side by Bishop George Bell and others, this movement was intended to be under Catholic leadership but with interdenominational participation. Its aims were supported in public meetings and in a letter in *The Times* of 21 December 1940 signed by Hinsley, Archbishops Lang and Temple, and the Revd W. H. Armstrong, Moderator of the new Free Church Federal Council. But a properly unified movement did not materialize. Amongst Roman Catholics, who, confident in their continued expansion, had little interest in ecumenical cooperation, there was much suspicion of the movement.[6] Bishop Bell had to be content with a result similar to his own suggestion in a 'Chichester memorandum' of 1941, that there should be parallel Catholic and Protestant bodies with a single joint committee. The latter committee, formed in mid-1942, was chaired by Geoffrey

[4] A. Macarthur, 'The Background to the Formation of the United Reformed Church (Presbyterian and Congregational) in England and Wales in 1972', *Journal of the United Reformed Church History Society*, 4/1 (1987), 6.

[5] R. C. D. Jasper, *George Bell, Bishop of Chichester* (London, 1967), 316–20.

[6] A. Hastings, *A History of English Christianity, 1920–85* (London, 1986), 393–6; S. P. Mews, 'The Sword of the Spirit: A Catholic Crusade of 1940', in W. J. Sheils (ed.), *The Church and War* (Studies in Church History, 20; Oxford, 1983), 409–30.

Fisher, Bishop of London, and many joint meetings were held by the parallel bodies.[7]

In spite of the challenge and stimulation of war, Christians were often reluctant to be engaged in it and regarded its outbreak as the failure of a careful and persistent peace policy. A correspondent in the Church of England *Guardian* in May 1938 expressed his dismay that 'many bishops' had been advising the population to enrol in the Government's Air Raid Precaution scheme:

How can they sincerely support the policy of our Government on this issue when the spirit behind air-raid precautions and the spirit of the Christian gospel are so fundamentally opposed? . . . Either we stand for a policy of friendship, understanding, mutual aid, freedom, and considerate affection for all men, and take the risks of such a way of life; or we surrender to our fears, and take the way of gas-masks and preventive drill and running for bomb-proof and gas-proof shelters, and the heathen satisfaction of reciprocal massacre and revenge.[8]

A year later, in mid-1939, the Moderator of the Congregational Union of England and Wales, the Revd Ernest James, also expressed the fundamental Christian desire for peace when addressing his Annual Assembly:

That the people of this country and empire carry no hatred in their hearts for the people of Germany and Italy is manifest to all who are not wilfully blind. That we have no desire to encircle or cripple or crush any other nation has been made clear by our military unpreparedness. That nearly two millions have joined the League of Prayer and Service is a clear indication where our heart is . . . It is the task of world-wide Christianity to preach and embody this vision of world Brotherhood.[9]

At the Baptist Annual Assembly taking place at about the same time, it was resolved that 'we gratefully acknowledge the deep desire of our Government, even in the face of provocation, to exhaust all honourable means of averting the incalculable tragedy

[7] Jasper, *Bell*, 245–54; T. M. Moloney, 'The Public Ministry of Cardinal Hinsley, 1935–43', Ph.D. thesis (London, 1980), 202 ff.; Barbara Ward to Bishop Bell, 7 Nov. 1940, BP 71, fo. 7; A. Wilkinson, *Dissent or Conform?: War, Peace, and the English Churches, 1900–45* (London, 1986), 256–8.

[8] Letter from Hugh Goodrich, *G.*, 20 May 1938, p. 320. Cf. Church of Scotland Dundee Presbytery Minutes, 1 Sept. 1939, for an example of how ministers armed themselves with ARP helmets, respirators, and anti-gas clothing, and protected their churches and congregations against air raids (CH2/103/43, pp. 24–5).

[9] *CYB* (1940), 76.

of armed conflict between the nations'.[10] In the same month Bishop Bell successfully moved in the Canterbury Convocation 'that Christian people of all nations should respond to the recent calls for prayer for the guidance of the Holy Spirit for the attainment of justice and peace among nations issued by the Archbishop of Canterbury jointly with others, and also by His Holiness the Pope'.[11]

Such hopes, explicit or implied, were disappointed. When war did break out, no Church opposition was voiced. The overwhelming majority of Christians engaged either actively or passively in the fight, though Christians were also among the small band of conscientious objectors.[12] It was at least much clearer than it had been in 1914 that the main enemy was an evil regime—or, as the Church and Nation Committee of the Church of Scotland stated, 'demonic forces of evil which have captured the soul of a people'.[13]

The war brought its own special social effects. During the Second World War the civilian population was affected for a longer period and more systematically than in the First by food and clothes rationing and compulsory conscription. It was also affected, to a much greater degree, by air raids, bombing, and the consequent widespread deaths and destruction. For the first time it experienced the large and systematic evacuation of children from the vulnerable centres of cities. These matters sometimes affected the Churches and their members directly, and were often the subject of comment in Church assemblies and newspapers.

Churches and the homes of their members and adherents were frequently damaged or destroyed in the blitzes, which occurred chiefly in 1940 and 1941. The *Church Times* reported in January 1941 that in Birmingham air raids

> many churches have been greatly damaged. Others have received only minor injuries, and some, as by a miracle, have escaped all damage. The people have met this time of testing with the same admirable courage and calm determination as has marked the conduct of people in even more stricken cities. Great demands have been made on the clergy, to which they have responded with courage and devotion.[14]

[10] *BH* (1940), 213.
[11] *Year Book of the National Assembly of the Church of England* (1940), 257.
[12] *CYB* (1940), 68.
[13] *RGACS* (1940), p. 377.
[14] *CT*, 24 Jan. 1941, p. 48.

The same issue of this paper contained an advertisement which showed the effect of bombing raids on some churches. The church and vicarage of Holy Trinity, Rotherhithe (East London), said the advertisement, had been 'completely burnt out':

> Who will help us? We should be grateful for gifts to replace what we have lost: church ornaments, vestments, pictures, books, etc. We shall need help if the Tradition of Public Worship and the Family Life of the Church are to be maintained . . . Please send money, blankets, clothes (old or new), toys, food, etc., to Canon Joseph Thrift, Vicar.[15]

Similarly, the Dean and Canons of Manchester Cathedral opened a restoration fund after 'a heavy bomb fell in the north-east corner of the churchyard, and demolished the Lady Chapel, the Ely Chapel, and the two eastern bays of the Regimental Chapel'.[16] The Congregational Union commenced a War Emergency Fund to deal with restoration needs: it was reported that, up to the end of 1941, ninety-four churches in the Union had been destroyed or made unusable, eighty had been badly damaged, and 193 slightly damaged.[17] Lambeth Palace received a bombing attack, and Archbishop Lang wrote to Cardinal Hinsley in May 1941: 'I thank your Eminence for your sympathy about Lambeth Palace. May 10th was certainly a very distressing night, hearing the explosion of these bombs and seeing the fire spreading over buildings full of such historical associations.'[18]

On 28 May 1941 the Upper House of Canterbury Convocation debated and unanimously carried a motion of Bishop Bell, expressing 'its deep sympathy with the sufferers in those towns and districts in Great Britain which have been the victims of bombing attacks from the air during recent months, and its admiration at the courage and endurance which men and women of all classes have displayed'.[19] In his opening speech Bell noted that 34,284 civilians had been killed in bombing attacks from October 1940 to April 1941, and that 46,119 had been badly injured. He also referred to 'the huge multitude of those who spent sleepless nights in shelter and tube in all sorts of conditions,

[15] *CT*, 24 Jan. 1941, 49.
[16] Ibid., 14 Feb. 1941, p. 98.
[17] *CYB* (1942), 29, 40.
[18] Lang to Hinsley, 24 May 1941, LP 184, fo. 313.
[19] *CCC*, 28 May 1941, i. 9, pp. 101–5.

sometimes going far from their town habitations and lying in the open'.[20]

The evacuation of children from inner-city areas, which were expected to be the most liable to attack, was planned in 1938–9 as part of the Air Raid Precautions. The country was divided into three kinds of area—evacuation (those to be evacuated), reception (those to receive the evacuees), and 'neutral'. Evacuees would be placed in private homes, and the receiving persons would obtain a government allowance. From the end of June to early September 1939, immense numbers of children (amounting to at least three millions) moved in accordance with these intentions. By the following spring many of these had returned home, as the war appeared to be a 'phoney' one until the fall of France and the Battle of Britain.[21] The subsequent sharp intensification of the conflict resulted in renewed evacuation, much of it from coastal areas.

Some clergy and ministers, like many others in the population, were involved in receiving evacuees, and they seem (like others) to have responded in varying ways to their task.[22] Some were welcoming 'receivers', others reluctant. Bishop Bell of Chichester was an enthusiastic receiver, providing his palace rent-free (in exchange for promised payment for damage and wear and tear) for the housing of evacuees from Streatham and Tooting in south London.[23] The *Universe* reported that, thanks to the determined efforts of priests, few of the Catholic children who had been evacuated from Liverpool and other cities to Wales 'have been deprived of Mass and the Sacraments from the earliest days of their arrival. Children who had been sent to districts where no [Catholic] religious facilities could be provided were moved by the persistent efforts of priests to places where they could live as Catholics.'[24]

Other social concerns of the Churches in the war were more familiar. They included drinking, gambling, divorce, and birth control. The last two, however, were related to worries over increased sexual activity and promiscuity encouraged by the particular

[20] Ibid. 102.

[21] B. Wicks. *No Time to Wave Goodbye* (London, 1988), 23–43, 101. See also R. M. Titmuss, *Problems of Social Policy* (London, 1950), 23–44, 101–82, 355–69, 424–61.

[22] Wicks, *No Time*, 83, 97.

[23] Jasper, *Bell*, 87.

[24] *U.*, 12 June 1942, p. 1.

pressures of wartime. The divorce legislation of 1937 and 1938 would have been expected to increase the number of divorces, but the disruption and new associations brought about by the war increased them much more than had been anticipated. The number of divorces compared with the number of marriages in Britain was 1:100 in 1939, but 5:100 in 1945; and after 1942 the number of petitions for divorce on account of adultery rose by 100 per cent each year (until 1945) above the average for 1939–42.[25]

In October 1944, at the behest of the Mothers' Union, which was very concerned about this trend, the Bishop of Bristol (Clifford Woodward) moved a resolution in the Upper House of Canterbury Convocation (carried after amendment) that 'in view of the alarming increase in divorce', parents and others should be urged of the need for more definite teaching on marriage as a lifelong relationship.[26] Woodward's speech emphasized the need to make marriages more stable. About two-thirds of all marriages in England took place in an Anglican church: bishops should constantly impress on their clergy 'the positive duty of preparing those who came to them for marriage and instructing them as to the demands which marriage would make upon them'. Parents should also take much more responsibility for advising their children about marriage, and organizations particularly concerned with this matter should increase their activities:

> Something in the nature of a nation-wide campaign was called for, conducted by those organizations which were in close touch with married women and mothers. One thought primarily of the Mothers' Union, but there was the great Women's Institute movement, the 'Inner Wheel' connected with the Rotary movement . . . The Mothers' Union ought to take the lead in trying to get a conference of the leaders of these various movements to bring home to their members the tremendous importance of doing what they could to train their children for marriage.[27]

The first Marriage Guidance Council had been formed in London in 1938, with the Bishop of London as its president, and the example was being followed in other large towns: 'this was surely one of the many spheres in which Churchmen could wholeheartedly combine with those who were members of other Churches or of

[25] J. Costello, *Love, Sex, and War: Changing Values, 1939–45* (London, 1985), 274–5.

[26] *CCC*, 12 Oct. 1944, i. 17, p. 268.

[27] Ibid. 270–1.

no Church at all.'[28] Bishop Herbert of Norwich, seconding Woodward's motion, referred to a need to strengthen the basis of marriage and domestic life as part of a post-war social reconstruction which would be based not only on material improvement but also on religious principles.[29] In the course of the debate E. W. Barnes, Bishop of Birmingham, pointed out the sometimes devastating effects of the war on the home and family:

> There was not the high seriousness in the approach to matters of sex which the Christian rightly wished to see. But it must be remembered that our people . . . had been the victims of a state of affairs unprecedented in our national life. Totalitarian war, as it had developed, was the enemy of social morality. The State, believing that such action was necessary, had virtually destroyed family life as it normally existed. Millions of families . . . had been disintegrated. Fathers were absent on war service. Mothers had entered munitions factories, and so were unable to give due care to the training of their children. Young women had been taken from home and billeted under conditions which encouraged promiscuity. It was a disastrous state of affairs; and the only way in which they could hope for a remedy of evils of which they were all too conscious was that national home life should be re-established as rapidly as possible.[30]

Commenting on the debate, the *Church Times* said that what was needed was 'general re-education in the principles of a Christian civilization, and reassertion of a comprehensive Christian outlook on life'.[31]

Artificial contraception continued to be a matter of some controversy during the war, although the next major Church declaration on the subject did not occur until 1958. When the Government issued a Rubber Control Order in 1942, there were complaints, for example from the Secretary of the Catholic Pharmaceutical Guild, that the order did not include reduction of the distribution of rubber contraceptives.[32] In reply to a lady correspondent who wrote to her 'dear Father-in-God' against artificial contraception, Archbishop Temple said that

> we should learn to master the bad tendencies that are so easily connected with the use of contraceptives. But I must be quite honest with you and

[28] Ibid. 271.
[29] Ibid. 272–3.
[30] Ibid. 274.
[31] *CT*, 20 Oct. 1944, p. 555. Cf. ibid., 3 Nov. 1944, p. 583.
[32] Ibid., 27 Mar. 1942, p. 194.

make it clear that I am not among those who are able to regard the use of contraceptives as necessarily wrong in principle . . . Unless the medical profession comes to the conclusion that all forms of them are in fact harmful in a medical sense I do not think they can be universally condemned on grounds of Christian morals.[33]

The correspondent, however, remained '"driven by the spirit" to fight for a time when Christian people will rise up and drive out the false claims made by Marie Stopes, Leslie Weatherhead and others of their way of thinking'.[34] Marie Stopes, for her part, ridiculed the desire of Michael Furse, Bishop of St Albans, to restrict the sale of contraceptives to married persons who could produce a medical certificate:

the best contraceptive in the world is olive (ordinary salad) oil. Is your Lordship proposing to have a Bill passed that olive oil shall only be sold to married women on the production of a medical certificate? In these fantastic times you may succeed but you won't be able to stop me telling women that castor oil and margarine remain, and even your Lordship cannot prohibit the sale of margarine, nor its use as a contraceptive by married women without any doctor's certificate.[35]

The internal use of tampons was also seen as a possible means of contraception as well as potentially causing physical harm. Cardinal Hinsley commenced a concerned correspondence on this matter with the Archbishops of Canterbury and York and the Moderator of the Free Church Federal Council, and the question of making official approaches to the Ministry of Health was discussed.[36]

In spite of the widespread use of contraceptives, illegitimacy increased during the war from an annual pre-war average of 5.5 illegitimate births per 1,000 to 16.1 per 1,000 in 1945.[37] The calling of many women into factory work and the auxiliary branches of the armed forces was thought to be partly responsible, as also were the departure and long absence, under military orders, of husbands

[33] Temple to Marjorie Hayter, 8 June 1942, TP 5, fo. 41; also 15 June 1942, ibid., fo. 45.

[34] Hayter to Temple, 11 June 1942, ibid., fo. 35; also 20 and 26 June 1942, 28 Feb. 1943, ibid., fos. 46, 49–53, 55–6.

[35] Draft of 'an open letter to the Bishop of St Albans' by Marie Stopes, 1 June 1943, SP BL Add. MS 58552 (unfoliated when seen).

[36] Hinsley to Lang, 7 Apr. 1941, LP 184, fo. 298; Lang to Hinsley, 9 Apr. 1941, ibid., fos. 299ff.; Hinsley to Lang, 23 May 1941, ibid., fos. 307–8.

[37] Costello, *Love, Sex, and War*, 277; *U.*, 16 Jan. 1942, p. 6.

and boyfriends. Another supposed contributory factor was thought to be the arrival of large numbers of foreign troops—notably the American GIs, whose natural charm was (it was commonly alleged) much enhanced by their superior wages.[38] The prospect of meeting sudden death in an air raid also allegedly played its part in heightening a desire for emotional and physical intimacy.

Prostitution and cases of venereal disease became much more frequent, especially at seaports.[39] Bishop Geoffrey Fisher, President of the PMC, said at a meeting of this body in October 1943 that 'the moral disease' behind venereal infections was much worse than the physical manifestations. An address by the Archbishops of Canterbury and York, he said, had

> put it with complete bluntness in one sentence: all sexual intercourse except between man and wife is a sin. Promiscuity . . . devastates both personal and social life . . . and there is no kind of doubt that promiscuity is being accepted by a large number of persons to whom before the war it would have been altogether out of the question.[40]

Late in 1942 the Ministry of Health launched a strong campaign against venereal disease. The Ministry persuaded the Government to apply a measure which had been used in the First World War and was authorized in Section 33B of the Defence of the Realm Act of 1939. This provided for the compulsory examination of persons suspected of carrying venereal disease, with, if necessary, treatment to follow. Archbishop Temple and others considered such a measure to be highly inadequate, on the grounds that it might have the effect of increasing irregular sexual intercourse through ignoring the question of morality.[41] Bishop Fisher wrote that 'the subject should *not* be treated as a purely medical subject but as involving the whole man and society . . . The War Office makes it a medical subject because it wants to avoid the *moral* issue.'[42] Temple informed General Sir Bernard Paget, Commander in Chief of the Home Forces, about his fears that advice to recruits on the subject

[38] Bishop A. C. Headlam to Temple, 11 May 1943, TP 34, fos. 15–17; D. Reynolds, *Rich Relations: The American occupation of Britain, 1942–5* (London, 1995), 200–8.

[39] Costello, *Love, Sex, and War*, 17–18, 82, 87–8, 127, 328.

[40] G. Fisher, *Thorny Problems* (PMC booklet; London, 1943), 81.

[41] Temple to Bishop of Norwich (P. M. Herbert), 29 Nov. 1942, TP 40, fos. 160–1; Ernest Brown, Minister of Health, to Temple, 22 Dec. 1942, ibid., fo. 204. Cf. pamphlet on 33*B and the V. D. Situation: A note to Members of Parliament from the British Social Hygiene Council* (copy ibid., fos. 170–3).

[42] Fisher to Temple, 24 Dec. 1942, TP 40, fo. 199.

was, in effect, instructing them 'how to be incontinent with the greatest possible safety. Many of us want to urge that something much more is needed and that it is a great mistake to treat the question as primarily medical.'[43] A special meeting to discuss Regulation 33B was held by the new British Council of Churches in January 1943. It was agreed that the Council would perform a great service if, through its Department of Social Responsibility, it would help to coordinate the Christian forces fighting venereal disease.[44]

A need to escape the fears and tensions of wartime, together with the earning of substantially increased real wages during the conflict, encouraged the British population to espouse leisure opportunities at perhaps a greater rate than ever before. Between 1938 and 1944 the amount of money spent on leisure grew by an enormous 120 per cent.[45] Much of this leisure spending went on cinema attendance. Although cinemas were vulnerable to bombing (10 per cent of them were demolished during the war), attendances rose steeply.[46] The Churches continued to be very interested in film, both as a means of spreading the Gospel and as a possible danger to morals and religion. Sometimes 'film services' were held, the film being central to the service; and sometimes cinemas were hired for services without films.[47] But, in regard to cinema attendance as a whole, the *Church Times* alleged in 1940 that there was 'a lamentable tolerance of degrading entertainment, which in its way is quite as anti-Christian as the cruelty of the concentration camps'.[48] Nudity in the theatre—a threat posed by, among other items, a review called *Fig Leaves*—was equally worrying, being certainly (in the view of the *Church Times*) 'incompatible with the claim that the war is being fought for the things that matter most in human life'.[49] Even the wartime BBC was not immune from banality. 'It is an affront to break off a beautiful service, if it is a few minutes too

[43] Temple to Paget, 28 Dec. 1942, ibid., fos. 202–3.

[44] Miss J. E. Higson (of the Church of England Moral Welfare Council) to Temple, 23 Feb. 1943, ibid., fos. 230–1. Cf. resolutions of twenty Chaplains to the Forces, 19 May 1943, ibid., fo. 325.

[45] J. Walvin, *Leisure and Society, 1830–1950* (London, 1978), 146–7.

[46] Costello, *Love, Sex, and War*, 184.

[47] *BW*, 28 Mar. 1940, p. 356; Church of Scotland Edinburgh Presbytery Minutes, 5 May 1942, CH2/121/61, pp. 96–7.

[48] *CT*, 19 Jan. 1940, p. 39.

[49] Ibid.

long, to make way for some dreadful crooner'; while radio comedians were more often vulgar than funny, giving the public an unhealthy taste for 'dirt'.[50] There were worries about the 'irreverence' in a broadcast play about Christ, *The Man born to be King* by Dorothy Sayers (herself an active Christian). Television broadcasting was stopped for the duration of the war, otherwise its developing transmissions might have been open to similar criticisms.

Betting showed some decline in the war years, though far from sufficient to satisfy anti-gambling opinion.[51] Anti-gamblers were encouraged by the Government's suspension of football pools when war broke out, with the aim of encouraging people to subscribe instead to Defence Bonds and War Savings Certificates.[52] The pools were soon allowed to resume in a somewhat restricted form, but in 1942 the Churches' Committee on Gambling was able to say that the population was spending less than eight million pounds a year on football pools, compared with nearly fifty millions before the war.[53] In reply to an attempt by Archbishop Lang to persuade him that the pools should be prohibited during the war on the ground that the Government needed more money, the Chancellor of the Exchequer (Sir John Simon) said he had already placed some limits on them. He did not believe that they 'reproduce all the evils of gambling in the way that betting on horses may do . . . there is not the temptation to double your stake when you lose, and to venture more money than you had originally intended, which is one of the very worst features of betting at a race meeting, or gambling at Monte Carlo'.[54] But Lang was not convinced, saying in his reply: 'I expect you may have to reconsider your attitude when your need of money becomes even greater than it is.'[55]

Though the need for money did become greater, football pools were not further disturbed during the war. There were continued efforts to have them suspended, but these were unsuccessful. Neville Chamberlain as Prime Minister agreed to receive a deputation on the subject, organized by Lang and Bishop A. A. David of

[50] Ibid., 3 Jan. 1941, p. 3. Cf. *RGACS* (1942), 374–5.

[51] *Thorny Problems*, 7; *PAGAFCS* (1940), 620.

[52] A. C. Don (Archbishop Lang's chaplain) to Bishop of Liverpool (A. A. David), 25 Nov. 1939, LP 176, fo. 162; Bishop David to Don, 29 Nov. 1939, ibid., fo. 163.

[53] Report of Church and Nation Committee to General Assembly of Church of Scotland, May 1940, *RGACS* (1940), 388–90; *CT*, 4 Sept. 1942, p. 480.

[54] Simon to Lang, 21 Dec. 1939, LP 176, fos. 167–8.

[55] Lang to Simon, 27 Dec. 1939, ibid., fo. 169.

Liverpool and including Benson Perkins, the Methodist chairman of the Churches' Committee on Gambling. But the deputation did not take place before Chamberlain was replaced by Churchill in May 1940, and after this Lang said that the war situation was too critical to broach such a matter to the premier.[56] In October that year a correspondent in the *British Weekly* said that he had approached politicians of different parties on the desirability of suspending the pools, but to no avail.[57]

Four years later, in October 1944, the *Church Times* noted that gambling was on the increase. The paper ascribed this to the earning of higher wages and to a dearth of goods in the shops, and feared that the increase would continue after the war: 'If the craze does not subside, and if the plans for a post-war boom in dog-racing are realized, there is every chance that gambling will become an even uglier social menace than it was in the twenties and thirties.'[58]

Fears about the growth of gambling were repeated in the case of drink. In this respect an increase had been noted in the few years before the war, seriously undermining the steady gains made by the temperance movement during several decades before the mid-1930s. The total expenditure on alcohol in Great Britain was estimated at £257,050,000 in 1938, showing an increase of more than £32,000,000 since 1933. The Public Questions Committee of the Free Church of Scotland, which gave these figures in 1940, noted also that the Government had so far taken no action, as it had in the First World War, to reduce the levels of drinking. During a brief four-week experiment in Glasgow, however, when the licensed trade closed its premises at 8 p.m. instead of two hours later, the number of road casualties in that city had dropped considerably. This seemed to prove, said the Public Questions Committee, that 'drink is certainly one contributory cause towards the slaughter that goes on week after week on our roads'. Licences to sell drink in Scottish hotels on Sundays were unfortunately increasing, 'to meet the demands of the travelling public and especially to cater for the hordes of restless pagans who disturb the peace of the countryside on the Lord's Day'.[59]

[56] Bishop David to Lang, 22 Feb. 1940, ibid., fos. 170–2; Lang to David, 21 Mar. 1940, ibid., fo. 175; David to Lang, 27 Mar. 1940, ibid., fo. 176; Lang to David, 18 May 1940, ibid., fo. 179.

[57] *BW*, 3 Oct. 1940, p. 4 (letter of F. Norton Bell).

[58] *CT*, 27 Oct. 1944, p. 571; cf. ibid., 3 Nov. 1944, p. 583 (letter of H. McNaught).

[59] *PAGAFCS* (1940), 619–20.

Complaints about government inaction over the drink trade were widespread during the war.[60] Among various efforts to reduce drinking were religious exhortations for personal restraint. For example, a letter in *The Times* towards the end of 1939, signed by Archbishop Temple, Cardinal Hinsley, and others, urged that the abnormal social conditions caused by war—such as 'the darkened streets, the increased peril of the roads, the gathering of young men in camps, and the widespread upheaval of family life'—should be met by restraint in the consumption of drink.[61] In January 1942 a deputation from the TCCC saw the Home Secretary, Herbert Morrison, to express concern about a government proposal to authorize the sale of drink in the canteens of munitions factories. Henry Carter, who was a member of the deputation, urged that the Government should establish a National Liquor Control Board as in the previous war. But this plea was unsuccessful.[62] The *New Campaigner*, which was issued by the TCCC, found the Government's attitude very disappointing compared with the actions taken in the 1914–18 conflict:

> At the outset of every war a wise administration should in the common interest establish temporary special safeguards with regard to liquor control. In marked contrast with the salutary measures taken by Mr Lloyd George in the last war, many persons view with concern the apparent apathy of H. M. Government as to this important matter at the present time.[63]

Cyril Black, addressing the Baptist Assembly, 'drew striking contrasts between the Government's desire for war savings, its concern for health and housing, food and education, and the paradox of support for a (drink) trade that undercut all these things'.[64]

In May 1943 the Temperance Committee of the Edinburgh presbytery of the Church of Scotland suggested that alcoholic drink should join the list of rationed commodities: 'this might be done by

[60] e.g. NFCC Minutes of Executive Committee, 22 Sept. 1939, bk. 6, p. 383; 15 Apr. 1940, p. 390; *BW*, 22 Feb. 1940, p. 283; *CYB* (1940), 200–1; Church of Scotland Dundee Presbytery Minutes, 3 Dec. 1941, CH2/103/43, p. 155; *PAGAFCS* (1942), 374.

[61] *New Campaigner* (Autumn 1939), 9.

[62] Ibid. (Spring 1942), 3–7.

[63] Ibid. 11. Cf. FCFC Minutes, 26 Oct. 1942, p. 32; *PAGAFCS* (1944), 146.

[64] *BT*, 10 May 1945, p. 6.

rationing the quantities of grain and sugar to be used, or through the quantities of liquor supplied by manufacturers or wholesalers to their customers, or by rationing to the customer by registration and/or coupons.'[65] This suggestion failed, as did other proposals for wartime restrictions on drink. By May 1945, when the war in Europe ended, the Church of Scotland General Assembly's Committee on Temperance lamented that drinking had considerably increased during the armed struggle: 'during the war the beer consumed in this country has risen in bulk from roughly 25,000,000 barrels to 31,000,000 barrels a year, as against a decrease in the last war from 36,000,000 barrels to 12,000,000 barrels.'[66] The tendency to consume more drink had been inflated by the presence of large numbers of foreign troops in the country. Nevertheless, it did not seem that temperance advocates were going to be complacent in the post-war years.

Drinking and gambling, the cinema, and other entertainments clearly threatened efforts to preserve Sundays from further secularization. During the Second World War, fears of further encroachment were continually present, and sabbatarians remained constant protesters. In May 1940 the Dundee presbytery of the Church of Scotland resolved that all Christians should consider deeply their manner of keeping the Lord's Day, on the basis of a motion that

> The Presbytery, recognizing that the Nation has been mobilized for the prosecution of a War for the preservation of the eternal verities of the Christian Faith, views with alarm the rapidly growing secularization of the Lord's Day, which, already acute, is being greatly increased by wartime conditions.[67]

'The attitude which a nation adopts towards the Lord's Day is an acid test of its moral and spiritual condition,' said the Public Questions Committee of the Free Church of Scotland in May 1944.

> Judged by that acid test, Scotland is today in a parlous state. The process of secularizing the Lord's Day proceeds apace . . . It is greatly to be feared

[65] Church of Scotland Edinburgh Presbytery Minutes, 4 May 1943, CH2/121/62, p. 48; also 4 Jan. 1944, ibid., pp. 133–4; 4 July 1944; ibid., p. 221.

[66] *RGACS* (1945), 285–6.

[67] Church of Scotland Dundee Presbytery Minutes, 13 Mar. 1940, CH2/103/43, pp. 50, 63. Cf. *RGACS* (1940), 386–7.

that such profanation of the Lord's Day will not cease, but will rather be intensified when the war is over, once a taste for such unprofitable wasting of the day has been created and sedulously nurtured.[68]

Using Sundays for cinema-going, factory work, harvesting, and golf-playing received condemnation in various quarters.[69] But wide differences on these matters had developed among Christians. The Catholic *Universe* objected in 1942 to an 'unreasonable' protest organized 'with large-scale advertisements' by the Lord's Day Observance Society against the broadcasting of plays on the life of Christ in 'Children's Hour':

The Society denounces the whole undertaking on grounds which we do not in the least accept . . . Far from disapproving of the use of either plays or the wireless for religious purposes on Sunday, we welcome any such enterprise most cordially. In this case we express our most sincere thanks to the BBC.[70]

It was particularly difficult to object to the use of Sundays for helping the war effort. Home Guard units often drilled on Sunday mornings, the Army and the Air Force held parades on that day, and there was strong pressure to keep factories at work on Sundays in order to expedite war production.[71]

The Sunday opening of cinemas was extended during the war, even in Scotland, in order to assist members of the armed forces to occupy their leisure time. But attempts to allow theatres and music halls to open on Sundays did not succeed. Many actors opposed the Sunday opening of theatres because they did not wish to work on that day. In anticipation of a House of Commons motion in 1943 to permit this opening (the motion was unsuccessful), Archbishop Temple was the recipient of letters from actors who held differing views on the question. Ronald Keir, Dorothy Dewhurst, Hugh Sinclair, and Athene Seyler wrote to him stating their objections to the proposed opening. As part of a group of actors at the Intimate Theatre, Palmers Green, London, Keir and Dewhurst told the Archbishop that 'the present emergency [i.e. the war] is being exploited by vested interests on the one hand who see great

[68] *PAGAFCS* (1944), 144.

[69] e.g. Church of Scotland Dundee Presbytery Minutes, 2 Apr. 1941, CH2/103/43, p. 116; *BW*, 5 Dec. 1940, p. 98; *CCC*, 28 May 1941, i. 9, pp. 136–8, 140–3.

[70] *U.*, 9 Jan. 1942, p. 6.

[71] *CCC*, 28 May 1941, i. 9, pp. 136–7, 141.

financial gain to be acquired, and the Communist element on the Council [of the British Actors' Equity union] who wish to see the end of Sunday as soon as possible'. They solicited Temple's aid 'to protect the theatrical profession against the serious possibility of a seven-day working week and to preserve for us our ancient heritage to pass our Sundays in peace and quiet'.[72] A letter to Temple from Hugh Sinclair, Athene Seyler, and others also informed him that the desire for Sunday opening came chiefly from the theatre proprietors and managers: 'a considerable section of the theatrical profession opposes it, not on the grounds taken by the Lord's Day Observance Society, but because of their desire to continue to share in the weekly rest-day common to most citizens.'[73] Dame Sybil Thorndike, on the other hand, wrote to the Archbishop strongly favouring Sunday opening:

> I don't think the question of numbers employed should be considered if it [theatre-opening] is for the service of the community, and we cannot seriously bring up the religious side as it wouldn't interfere with one's early communion or any other service; nor do I think the wider question of the religious life of the whole community comes into the argument, as we allow, without protest, munition workers, bus drivers, railway servants [*sic*] etc., to work on Sundays—and their work is no more necessary surely than the cultural services . . . I think Sunday opening of theatres should be allowed . . . the majority of British Actors' Equity is in favour of it . . . As a regular communicant I know Sunday opening wouldn't interfere with church-going, and many of us already work very hard on Sundays, only without pay . . . For many of the public Sunday night is the only night when they are not tired out—and it is the working class that likes the finest plays.[74]

In response to these urgings Temple wrote to *The Times*; his letter was published on 18 January. He said that

> every stage in the direction of commercializing Sunday is to be regretted. It may interfere with worship, the primary religious obligation of the day,

[72] Ronald Keir, Dorothy Dewhurst, *et al.* to Temple, Jan. 1943, TP 42, fo. 292.

[73] Hugh Sinclair, Athene Seyler, *et al.* to Temple, 6 Jan. 1943, ibid., fo. 255. Cf. Revd William Paton to Temple, 8 Jan. 1943, enclosing a letter he had received from Valerie Taylor and Hugh Sinclair (ibid., fos. 256–7), citing the support of 116 actors including Peggy Aschroft, Cecil Parker, Alistair Sim, and Phyllis Calvert; also H. H. Martin (Secretary, Lord's Day Observance Society) to Temple, 16 Jan. 1943, ibid., fo. 269; *BW*, 21 Jan. 1943, p. 210.

[74] Sybil Thorndike Casson to Temple, 12 Jan. 1943, ibid., fos. 260–3. Cf. *CT*, 28 Feb. 1941, p. 119.

though this is perhaps not inevitable. But it will certainly, for many people, interfere with the freedom for family and social intercourse, and it will for all involve a regrettable change in the moral atmosphere or feeling of the day.[75]

During the armed conflict the formidable social challenges to the Churches in the inter-war years were intensified. Drinking, divorce, and the use of artificial birth control increased. Much of this growth, however, occurred on account of the pressure of wartime conditions and events. It was by no means inevitable that the growth would continue when peace was restored, and in at least some ways it did not. The wartime social trends subsided in several respects into tamer and more cautious paths. On no account did the unprecedentedly large use of divorce and birth control in wartime, and perhaps unprecedented rates of adultery, commence a lengthy and continuous introduction to the marked permissiveness of the 1960s. The permissive developments of the 1960s emerged from previous changes and desires stretching back at least to the beginning of the century. But they were not continuously linked to the experiences of the war years, because no continuing escalation of permissive developments took place after the war. The later 1940s and 1950s were, on the whole, a quieter period in regard to social behaviour, during which innovation and change receded until the appearance of stronger transforming winds by 1960. But this quieter period was far from heralding the introduction of the new, moral social order desired by the Churches as the major aspect of post-war reconstruction.

Reconstruction of various kinds, based on the hope that Britain would emerge from the struggle victorious, was a constant theme of British thought and expression and motivated some government enactments during the Second World War. Some aspects of the desire for reconstruction were related to the need to curb or alleviate developments taking place in the war or before it, such as increased alcohol consumption and gambling, increased divorce rates, and the need for new housing in an attempt to repair the effects of enemy bombing. Other aspects were related to the opportunity sought from the anticipated victory to adopt and implement

[75] *The Times*, 18 Jan. 1943 (draft letter in TP 42, fos. 271–5). Cf. Sinclair to Temple, 18 Jan. 1943, ibid., fo. 280; Ivor Thomas, MP, to Temple, 20 Jan. 1943, ibid., fos. 288–9; Temple to Dame Sybil Thorndike, 21 Jan. 1943, ibid., fo. 290.

plans of public policy—such as a reformed and extended education system, a national health service, and perhaps nationalized industry—which had been in incubation for a generation among various planning groups. Added to these large domestic concerns was the supreme aim of establishing an international order in which peace would last.

Many organizations saw renewed temperance campaigning as an essential contribution to social reconstruction, especially on account of the high drink consumption of wartime. Among resolutions placed before the fourth annual congress of the FCFC in 1944 was a plea that education authorities should be urged to include, in lessons on citizenship, warnings about the dangers of drinking.[76] In 1945 the Church and Nation Committee of the Church of Scotland expressed the emphatic hope that community centres in new housing schemes built after the war would be kept alcohol-free, and that the new housing areas would be 'permitted to develop their social life without the introduction of the thwarting influence of the public house'.[77]

The building of new houses in devastated areas—in order to meet 'an urban housing problem of gigantic proportions', as Cyril Garbett (now Archbishop of York) stated[78]—was the most basic aspect of post-war reconstruction needs. On this there was considerable emphasis in the discussions and resolutions of Church bodies. In a Canterbury Convocation debate in May 1942, the Bishop of Exeter (C. E. Curzon) disclaimed any wish to become involved in technical details which required expert knowledge, but opposed the idea of 'zoning' to which many town planners adhered. Zoning denied the fellowship of 'all sorts and conditions of men' living together: 'it destroyed community, it created snobbery, and it was distinctly un-Christian . . . As a former Bishop of Stepney . . . he had great hopes that this unrivalled opportunity would not be missed and that the London County Council would provide for and seek to direct all kinds of residents into East London.' In the same debate Bishop Barnes of Birmingham advocated the building of 'satellite towns . . . where the dwellers were so situated that they could obtain easy approach to nature . . . with the wholesome

[76] FCFC Minutes of General Purposes Committee, 6 Mar. 1944, p. 62; 28 July 1944, p. 69.

[77] *RGACS* (1945), 290–2.

[78] *CT*, 2 Oct. 1942, p. 537.

health to body, mind and spirit which nature gave'. The Upper House of the Convocation unanimously resolved that the planning authorities should 'discourage the segregation of citizens in different parts of towns according to differences in their income or occupation', and, in the siting of new towns, that they should have 'reverent regard to the preservation of the beauty of the countryside and the fertility of the soil of Britain'.[79]

Social planning for the country after the war ran from 1940 in almost uninterrupted sequence with the planning which had characterized the 1930s and before. Christians made a large contribution to the suggestions for post-war society, as authors of books and as participants in conferences, political organizations, and Church assemblies and committees. But the proposals for reconstruction and the large extent to which they were implemented cannot be seen as a Church or a Christian activity alone. They did involve many Christians, but also many non-Christians such as Keynes and Beveridge, two of the leading apostles of reconstruction through State management supplemented by voluntary giving.

Both established Churches were to the fore in initiating discussions and proposals on social change. The Church of Scotland General Assembly launched in 1940 a Commission for the Interpretation of God's Will in the Present Crisis. This issued five reports during the remainder of the war, wide-ranging in overall scope, widely circulated, and including (in the reports of 1942 and 1944) recommendations on social policy. The 1942 report emphasized the unchanging evangelical condemnation of sin, which was seen as embracing undue regard for self-interest and class interest and neglect of social and communal obligation. A section of the 1944 report recommended that there should be some public ownership of the means of production and distribution.[80] Reconstructive action of this kind was seemingly more resolute in the Church of Scotland than in its sister-establishment of England. It was only by twenty-nine votes to twenty-two that the Lower House of Canterbury Convocation agreed in May 1941 that a committee should be appointed, preferably in cooperation with other bodies, to 'draw up a statement of Christian principles necessary for social

[79] *CCC*, 19–20 May 1942, i. 10, pp. 176–80; *Year Book of the National Assembly of the Church of England* (1943), 99–100.
[80] Donald C. Smith, *Passive Obedience and Prophetic Protest: Social Criticism in the Scottish Church, 1830–1945* (New York, 1987), 373–8.

reconstruction after the war'. Misgivings about the practicality of trying to conduct such a committee in wartime were expressed by the Dean of Chichester (A. S. Duncan-Jones) in the debate, and the preferability of leaving such questions to 'economists, politicians, and statesmen' was raised.[81]

No such reticence, however, marked the attitude of Temple and the ICF. P. T. R. Kirk of the ICF suggested, and the Christendom Group helped to organize, an Anglican conference at Malvern College, Worcestershire, from 7 to 10 January 1941. Temple presided. T. S. Eliot, Dorothy Sayers, Sir Richard Acland, Kenneth Ingram, Donald Mackinnon, V. A. Demant, and W. G. Peck were among the distinguished speakers, most of whom represented the viewpoint of the Anglo-Catholic Christendom Group. Another of this school of thought, Maurice Reckitt, could not attend on account of illness, but sent his paper, which was read by Temple to the gathering. Many of the participants, perhaps most of them, favoured more State intervention in order to reform society. But, while some participants were socialists, others were clearly not, and the question of nationalized industry caused differences among them.[82]

The Malvern Conference was only a partial success. It was far smaller than Copec, having 400 participants, and the proceedings were overloaded and rushed. Malvern did not produce anything like Copec's volume of reading matter, but this was far from being the intention. The event produced only one report, drawn up through the Broad Church Temple's coordinating skills, entitled *The Life of the Church and the Order of Society*.[83] This report, which was not supported by all present, advocated rejection of the economic motive as the foundation of national life, and suggested tentatively that the main industrial resources should be taken into public ownership. The report laid down a role for the

[81] *CCC*, 27 May 1941, i. 9, pp. xi, 78–80 (esp. speech of Dean Duncan-Jones).

[82] R. Lloyd, *The Church of England, 1900–65* (London, 1966), 309–10; F. A. Iremonger, *William Temple, Archbishop of Canterbury, his Life and Letters* (1948; new impression, 1949), 428 ff.; S. Mayor, *The Churches and the Labour Movement* (London, 1967), 372; E. R. Norman, *Church and Society in England, 1770–1970* (Oxford, 1976), 365–7; J. S. Peart-Binns, *Maurice B. Reckitt, a Life* (Basingstoke, 1988), 140–3; J. Kent, *William Temple: Church, State and Society in Britain, 1880–1950* (Cambridge, 1992), 150–1, 155–65.

[83] *Malvern, 1941. The Life of the Church and the Order of Society, Being the Proceedings of the Archbishop of York's Conference* (London, 1941).

Churches as advisers on the broad principles of legislation, before specific proposals were suggested by professional experts and debated by Parliament.[84]

'Since the Malvern Conference of 1941', Reckitt wrote in 1945, 'there has certainly been a revival of interest in the social applications of Christianity. It has gripped the minds of many both of the clergy and of the laity.'[85] Two hundred thousand copies of the Malvern conclusions were issued by the ICF, and the conference had offshoots, amongst which might be numbered Temple's widely read Penguin Special, *Christianity and the Social Order*, published in 1942. One of Malvern's offshoots was a Council of Clergy and Ministers for Common Ownership, started after a two-day Whitsuntide conference at Leicester in 1942. Alfred Blunt, Bishop of Bradford, was unanimously nominated president of the new council, and Dean Hewlett Johnson (who succeeded Blunt as president) and J. C. Putterill, successor of Conrad Noel as Rector of Thaxted, were among the members. The first pamphlet issued by the Council, *Christians in the Class Struggle*, written by Gilbert Cope and with a foreword by Bishop Blunt, was extremely controversial and involved Blunt in much correspondence. The aims of the Council included a commitment to the ideal of nationalization, which was only partially satisfied by the post-war Labour Government:

> We believe that the private ownership of the great productive resources of the community is contrary to Divine Justice, and inevitably involves man in a self-centred way of life. We believe that the common ownership of these resources, with due regard for the freedom of the individual, more nearly expresses the will of God for man's life on earth as revealed by Jesus Christ. We pledge ourselves, as an essential part of our Christian duty, to work for this end.[86]

The ICF engaged in further notable activities. It organized a vast gathering in the Albert Hall on 26 September 1942, attended by 7,000 people and having to refuse admission to another 13,000 on account of lack of space. The audience was in effect called on, as the *British Weekly* put it, 'to share a crusade to establish a sort of

[84] *CT*, 17 Jan. 1941, pp. 27, 31; 31 Jan., p. 64; 14 Feb., p. 96; 21 Feb., p. 103; 23 Jan. 1942, p. 54.

[85] M. B. Reckitt (ed.), *Prospect for Christendom: Essays in Catholic Social Reconstruction* (London, 1945), 234.

[86] J. S. Peart-Binns, *Blunt* (Queensbury, Yorks., 1969), 190–2.

superior and Christian socialism'.[87] Almost inevitably Temple was a prominent speaker. Others included Archbishop Garbett, who spoke on his favourite subject of housing needs, and Sir Stafford Cripps, a Labour member of Churchill's War Cabinet. It was, said Cripps, fundamentally important that Christians should insist that

the Church undertook here and now its task of social salvation as the means of perfecting the rule of God on the earth. It was not, however, the function of the Church to enter the lists of political parties, but to provide the moral force and the driving power for social and economic development.[88]

Temple, as Archbishop of Canterbury, sustained the reputation he had developed as Bishop of Manchester and Archbishop of York as the leading ecclesiastical proponent of the extension of social welfare through State intervention. At the numerous meetings he attended he made either broad statements of intent or commented on practical social or religious action. He referred to an example of the latter, taking place in a heavily bomb-damaged area, at a Convocation meeting in May 1942:

We have been able in Hull, through the Hull section of the Diocesan Reorganization Committee, working in concert with the Free Churches, to present a plan for meeting what we take to be the spiritual needs of the rebuilt areas, and this has been received with great sympathy and cordiality by the (local) authorities.[89]

Temple's most famous contribution to reconstruction during the war was his slim volume *Christianity and the Social Order*, published by Penguin in February 1942 and selling 140,000 copies. This was basically a historical survey of the development of Christian involvement with social reform, with a brief section on reconstruction—curiously brief, considering the importance and popularity of the subject—entitled 'The Task Before Us', to which was appended 'A Suggested Programme'. The programme recommended a State policy to improve housing and leisure provision (the working week should be no more than five days), and the control of unemployment through public works and other means. Educational improvement should be sought through the development of smaller classes and a later school-leaving age. Wage levels should be adequate 'to

[87] *BW*, 1 Oct. 1942, p. 10; *CT*, 2 Oct. 1942, pp. 536–8.
[88] *BW*, 1 Oct. 1942, p. 10.
[89] *CCC*, 2 May 1942, i. 10, p. 229.

bring up a large family in proper decency and comfort', and a family allowance should be paid for every child after the first two. The involvement of workers in the management of their industry should be developed.[90]

Temple made it clear that he was stating these aims as an individual and did not seek in any way to have them adopted as official Church policy. Nevertheless, he wrote in the book, 'the first necessity for progress is more and better Christians, taking full responsibility as citizens for the political, social, and economic system under which they and their fellows live'.[91] To his first Canterbury diocesan conference in July 1942 he said that Christians should influence 'in a profound and penetrating way the State itself in . . . fields of activity for human welfare'.[92] Temple's book was acclaimed by people and newspapers of similar opinion across the denominations. The Roman Catholic *Universe* said that in Temple 'we recognize an extremely able and earnest churchman whose deep interest in social reform should find full scope in the years of recovery'.[93] But the only enactment of reconstruction that Temple lived to see was the Butler Education Act of 1944. When he died in October that year, nearly all the period of reconstruction and recovery was still to come.

The year 1942 saw the appearance not only of Temple's book but of the more broadly and directly influential Beveridge Report. Beveridge and Temple, the agnostic and the archbishop, were in touch over social reconstruction—for example, about the possibility of Temple's becoming a trustee of a suggested non-party organization to be called 'New Britain'.[94] When the Beveridge Report appeared in December, advocating social welfare for all on national-insurance principles 'from the cradle to the grave', it was widely welcomed among organs of religious opinion. The Nonconformist *British Weekly* described it as 'an event of the first importance in our national history'. The Convocation of York resolved,

[90] W. Temple, *Christianity and the Social Order* (Harmondsworth, 1942), 73–80; Norman, *Church and Society*, 367–9; *CT*, 20 Feb. 1942, p. 116 (leading article). For Temple's views on family allowances, see also Temple to Eleanor Rathbone, 5 June 1942, TP 23, fo. 335.

[91] Temple, *Christianity*, 74, 75.

[92] Temple to conference, 13 July 1942, TP 69, fos. 54–5.

[93] *U.*, 27 Feb. 1942, p. 6. Cf. M. P. Fogarty, *Planning and the Community* (Catholic Social Guild Year Book, Oxford, 1942).

[94] Beveridge to Temple, 16 Nov. 1942, TP 5, fo. 19.

on the motion of Bishop Blunt, to approve the report and its system of social insurance. The annual assembly of the Congregational Union welcomed the report as 'a bold, if yet incomplete, proposal for providing economic security for every citizen against every form of undeserved calamity or cause of want'.[95] The Report also had opponents among Christians, however—for example, Major Sir Guy Kindersley, who wrote to Temple:

I do not see how your Grace can—in however personal a capacity—publicly support these proposals without, in the eyes of most plain people, appearing to commit the Church of England to the methods admitted by Sir William Beveridge himself to be necessary in order to implement them; and therefore surely taking a side, and, in my judgment, the wrong side, in the greatest political issue of the day . . . every encroachment on individual liberty by the State should be regarded by Christians with suspicion and not as necessarily a good.[96]

Kindersley, though an Anglican, preferred the view of the *Tablet* that the Beveridge Report was a threat to individual liberty and family initiative.[97] Temple replied that he believed the Beveridge plan could be 'so administered as to increase actual liberty, for it seems to me that the primary necessity for effective liberty is security'. 'Of course one knows', he said in the same letter, 'that *The Tablet* is on the extreme wing of Roman Catholic opinion in respect of such matters. A quite different emphasis is given by the *Catholic Herald*, and I do not think it would be possible to claim that one of these is more loyal than the other to the main stream of Catholic teaching'.[98]

Early in 1945 a Plan for Social Security was adopted by the Coalition Government, embodying the main provisions of the Beveridge Report. The plan was 'publicly supported by all political parties', reported the Church of Scotland's Church and Nation Committee to the General Assembly of May that year.[99] The verdict of the general election of July 1945, however, seemed to be that a Labour Government would provide the most effective endorse-

[95] *BW*, 10 Dec. 1942, p. 119; *Year Book of the National Assembly of the Church of England* (1944), 116; Peart-Binns, *Blunt*, 182–3; *CYB* (1944), 32.

[96] Kindersley to Temple, 1 July 1943, TP 5, fo. 29.

[97] Ibid. See P. Coman, *Catholics and the Welfare State* (London, 1977), 41–51.

[98] Temple to Kindersley, 2 July 1943, TP 5, fos. 30–1. See also Kindersley to Temple, 6 July 1943, ibid., fos. 32–3; Temple to Kindersley, 9 July 1943, ibid., fo. 34.

[99] *RGACS* (1945), 274.

ment of the Beveridge plan, and the Labour Party was returned strongly to power. 'If the [Coalition] security scheme succeeds', said the Church and Nation Committee report,

> it will eliminate the hard times resulting from trade cycles, secure employment without the loss of personal freedom, and avoid the miseries and frustration of years of depression after the war . . . The Church ought to cultivate within her own borders and in society a spirit of goodwill and self-sacrifice to make the scheme effective.

At the same time, however, overweening State power at the expense of individual liberty had to be prevented:

> A word of warning is . . . needed. At a time when the community is assuming more and more responsibility for the physical, mental and social well-being of its citizens of all ages, there is an indubitable temptation for parents, employers, and others to hand over the function of the wise guardian and the good neighbour entirely to the State. This tendency might become calamitous. The Church ought to re-emphasize the basic importance of parental care, initiative and neighbourly generosity in any State that can be truly called Christian.[100]

Thus was stated the dilemma, or perhaps simply the desire for compromise, between State control and voluntary action, which characterized a great many in the Churches. Perhaps the majority of Church members and the majority of Christians in the country tried to hold to this compromise, though of course there were many who disagreed with it from either a 'left' or a 'right' way of thinking. Over the succeeding half-century much vocal Church opinion, especially among Church leaders, showed itself partial to this *via media*, issuing warnings against enthusiasts of either a pronounced 'left' or a pronounced 'right' tendency who sought to undermine it.

The same report of the Church and Nation Committee of the Church of Scotland showed that it had specific Scottish concerns in regard to reconstruction as well as general British ones. Not only afforestation and a strengthened fishing industry but also the development of hydro-electric power and commercial aviation were needed to revitalize the Highlands and Islands, while 'men of all parties have united in urging the claims of Prestwick as an international airport second only to London, the building of a road bridge

[100] Ibid.

over the Forth, and the retention of the dockyard and naval base at Rosyth'.[101]

The 1944 Education Act for England and Wales was in effect the first of the enactments which created the Welfare State, and it contained elements of vital importance to all who wished to preserve marked Christian elements in State education. The Act was based on proposals in a White Paper which appeared in mid-1943. Before this there had been much religious discussion in anticipation of change in public policy. In February 1941 a statement on Christian education was issued, signed by the Archbishops of Canterbury, York, and Wales. The statement had the full agreement of Free Church leaders, and followed consultation with the bishops of the Church of England and of the Church in Wales. The importance of a Christian education in all schools was emphasized, though it was recognized that parents had the right to withdraw children from the religious education offered. Five points were made concerning the quality and quantity of religious education, one of them being that there should be an act of worship by the whole school at the beginning of the school day. An agreed syllabus for religious education should also be adopted, with the right of withdrawal for special instruction if desired.[102] All five points were included in the White Paper of 1943.[103]

Roman Catholics were anxious to maintain their own schools, and disliked having to pay rates to support undenominational schools in addition to paying for the upkeep of their own.[104] Their dissatisfaction was not relieved in the 1944 Act. As a body they were the clearest opponents of this measure, but they were not alone in objecting to it. Among Anglicans, Bishop A. C. Headlam had stigmatized the existing dual system of 'provided' (council) schools and 'non-provided' (voluntary) schools as a threat to 'liberty and initiative'. He preferred something along the lines of the existing Scottish system:

> The only just system of religious education is to secure by statute the right for all children to be educated according to the beliefs of their parents, in

[101] *RGACS* (1945), 275–6.
[102] *The Times*, 13 Feb. 1941 (extract in BP 159, fo. 1).
[103] *CCC*, 27 May 1941, i. 9, p. vii; *Year Book of the National Assembly of the Church of England* (1942), 204; J. G. Lockhart, *Cosmo Gordon Lang* (London, 1949), 368–9; *CT*, 28 Aug. 1942, p. 471.
[104] *U.*, 27 Mar. 1942, p. 7; *The Times*, 26 Aug. 1943 (extract in BP 160, fo. 80).

all State-provided and State-aided schools. The method . . . would be partly by separate schools, partly by giving facilities either within or without (schools), as might be most convenient.[105]

But the dual system was maintained by the 1944 Act, and religious teaching was strengthened. In the State schools religious education became compulsory by law for the first time, although it had invariably been provided before by the decision of local authorities. The non-provided schools became either 'voluntary aided' or 'controlled'. In the former case, they would continue to provide denominational teaching in accordance with their trust deeds; in the latter, they had to open two-thirds of their management bodies to representatives of the local authority, and the management bodies would have control of religious education. The greater freedom of voluntary-aided schools was obtained in return for meeting half the cost of reaching the Ministry of Education's building standards. The Church of England had approved the principle of the bill before its passage, and the measure was accepted by the National Assembly as it was going through Parliament. There was also general Nonconformist satisfaction with it. There were some misgivings, however, among supporters of Anglican education—misgivings which were borne out later as the financial implications of voluntary-aided status came home to the Church of England and the Church in Wales.[106] Nevertheless, the settlement was a notable change from the hard battles between Church and Nonconformity over the Education Acts of 1870 and 1902.

Through this Act the State had confirmed its desire to maintain Christianity officially in society, and this no doubt contributed to the sense of cautious optimism with which the Churches faced a restoraton of peace.[107] Despite the four decades of numerical decline which most of the British Churches had now experienced—the Roman Catholic Church and, to a much lesser extent, the Church of Scotland being the main exceptions—there was now the hope that, through home-missionary efforts, post-war reconstruction might

[105] Letter from Headlam in *The Times*, 5 Nov. 1942 (extract in BP 159, fo. 30). Cf. Bishop George Bell to Cardinal Hinsley, 5 Nov. 1942, BP 159, fo. 29; Bell to Powell Edwards, 25 Nov. 1942, ibid., fo. 88; *The Times*, 21 Nov. 1942 (leading article; extract in BP 159, fos. 65–65*a*); *CT*, 3 Mar. 1944, p. 155; 17 Mar. 1944, p. 144; 14 Apr. 1944, p. 195; Norman, *Church and Society*, 401–6.

[106] *CT*, 11 Apr. 1947, p. 204.

[107] J. Wolffe, *God and Greater Britain: Religion and National Life in Britain and Ireland, 1843–1945* (London, 1994), 251.

come to include a halting of contraction in membership. Moral rejuvenation was also the hope of Christians, and generally speaking this meant (until at least the 1960s) the strengthening of traditional morality. 'We need to enter the post-war world with a great reserve of moral strength,' said a report of the PMC in October 1943.

The Free Church of Scotland's Commmittee on Public Questions was in no doubt that, more than mere material improvement, 'fresh tides of spiritual power' were necessary for national revival and well-being.[108] Similarly Bishop Bell had said in his Penguin book of 1940, *Christianity and World Order*: 'the supreme need is not schemes or constitutions or blue prints, but a new spirit, a conversion of human persons.'[109] As for the differing proposals for reform coming from political parties and other groups, 'the Church is the Mother of them all', said the *Church Times* in September 1941, and she should not give exclusive support to one or another; but the Church, though non-ideological in a secular sense, could support and even initiate schemes for housing reconstruction after the physical depredations of the war.[110]

On the motion of Malcolm Spencer, a leading social reformer among Congregationalists, it was resolved at an annual assembly to congratulate the Government on its policy for house-building.[111] In regard to moral reconstruction, the Church (urged Mervyn Stockwood, later Bishop of Southwark, in a letter to Temple) should engage in industrial mission—for example, by sending clergy to work in factories.[112] It was announced in the *British Weekly* in May 1945 that the Church of Scotland had resolved to raise a million pounds in ten years, in order to build churches and halls for many of the Scots who were expected to be resettled in new housing areas after the war.[113] Whether they were interested in their own internal plans for reconstruction and expansion, or in these objects on a wider basis, the Churches were going to be deeply concerned with social policy and social behaviour in post-war Britain.

[108] *PAGAFCS* (1945), 352.
[109] G. K. A. Bell, *Christianity and World Order* (Harmondsworth, 1940), 102.
[110] *CT*, 5 Sept. 1941. Cf. Church of Scotland Edinburgh Presbytery Minutes, 7 Mar. 1944, CH2/121/62, p. 165, and Church of Scotland Dundee Presbytery Minutes, 5 Apr. 1944, CH2/103/44, p. 269.
[111] *CYB* (1945), 33.
[112] Stockwood to Temple, 5 May 1944, TP 42, fos. 222–6.
[113] *BW*, 24 May 1945, p. 100.

5
Churches and Social Issues, 1945–1960

The Churches had been thoroughly bound up with the British war effort, and were equally involved with the victory celebrations. Not surprisingly, they hoped that peace would bring their own revival and victory to parallel the new boost to British morale bestowed in some ways by the outcome of the war. But, just as the country as a whole had soon to face unavoidable facts regarding its position in the world—the loss of empire and of foremost world-power status—the Churches as a whole had to face the probability that they were not likely to return to the position of strength they had possessed up to the 1920s. Christian revival seemed to become limited to brief spurts—the continuance of the wartime Commando Campaign until 1947, the launching of industrial missions, the Billy Graham crusades of the 1950s, and the sporadic rise of religious groups among the young—rather than being sustained by consistent and long-term growth. The only exception to this seems to have been the church-building programmes in new towns and housing areas.

In a survey of churchgoing in York in 1948, Seebohm Rowntree and G. R. Lavers found that overall attendance had not declined much since a previous inquiry in 1935, but that the current and potential prosperity of Churches in the city varied widely on account of their differing success in attracting the young:

> It follows [from figures given] that the Roman Catholics have an excellent chance of maintaining a vigorous and expanding congregation for some decades, because the proportion of younger adults attending their churches is substantially higher than the proportion in the nation as a whole. No particular change in attendances is to be expected in the Anglican Church and Salvation Army arising solely from the distribution in age groups of their attendances, but the long term prospect for the Nonconformists in York appears to be distinctly bleak, for

these figures indicate that they are not attracting sufficient of the younger age groups.[1]

Between 1945 and 1960 formal membership of the Church of England and the Church of Scotland remained stable, while the Roman Catholics continued to grow rapidly and the Nonconformists (taken collectively) continued to decline steadily.[2] It was perhaps premature to describe the age as 'post-Christian', a term which was already coming into use.[3] But the age (as far as Britain was concerned) could hardly be described as sturdily and clearly Christian. Nor—for various reasons, including the expanding presence of other faiths through immigration—could it be credibly predicted that the country was likely to become so again. The Christian beliefs held by most of the population had become largely 'privatized'—maintained apart from demonstration at public services—and there was no sign that this situation would be reversed. Moreover, while a majority of the population was still Christian, perhaps at least a fifth was agnostic or atheist.[4] Churchgoing met not hostility but indifference from a vast section of the population. The prevailing attitude was perhaps encapsulated in the remarks of a bus conductress recorded in Rowntree and Lavers's *English Life and Leisure*, published in 1951: 'when she brings people home from church on Sunday they don't look any different to her from what they did when she took them there, and she hears them gossiping about one another just as spitefully as usual.'[5] Such remarks indicated that the general populace expected too much from its churchgoers, as it apparently did also from its clergy and ministers. Rowntree and Lavers concluded that, 'despite the devoted adherence to the Churches of millions of ordinary men and women, who make up church membership, it remains true that in the lives of a large majority of people of all classes of the community the Church is no longer relevant'.[6] They also concluded, however, that 'people to-day still believe that Christianity is a

[1] B. S. Rowntree and G. R. Lavers, *English Life and Leisure, a Social Study* (London, 1951), 344–5.

[2] R. Currie, A. Gilbert, and L. Horsley (eds.), *Churches and Churchgoers: Patterns of Church Growth in the British Isles since 1700* (Oxford, 1977), 32.

[3] E. R. Norman, *Church and Society in England, 1770–1970* (Oxford, 1976), 394.

[4] See the analysis of religious affiliation, on a regional and denominational basis, in G. Gorer, *Exploring English Character* (London, 1955), 237–53.

[5] Rowntree and Lavers, *English Life and Leisure*, 346.

[6] Ibid. 352.

relevant and vital force, although they no longer accept the idea that the Church is the "chosen instrument" for the expression of that force'.[7]

The ecumenical movement, which was clearly growing in the 1950s, conferred many religious benefits, including the sharing of buildings and services. But only one inter-Church union emerged, that between the Congregationalists and Presbyterians in England in 1972. In other promising cases, notably that of the Anglicans and Methodists, doctrinal differences proved too strong. In 1972 the effort at Anglican–Methodist union failed.[8] Little emerged from the ambitious hope of achieving 'the re-integration of the whole Church of Christ'.[9]

Some of the social planning of the Second World War and before was realized in the rapid erection of a Welfare State by the Labour Government of 1945–50, with the wide agreement of opposition parties. The adoption of universal social security was the culmination and extension of forty years of intervention. The finished product provided family allowances, sickness and unemployment insurance, old age pensions, a National Health Service, and free primary and secondary education. These innovations could be seen as the satisfactory realization of the collectivist trend of social thinking among many Christians. But amidst the enthusiasm for the Welfare State some cautionary notes were sounded in religious quarters. The *Church Times* tempered its satisfaction by warning that 'the Socialist State is not the same thing as the Kingdom of God'.[10] From some Roman Catholic individuals and publications, and from the Catholic Social Guild, there was pronounced criticism of the Welfare State over a period of some fifteen years, on the grounds that it would undermine individual initiative and family responsibility.[11] The economic crises of the later 1940s added fuel to the criticism because the Government could be accused of being too free with much-needed resources. What Britain needed in its critical economic state in 1947, said a Jesuit writer, Paul Crane, was not expensive social services so much as hard work, sacrifice, and

[7] Ibid. 367.

[8] *CT*, 10 July 1959, p. 9, and 31 July 1959, p. 8, emphasizing theological difficulties in the way of Anglican–Methodist reunion.

[9] *LW* (May 1957), 110.

[10] *CT*, 19 Oct. 1951, p. 711.

[11] See P. Coman, *Catholics and the Welfare State* (London, 1977), 41–85.

faith in God.[12] Among Anglican Church leaders, however, there was by the late 1940s no clear dissent from the view expressed in a publication of 1947 by J. W. C. Wand, Bishop of London, that the Welfare State was 'an expression at the national level of the humanitarian work of the Church'.[13] Arthur Headlam resigned his bishopric in October 1945 and died in January 1947, Hensley Henson had resigned his see in 1939 and died in September 1947; and for many years they had no clerical successors in the Church of England as prominent critics of State intervention.

The great many Christians who welcomed the Welfare State did not, however, want it to become so universally pervasive that it removed all scope for individual action. The triumph of collectivism must not be allowed to become too all-embracing. If Headlam and Henson were soon to leave the scene, Temple with his very different ideas had already departed. His successor as Archbishop of Canterbury, Geoffrey Fisher, has been described as 'inherently conservative' by instinct but independent in his actions from any political party line: 'in domestic questions, Fisher was conciliatory but in general unmoved by the sort of passions which had occupied his predecessor.'[14] Garbett, Demant, Reckitt, and other reformers warned against the growth of an overmighty State, though the actual policies implemented by the Labour Government were generally in accordance with their own advocacy. The potential conflict between State growth and the individual's scope for action was mentioned not infrequently in Church gatherings. The Methodist Conference in 1949, for example, declared that the growth of State power 'threatens to become a totalitarian colossus to which the individual person is completely subordinate'.[15] A report of the Lambeth Conference of 1948, entitled *The Christian Doctrine of Man*, said that the Church must remain the guardian of personal freedom against 'the natural bias of the State towards totalitarianism', and that the Church must preserve the spirit of voluntary social service.[16] Archbishop Fisher, speaking at Brisbane in 1950, said that the Welfare State, though it was welcome and firmly based

[12] P. Crane, *Britain's Crisis: A Personal Opinion* (Glasgow, 1947), 7–9, 20–2, 43–50. Cf. *The Tablet*, 23 Apr. 1950, pp. 303–4.
[13] Quoted in Norman, *Church and Society*, 375.
[14] Ibid. 373.
[15] Ibid. 375.
[16] Ibid. 377.

in Christian thought, had 'to deal with men's material needs, in bulk':

It may come to think that is all a man is—a mouth, a body, an end in himself—unless somebody is going to keep another idea alive, that man has a greater end to serve than himself and a higher law to live by and deeper ends to be fostered and fed. In fact, the Welfare State calls at every point for a far higher level of citizenship from all of us than ever before. It requires citizens who put what they do for others before what they get for themselves; who are keen to put more into the common pool than they take out of it. This higher level of citizenship is essential if the Welfare State is to work; and if it does not, a successor state will almost certainly be some sort of tyranny.[17]

The *Church Times* had stated in 1946 that, in seeking to develop such a higher citizenship, 'the Welfare State knows that it stands to gain enormously by association with organized Christianity'; and Fisher said in 1958 that 'the Welfare State can only be made workable if its citizens become more Christian than they were before'.[18] Similarly the Church of Scotland's *Life and Work* magazine said in 1951 that

essentially it [the Welfare State] presents us with a call and a challenge. The call is to a common helpfulness, 'bearing one another's burdens'; the challenge is to united effort. These are spiritual contributions. If it is to succeed—and all of us must see that it does succeed—it will be only through the exercise of the Christian virtues.[19]

That the Church wished to cooperate with the social services provided by the Welfare State was shown, on a local basis, at Gloucester in 1955, when a working party was established for this purpose, presided over by the bishop.[20] New housing was a development particularly encouraged by Church leaders in the post-war years. Cardinal Griffin, Archbishop of Westminster, said at a rally of the Catholic Social Guild in 1947 that

the provision of houses suitable for families ought to be the main concern of those who direct affairs in this country . . . And once the houses are

[17] Quoted in W. Purcell, *Fisher of Lambeth: A Portrait from Life* (London, 1969), 210.

[18] *CT*, 20 Sept. 1946, p. 564 (cf. ibid., 7 Sept. 1951, p. 606); *CEN*, 14 Mar. 1958, p. 1.

[19] *LW* (July 1951), 153 (quoted in G. I. T. Machin, 'British Churches and Social Issues, 1945–60', *Twentieth Century British History*, 7/3 (1996), 348–9).

[20] *CT*, 27 May 1955, p. 12.

erected the occupants should be encouraged to purchase them . . . We should like to see people of every class owning their own house and having their own little property.[21]

Churches in general wished to maintain their own voluntary endeavours in social aid as a supplement to the operations of the Welfare State, and not to diminish the former because of the extension of the latter. In 1955 the Bishop of Durham, A. M. Ramsey (later Archbishop of York and of Canterbury), stated when opening the thirtieth Summer School of Christian Sociology at Oxford that the numerous ramifications of the Welfare State were weakening Christian social initiative: 'too many Christians appeared to think that the Welfare State had usurped the role of the Church to the extent that there was little left to do but to try to prevent atomic annihilation by retiring into Pacifism.'[22]

Whereas the value of the Welfare State was not seriously questioned among the leaders of most Churches, the question of nationalizing industry aroused more controversy. There were differing views on this question within the respective Churches, as there were in society at large. The fearful could easily present the nationalization of some major industries as the gateway to totalitarian control such as was being imposed in Eastern Europe. The *Church Times* was quite favourable to the Labour Government's industrial programme.[23] But the *Universe* said in March 1947 that, while it had no objection to nationalization in moderation, the unrestricted State takeover of industry might lead to 'the subjection of each and every individual' to the State.[24] The *Methodist Recorder* said that the general election of 1950 was mainly concerned with 'whether the life of the people is to be brought more and more under governmental direction and control. The nationalization of practically all main industries, of the means of production and distribution, is plainly foreshadowed, and indeed asserted, in the declarations of members of the present Government.'[25]

The Labour Governments of 1945–51 bestowed a good deal on their citizens, supplementing universal social security with town-

[21] *U.*, 24 Oct. 1947, pp. 1, 3.
[22] *CEN*, 5 Aug. 1955, p. 3.
[23] *CT*, 28 Mar. 1947, p. 171.
[24] *U.*, 7 Mar. 1947, p. 6.
[25] *MR*, 23 Feb. 1950, p. 8.

and-country-planning initiatives, a housing programme, and implementation of educational extension. But, despite generally full employment, the ministry had severe and repeated economic difficulties. Wartime restrictions—for example, food rationing—lasted for an uncomfortably long time into the peace (or Cold War) era. A longed-for boost in personal consumption, building on the improving conditions of the 1930s which had been halted during the war, did not clearly materialize until the 1950s, although there was a growth in leisure spending in the later 1940s.[26] The initial post-war popularity of Labour became weaker, and in the 1951 election the Conservatives obtained a small majority and commenced a thirteen-year period in power. During this period the Welfare State and most nationalized industries were maintained, and house-building increased. There was general consensus between the Conservative and Labour leaderships over domestic policy, and the main political disputes of the 1950s occurred within the Labour Party. The Conservatives, moreover, were able to add to the benefits of the Welfare State the related benefits of rapidly rising consumer power. Growth in popular prosperity was a dominant feature of the 1950s and 1960s, and gave the Churches cause for both pleasure and concern.

From 1952 a wave of economic prosperity produced an unpecedented rise in consumer spending, which almost doubled in the 1950s. The purchase of cars, television sets, and holidays both at home and abroad were among the manifestations of the new consumer power. The trend continued in spite of the failure of the economy to perform consistently. In 1955 boom gave way to recession, which was in turn replaced by expansion after remedial measures by the Government. A 'stop–go' cycle thus commenced which has characterized the British economy up to the late 1990s. In the late 1950s inflation and rising unemployment were being widely condemned by the Churches.[27]

The Churches gave a restrained welcome to the increasing prosperity of the people, but consistently warned of the need for caution in pleasure and consumption. Children should not be given the large amounts of pocket money that many now received, warned an article in the *Church of England Newspaper* in March

[26] J. Walvin, *Leisure and Society, 1830–1950* (London, 1978), 149.

[27] *LW* (Nov. 1957), 271; *RGACS* (1958), 372; *U.*, 8 May 1959, pp. 1, 20; *MR*, 23 July 1959, p. 8; *CYB* (1960), 82–3.

1957.[28] Teenagers should not use their surplus earnings to parade as 'Teddy Boys' and become a social menace.[29] The dangers of entering into hire-purchase agreements which might overtax personal resources were frequently emphasized by Church bodies. Restrictions placed on hire purchase in the recession of 1955 were welcomed by the Church and Nation Committee of the Church of Scotland, which stated that 'the enormous recent increase in buying by such methods has both financial and moral risks. A very large number of commodities are now bought in this manner, often with little foresight or responsibility.'[30] There was naturally a temptation to do overtime work in order to boost spending power, and this could reduce both time spent in the family circle and energy spent on social pursuits—'injurious tensions' could be caused in human relations.[31] The new prosperity was likely to cause well-being to be assessed 'in terms of material comfort and physical enjoyment': 'more than ever in such a situation is it necessary for the Church to proclaim the teaching of Christ that "a man's life consisteth not in the abundance of things which he possesses" '.[32]

Some objects of the increased consumer power were viewed by the Churches as more innocuous than others. Among the more harmful, and the more familiar, results of prosperity was the tendency to spend more on drinking and gambling. In regard to drink, the country emerged from the Second World War in an apparently less respectable state than it had from the First. The consumption of beer had dropped during the earlier conflict, to only twelve million barrels a year, but during the later one it had increased, to thirty-one million barrels a year.[33] The country seemed to have revived its taste for alcohol, only too much in fulfilment of the determined brewers' campaign of the 1930s. The new comparative affluence of the 1950s was likely to act as a further incentive to drink.

Post-war protests against encouragement to drink came frequently from Church organizations. Among the protests were objections to the insertion in a Civic Restaurants Bill of permission to

[28] *CEN*, 22 Mar. 1957, p. 9.
[29] Ibid., 14 Mar. 1958, p. 6.
[30] *RGACS* (1955), 303. Cf. ibid. (1958), 366–7.
[31] Ibid. (1955), 303.
[32] Ibid. (1955), 351. (quoted in Machin, 'British Churches and Social Issues').
[33] *RGACS* (1945), 286. Cf. *BT*, 3 May 1945, p. 9; *Focus on Drink and Gambling* (TCCC, n.p., 1977), 3.

sell liquor at these establishments; and expressions of disappointment when ratepayers in Scotland voted to overturn pre-war decisions against drink sales.[34] The Dundee presbytery of the Church of Scotland objected to the provision of drink by the local town council at municipal functions; and a committee of the FCFC supported the opposition of the Workers' Temperance League to holding trade-union meetings in licensed premises.[35] Practical public action was taken by religious temperance organizations; for example, the London Church of England Temperance Society collaborated with the Society for the Study of Addiction to establish the first outpatient clinic giving free treatment for alcoholics.[36]

A clear manifestation of rising prosperity was a rapid increase in the number of cars (from one and a half millions to five and a half millions between 1945 and 1960). Hence, a natural concern of temperance advocates at this time was the effect of drink on driving and road accidents. The General Assembly of the Church of Scotland advocated stiffer penalties for people found to be under the influence of drink when in charge of a car, and applauded the warnings in the *Highway Code* against the dangers of drinking before driving.[37] The executive committee of the FCFC praised the decision of the Minister of Transport in 1959 that restaurants on the new motorways should not sell alcohol.[38] Beyond the question of drinking and driving, Christians were urged to drive safely and to respect their fellow road-users. 'Christian good manners on the roads', said the *Church Times*, should be practised at all times, as 'religion can be practised sitting by the gearbox as well as occupying the pew'.[39]

Differences of opinion continued to be shown among Christians about the precise degree of temperance to be urged. Moderate

[34] Church of Scotland Edinburgh Presbytery Minutes, 7 Jan. 1947, CH2/121/62, pp. 600–1; 4 Nov. 1947, CH2/121/63, pp. 39–40; Church of Scotland Dundee Presbytery Minutes, 8 Jan. 1947, CH2/103/45, p. 98; *CYB* (1948), 91–2.

[35] Church of Scotland Dundee Presbytery Minutes, 2 Feb. 1949, CH2/103/46, p. 12; FCFC, Minutes of General Purposes Committee, 6 Sept. 1946, bk. 1, pp. 107–8.

[36] *CT*, 6 May 1955, p. 21.

[37] *RGACS* (1955), 325–6. Cf. ibid. (1952), 267–74; *PAGAFCS* (1951), 342; Church of Scotland Edinburgh Presbytery Minutes, 4 Nov. 1947, CH2/121/63, p. 39.

[38] FCFC, Minutes of Executive Committee, 11 Dec. 1958, 23 Apr. 1959, bk. 2, pp. 64, 115.

[39] *CT*, 22 Apr. 1955, p. 3. Cf. *RGACS* (1958), 410: 'fundamentally the road safety issue is a religious one . . . The General Assembly . . . call upon all who frequent the Queen's highway to humble themselves under the mighty hand of God.'

drinking was probably condoned by the majority, and abstinence was probably the avocation of a small minority. The Church of Scotland General Assembly of 1956 decided not to recommend total abstinence to the members of the Church; this brought a protest, in the columns of *Life and Work*, from an advocate of abstinence.[40] As for the temperance cause as a whole, a spokesman of a Church of Scotland committee on temperance education believed that support was weakening: 'it is becoming more and more difficult to interest people in the cause of temperance; as for temperance rolls and temperance associations and Bands of Hope, very few of them are still functioning; and little, if anything, is being done as regards teaching of temperance in Sunday Schools.'[41]

The rival and similarly addictive temptation of gambling also continued to incur strictures from the Churches. A leading anti-gambling writer, the Methodist minister E. Benson Perkins, stated in his book *Gambling in English Life* in 1950 that the amount of betting on horses, dogs, and football pools was some £650,000,000 p.a., equalling about 9 per cent of total private expenditure.[42] All forms of gambling did increase in the few years after the war, but then generally declined from the later 1940s for about ten years.[43] Thus in the case of gambling more popular spending power does not seem to have brought more indulgence in the 1950s; consumer goods and holidays were a greater lure. The Free Church of Scotland General Assembly of 1951 expressed satisfaction that 'the total sums spent on betting and gambling and on intoxicating liquor show a substantial decrease'. But a report to this Assembly deplored that 'commercialized sport has become a form of idolatry which prevents people from reflecting on important questions in Church and State'.[44]

While the post-war gambling spree was still unspent, the *Church Times* of 6 August 1948 published an article on 'The Menace of

[40] *LW* (July 1956), 179. Cf. *The Methodist Conference, Liverpool 1949* (London, n.d.), 29, for references to the disappointing response to a Methodist appeal for a Total Abstinence Campaign in 1948.

[41] Church of Scotland Edinburgh Presbytery Minutes, 8 Sept. 1953, CH2/121/65, pp. 127–8.

[42] E. Benson Perkins, *Gambling in English Life* (London, n.d. [1950]), 25–8; cf. Rowntree and Lavers, *English Life and Leisure*, 122ff.

[43] R. McKibbin, 'Working-Class Gambling in Britain, 1880–1939', in R. McKibbin (ed.), *The Ideologies of Class: Social Relations in Britain, 1880–1950* (Oxford, 1991), 112; *CT*, 22 Feb. 1957, p. 10.

[44] *PAGAFCS* (1951), 214, 342.

Gambling' which stated that a majority of working men attended greyhound races, that a third of all adults did the football pools, and that a recent survey had shown that 'eighty-six per cent of the population in these islands admit to gambling in some way, if not on horses, dogs, or football pools, then on raffles, cards or some other forms of gambling'.[45] 'Some other forms of gambling' probably included church raffles, one of the smaller but quite frequent manifestations of the activity, and one of several which were 'in aid of a good cause'. The holding of church raffles showed something of the differences of opinion in religious circles on the question of gambling. They were often condemned in Church assemblies,[46] but nevertheless persisted under the auspices of clergy and ministers who were apparently unconvinced of the 'evil' in the practice (or more fully convinced, perhaps, of the need to raise funds urgently to repair the church roof).

As over drink, there was division of opinion on whether to condemn gambling as a whole or only excess in the practice which was likely to cause harm. A statement by a Social and Industrial Commission of the Church of England National Assembly in 1951 that gambling was only evil when indulged in excessively was not thought worthy of adoption by the National Assembly, and was said by an FCFC committee to be 'quite contrary to the traditional standpoint of the Free Churches'.[47] The same Free Church committee, together with the Committee of the Churches on Gambling, opposed a suggestion in 1951 by a Royal Commission on Betting, Lotteries, and Gaming that betting shops should be allowed to open in order to cater for cash betting, which would be legalized.[48] The attitude of the Roman Catholic Church, that betting in moderation was harmless, was contrary to the conviction of some leading Christians that there should be total abstinence from it.[49]

Religious differences over gambling sometimes appeared in parliamentary debate. This was notably the case in April 1956, when the third reading of a Small Lotteries and Gaming Bill, seeking to

[45] *CT*, 6 Aug. 1948, p. 443.
[46] e.g. Church of Scotland Edinburgh Presbytery Minutes, 14 Jan. 1958 (CH2/121/66, p. 328); *LW* (Jan. 1956), 19.
[47] FCFC, Minutes of General Purposes Committee, 25 May 1951, bk. 1, p. 205.
[48] Ibid., 27 July 1951, p. 208. Cf. *CT*, 20 Apr. 1951, p. 267; *CYB* (1953), 101; *PAGAFCS* (1952), 535; speech of Leslie Hunter, Bishop of Sheffield, in Lords, 8 Feb. 1956 (HL Deb., 195, 813–17).
[49] *RGACS* (1952), 256–7, 260; *LW* (Jan. 1956), 19.

remove restrictions on small lotteries in the Betting and Lotteries Act of 1934, was debated in the Commons. The question of whether or not church raffles were widely held was a feature of the discussion. Harold Wilson said that, though a Nonconformist, he supported the bill because the current law was derided and evaded. Another Labour MP, Robert Mellish, who was a Roman Catholic, also gave his support. He said that his Church had large debts because of its commitment to maintain an educational system and would welcome the chance of raising money by means which the bill proposed to legalize. His Church, he said, believed 'that small lotteries create no great harm, and that they are not an iniquitous evil because, obviously, if they were, the Church would not support them'. He thought that the bill would facilitate small gambling without causing any hardship to the participants, and he resented the strictures on gambling coming from some who had large investments in stocks and shares.

A fortnight later Archbishop Fisher denounced the bill in the Lords. He was more alarmed, however, by a recent budget proposal in March by the Chancellor of the Exchequer, Harold Macmillan (a devout Anglican), to introduce a national scheme of premium bonds. A scheme of premium bonds had first been considered by a Government in 1917, but a House of Commons Select Committee had not supported it. 'Premium bonds represent a degrading method of tax collection', said the Public Questions Committee of the Free Church of Scotland in a report of 1957—which also congratulated 'the local Public Library Committees which are careful to expurgate the results of horse and greyhound racing from the newspapers on display'.[50] Fisher described the premium-bond plan in his speech in the Lords as a direct State encouragement to engage in the squandering of money. Cabinet Ministers were neglecting their duty to 'restore the true coinage without which we cannot endure as a great people. They have chosen instead . . . a second-rate expedient, which may attract savings but which adds nothing to the spiritual capital of the nation.' The plan represented an 'undignified and unedifying adulteration of public duty by motives of private gain'.[51] But Fisher's outburst attracted very little parliamen-

[50] *PAGAFCS* (1957), 302, 303.

[51] Machin, 'British Churches and Social Issues', p. 354; HC Deb., 551, 619–35; HL Deb., 196, 1291–1324; Purcell, *Fisher*, 215–16.

tary support, and the undeniable existence of church raffles was used against him in the debate.[52] No bishop voted in favour of the Small Lotteries Bill, but its second reading in the Lords was carried by forty-seven to five. Fisher's opposition to the much larger matter of premium bonds, however, was supported by some religious bodies, including the British Council of Churches, the General Purposes Committee of the FCFC, and the annual Assembly of the Congregational Union.[53]

Thus in 1956 not only were small lotteries legalized but premium bonds were introduced. To add to the current anti-gambling worries, the Government stated in March that year that it would adopt the recommendation of the Royal Commission on Betting, Lotteries, and Gaming in 1951 to allow betting shops (if licensed by local councils) to be reintroduced after a hundred-year absence.[54] By the end of the decade, however, nothing had been done about the matter. Some establishments were fined for operating illegally as betting shops, and some continued operating unpunished.[55] In November 1959 a bill was before the Commons proposing to allow betting shops to be opened. This received opposition from some Church quarters;[56] but it became law in the following year, joining the Obscene Publications Act of 1959 as a herald of the legislative permissiveness of the 1960s.

In their continuing efforts to defend the marriage bond, the Churches were confronted with a steep rise in divorces during and immediately after the war. Standing at 1.5 per 10,000 of the population in 1938, the divorce rate increased to 13.6 per 10,000 in 1947. The increase resulted from the more liberal divorce legislation of 1937–8 and the effects of wartime disruption on many marriages.[57] The rise did not prove to be permanent, though it was resumed by the 1970s after a much more liberal Act in 1969. In the mid-1950s it

[52] HL Deb., 196, 1307.

[53] *LW* (June 1956), 140; FCFC, Minutes of General Purposes Committee, 27 Apr. 1956, bk. 2, p. 33; *CYB* (1957), 94. Cf. M. Clapson, *A Bit of a Flutter: Popular Gambling and English Society, c.1823–1961* (Manchester, 1992), 200–4.

[54] HC Deb., 549, 2503–94, esp. 2567–71; *CT*, 20 Apr. 1951, p. 267.

[55] *RGACS* (1958), 368; HC Deb., 601, col. 1697.

[56] FCFC, Minutes of General Purposes Committee, 27 Nov. 1959, bk. 2, p. 132. Cf. Clapson, *A Bit of a Flutter*, 68–73.

[57] P. Summerfield, 'Women in the Two World Wars', *Historian*, 23 (Summer 1989), 6.

was noted by the Bishop of Durham, Michael Ramsey, that a decrease had taken place since 1951.[58]

The Churches' concept of marriage as a lifelong union continued to be expressed repeatedly in the years from 1945 to 1960.[59] But there was a good deal of debate in the Church of England about the Convocation resolutions of 1938 that divorced persons should not be married in church, and about pastoral treatment of those who had been divorced (including the question of their admission to communion).[60] At the same time there was shown the desire of a liberal society to extend the legal provisions for divorce beyond the position reached in 1937–8. There was also a desire for the extension of marriage guidance to assist couples to stay together.[61]

The wish to establish new grounds for divorce did not succeed in the 1950s, despite efforts made in Parliament. In October 1950 Colonel Marcus Lipton, a Labour MP, raised in the Commons his desire to extend the grounds for divorce beyond the 'matrimonial offence' in order to establish the right to end a marriage after a separation of a certain number of years.[62] He wished to end 'a broken down system of matrimonial law' which had produced, in regard to divorce and separation, 'statistics of distressing magnitude and disastrous social implications': 'in what way have the social and moral interests of the community been served by this kind of living death?'[63] In March 1951 a second reading was given in the Commons to a private member's bill introduced by another Labour MP, Mrs Eirene White, proposing that separation for seven years should become an additional ground for divorce. Archbishop Fisher condemned this proposal as a palliative for the moral sickness of a society which was increasingly rejecting permanent marriage. Archbishop Garbett wrote that the proposal must be resolutely opposed, otherwise 'within a few years marriage will

[58] *CT*, 7 Oct. 1955, p. 21.

[59] Norman, *Church and Society*, 410–11; e.g. *U.*, 20 July 1945, p. 6; *RGACS* (1946), 316–17; *CCC*, 17 Oct. 1946, ii. 3, pp. 239–40; 12 Jan. 1950, ii. 12, pp. 27–40; 23 May 1957, ii. 5, pp. 174–5; *CT*, 12 Sept. 1947, p. 547, 20 Aug. 1948, pp. 467, 470; *CEN*, 24 May 1957, p. 10.

[60] *CCC*, 14 Oct. 1953, i. 4, pp. 238–44; 11 May 1954, i. 5, pp. 46–65; 9 Oct. 1956, ii. 4, pp. 221–35; *LW* (May 1956), 122; *CEN*, 31 May 1957, p. 3; *CT*, 4 Oct. 1957, pp. 11–12.

[61] J. Lewis, 'Public Institution and Private Relationship: Marriage and Marriage Guidance, 1920–68', *Twentieth Century British History*, 1/3 (1990), 253–4.

[62] HC Deb., 480, cols. 79–85.

[63] Ibid. 480, 83.

be treated as a temporary contract which can be broken after a brief experiment'.[64]

Mrs White's bill was withdrawn, and the question was diverted into the hands of a Royal Commission on marriage and divorce, appointed in September 1951. This, after long and thorough consideration, presented its report in March 1956.[65] Nearly all the nineteen members of the Commission wanted to retain the principle of 'matrimonial offence' as the basis of divorce. But nine members (opposed by most of the others) supported the addition of a new ground for divorce, that of 'breakdown of marriage'. This would allow divorce, on the petition of either party to the marriage, after 'proved' separation for seven years. One member wanted to replace the 'matrimonial offence' with 'breakdown of marriage' (after three years' separation) as the basis of divorce.[66] But this desire was not to be realized until the passage of the Divorce Law Reform Bill of 1969, which effected this replacement and thereby put divorce in Britain onto an entirely new and much easier track.

In the meantime there was some sign of relaxation of the ecclesiastical stand against divorce. Some Anglican clerics were prepared to disobey the Convocation ruling of 1938 that no divorced person, innocent or guilty, should be allowed to have an Anglican wedding. Fisher declared in 1957 that disobedience incurred spiritual peril, but this met with a strong protest from about forty clergy in the Birmingham diocese, who objected to Fisher's alleged interference with the exercise of the clerical conscience.[67] In May 1958 the General Assembly of the Church of Scotland approved of the remarriage in church of guilty parties to divorce, at the discretion of the minister, in addition to the permission already in force regarding the remarriage of innocent parties.[68]

[64] *CT*, 30 Mar. 1951, p. 209.

[65] FP 88, fos. 388–93 (evidence of Fisher to the Commission), and 105, fos. 32–40, 97–106; G. Fisher, *Problems of Marriage and Divorce* (London, 1955).

[66] *Marriage, Divorce and the Royal Commission: A Study Outline of the Report of the Royal Commission on Marriage and Divorce, 1951–5* (Church of England Moral Welfare Council; London, 1956), 1–13.

[67] *CT*, 25 Oct. 1957, pp. 6, 12. Cf. Bishop of St Edmundsbury and Ipswich (Richard Brook) to Fisher, 17 Mar. 1949, FP, 60, fo. 6; Fisher to Brook, 18 Mar. 1949, ibid, fo. 7.

[68] *CEN*, 30 May 1958, p. 1; Church of Scotland Edinburgh Presbytery Minutes, 5 Nov. 1957, CH2/121/66, pp. 298–300; 3 Mar. 1959, ibid. 67, pp. 30–1.

As well as divorce, the questions of artificial contraception, artificial insemination, and abortion were lively matters at this time. Towards the use of artificial contraceptive methods, a general distinction had emerged between the Roman Catholic Church and the Protestant Churches. Marie Stopes continued to press her opposition to the attitude of the former. 'I feel the menace of Rome has . . . increased dangerously in the last five years,' she wrote in January 1950.[69] A few years later she was in unfruitful correspondence with Cardinal Griffin, Archbishop of Westminster, who had condemned contraceptives in his enthronement sermon in 1944.[70] Griffin was unwilling, and of course unable, to give up the well-established Roman standpoint that only natural birth control (i.e. the use of the safe period) could be employed. He informed Stopes in March 1954 that the discussion between them could not continue with any advantage. But Stopes replied the following day (apparently without receiving an answer) that he should consider her suggestions, as 'the matter is of supreme importance' and 'I have God and Truth on my side'.[71] One of her supporters condemned 'that enemy of the human race, the Roman Church': 'it is infuriating to realise . . . that this malodorous menace can thus hinder and in some cases actually arrest the progress of such a worthy cause as yours.'[72]

The difference between Rome and the other Churches seemed to widen. The Lambeth Conference of 1958 recognized clearly and openly, without any of the marked inhibitions of the resolution of 1930, that family-planning methods were a matter for the individual conscience. Indeed, said the 1958 resolution, sexual intercourse could be of great human value in its own right, apart from the matter of procreation. Father W. Digby, a Roman Catholic priest, described this resolution as 'a shedding of traditional principles by Christian leaders to suit the demands of modern paganism'.[73] In

[69] Stopes to Revd C. Leopold-Clarke, 4 Jan. 1950, SP BL Add. MS 58552, fo. 147. Cf. Very Revd W. R. Inge to Stopes, 15 June 1953, ibid. 58548, fo. 146.

[70] Father Derek Worlock to Stopes, 12 Oct. 1949, FP 53, fo. 305.

[71] Griffin to Stopes, 2 Mar. 1954, SP BL Add. MS 58553 (unfoliated when seen); Stopes to Griffin, 3 Mar. 1954, ibid. Cf. Stopes to Canon H. C. Warner, 6 Apr. 1954: 'Today in many parts of the world efforts to help the world's population problems are constantly hindered by Roman Catholic opposition' (ibid. 58552, fo. 195); also Stopes to Canon Adam Fox, 24 May 1954, ibid. 58549, fos. 192–3.

[72] A. Almond to Stopes, 14 Dec. 1954, ibid. 58552 (unfoliated when seen).

[73] *CEN*, 5 Sept. 1958, p. 1; Norman, *Church and Society*, 413.

1959 a papal Apostolic Delegate, Gerald O'Hara, wrote to Mervyn Stockwood, Anglican Bishop of Southwark, objecting strongly to the support he was giving to the Family Planning Association. But the Apostolic Delegate found himself reproved in turn by Archbishop Fisher, to whom Stockwood had sent copies of the correspondence between O'Hara and himself. 'Is it in keeping with the duties of your office to address an official rebuke to one of the Bishops of my province without any reference to me?' asked Fisher.[74] The birth-control issue had clearly deepened the division between Canterbury and Rome.

Nevertheless there remained, in some Protestant ecclesiastical circles, considerable inhibitedness on the subject of contraception. This was shown, for example, by Archbishop Fisher in his correspondence.[75] Anglicans were often as concerned as Roman Catholics about the public advertisement of contraceptives for sale and the use of slot machines to dispense them. There was also, not surprisingly, strong Anglican objection to the quotation without permission, by contraceptive manufacturers, of favourable clerical opinions in their advertisements.[76] Fisher said in the full synod of Canterbury Convocation in 1949 that he did not object to adults obtaining contraceptives 'in an orderly way', but 'the indiscriminate and uncontrolled provision of them' was 'entirely evil'.[77] The Government had previously defended contraceptive slot machines as being likely to do well in the export market.[78] To the relief of Fisher and many others, however, the Government relented somewhat and recommended a by-law to local authorities which would prohibit the installation of these machines outside shops.[79] Before

[74] Correspondence between O'Hara and Stockwood, 21 June–3 July 1959, FP 228, fos. 228–31; Fisher to O'Hara, 14 Aug. 1959, ibid., fo. 237 (quoted in Machin, 'British Churches and Social Issues', p. 360).

[75] Fisher to Revd David Mace (a Secretary to the Marriage Guidance Council), 4 Apr. 1946, FP 17, fo. 34.

[76] Correspondence of Fisher in Sept.–Oct. 1949 with Basil Henriques, Dillon MacCarthy, Sir Ernest Graham-Little, and Rt. Revd Walter Carey, ibid. 53, fos. 287–308; protest by the Catholic Pharmaceutical Guild of Great Britain to the advertising director of *Reader's Digest* (extract from *Catholic Herald*, 9 Oct. 1959, ibid. 219, fo. 304); letter from the solicitors of SPCK to the managing director of the London Rubber Co. Ltd., 23 Oct. 1959, ibid., fo. 331; Revd H. Viney to Secretary of Lambeth Conference, 3 Nov. 1959, ibid., fos. 346–7.

[77] Ibid., fo. 305.

[78] Jack Jones, MP, to Sir Ernest Graham-Little, 23 Aug. 1949, ibid., fo. 291.

[79] Fisher to Home Secretary (James Chuter Ede), 21 Oct. 1949, ibid., fo. 317; Sir Henry Morris-Jones, MP, to Fisher, 22 Oct., ibid., fos. 320–1; extract showing

this concession was made one cleric said that he would be 'quite prepared to organise a smashing-machine campaign'.[80]

Not only artificial contraception for the purpose of limiting births, but artificial insemination for the purpose of increasing them, was a matter of controversy among the Churches. Particular attention was given to the subject of artificial insemination in 1945, but the controversy over it stretched on for many years. The practice had been in use for some thirty years.[81] But the method, whether in the form of artificial insemination by a husband (AIH) or artificial insemination by a donor (AID), was condemned as unnatural by 'a Catholic Sociologist' in an article of 1945. Natural law, argued this writer, insisted not only that sexual intercourse should take place exclusively within marriage, but that there should be 'direct and natural union' between husband and wife for the purpose of conception, without any artificial intervention or aid: 'an artificial means is a mechanical substitute for the natural instinct or passion.' Both AID and AIH could have bad results in family life; in regard to the former in particular, 'it is hard to exaggerate the damaging effects likely to accrue when an impressionable child learns that he is, in fact, the illegitimate son of an unknown donor, conceived by a syringe out of a test tube'.[82] The Pope expressed similar opinions at the fourth International Congress of Catholic Doctors in 1949.[83]

This official Catholic view found a sympathetic echo in many Protestants, at least in regard to AID if less so over AIH. An opinion coming from the Free Churches and expressed at a meeting of the PMC in April 1947 was that AID was 'to be discouraged even by the broad-minded'.[84] In 1958 the Church of Scotland magazine *Life and Work*, and in 1959 the Anglican *Church Times*, condemned AID as an invasion of the sanctity of marriage.[85] The Methodist Conference of 1958 resolved that: 'The exclusive sexual

printed by-law, ibid., fo. 330; Church of Scotland Edinburgh Presbytery Minutes, 1 Nov. 1949, CH2/121/63, p. 388; Fisher to Sir Ernest Graham-Little, 8 Nov. 1949, FP 53, fo. 334.

[80] Rt. Revd Walter Carey to Fisher, 11 Oct. 1949, ibid., fos. 303–4.

[81] *LW* (Mar. 1958), 59.

[82] Copy in FP 1, fo. 271.

[83] *The Times*, 1 Oct. 1949 (extract in FP 51, fo. 161); Fisher to Mrs Mayford, 5 Oct. 1949, FP 51, fo. 162.

[84] *CT*, 25 Apr. 1947, p. 237.

[85] *LW* (Mar. 1958), 59; *CT*, 10 July 1959, p. 8. Cf. *PAGAFCS* (1959), 115–16.

union of man and wife is the essence of marriage as the Christian understands the mind and purpose of God . . . It is because the exclusive union between man and wife is . . . invaded by the giving and receiving of the seed of the donor that AID is wrong.'[86]

There was clearly more Christian sympathy for the married couple who tried to overcome infertility by using the less radical method of AIH, but even AID gave rise to differing opinions among the members of Churches.[87] Archbishop Fisher stated in August 1945 that AID should be regarded as 'forbidden to the Christian conscience', while AIH was more permissible but needed further deliberation. Both of these judgements, he said, reflected 'the general opinion of my brother bishops'.[88]

In December 1945 Fisher appointed a commission of doctors, lawyers, and theologians, chaired by J. W. C. Wand (Fisher's successor as Bishop of London), to consider the morality of artificial insemination. The conclusions of this commission, published in 1948, condemned AID (the Dean of St Paul's, W. R. Matthews, dissenting) and suggested that it might be made a criminal offence.[89] In a presidential address to the Convocation of Canterbury ten years later, Fisher repeated this condemnation and said that, if AID could not be made a criminal offence, legal restrictions should be imposed on it, including compulsory public registration stating the name of the donor.[90]

As already indicated, Anglican opinions differed over AID. A lady who was the daughter of a clergyman and former secretary to a bishop wrote to Fisher protesting against his 'absolutely inhuman pronouncement' to Convocation, adding that her best friend was 'happily married with three children, all by AID'.[91] The Modern Churchmen's Union, a liberal Anglican body, stated in 1959 that it

[86] *BW*, 28 July 1960, p. 6.

[87] e.g. the different opinions expressed at a conference of the Church of England Moral Welfare Council, reported by Revd Gilbert Russell to Fisher, 9 Aug. 1945, FP 1, fos. 312–16; also Mrs Rosamund Fisher (Central President of the Mothers' Union) to Fisher, 1 May 1945, ibid., fo. 278.

[88] Fisher to Miss Tugwell, 13 Aug. 1945, ibid., fos. 318–19. Cf. Fisher to Sir H. B. Vaisey, 14 Dec. 1945, ibid., fo. 350.

[89] Purcell, *Fisher*, 213–14; E. Carpenter, *Archbishop Fisher, his Life and Times* (Norwich, 1991), 391–2; *CT*, 30 July 1948, p. 423.

[90] Purcell, *Fisher*, 214. See also FP 235, fos. 140ff.

[91] Mrs V. Flower to Fisher, 15 Jan. 1958, FP 199, fo. 173; Fisher to Mrs Flower, 20 Jan. 1958, ibid., fo. 174; R. C. Mortimer, Bishop of Exeter, to Fisher, 30 Jan. 1958, ibid., fo. 175.

did not regard AID as sinful but thought it should be used only as a last resort—an opinion resembling that of the Lambeth Conference of 1930 (but not that of the 1958 Conference) regarding artificial contraception.

The practice of abortion remained illegal during this period. The Abortion Law Reform Association had campaigned for the legalization of abortion since 1936, but did not succeed until 1967. In 1952 and 1954, and again in 1961, bills were introduced into Parliament in favour of this reform, but made little or no progress there. The subject was increasingly a matter of public interest. The first television programme on the issue, containing a plea for legalized abortion under certain circumstances, was in June 1958. Women's organizations and other associations sometimes supported the reform, but the Roman Catholic Church was as opposed to this 'unnatural' development as it was to 'unnatural' contraceptive devices. Among Protestants there was probably more disapproval of abortion than there was of artificial contraception.[92]

More progress was made at this time by a desire to remove the stigma of criminality from homosexual practice. This matter came to a head in the 1950s, largely through the reforming books of Eustace Chesser and (from a more specifically Christian viewpoint) Derrick Sherwin Bailey;[93] and through the recommendations of the Wolfenden Report of 1957 that homosexual acts between consenting adults should be legalized. Many Christians still took the traditional view of homosexual practice as an abnormal and despicable vice. This opinion was expressed as follows in a letter in the Church of Scotland magazine, *Life and Work*: 'Whatever our compassion for these unfortunate people born abnormal, homo-sexuality is no more or less than an unnatural vice, indulged in by certain abnormal people which . . . leads towards the moral decline of our nation.'[94] But other opinions were growing, extending even to acceptance of the common validity of the homosexual

[92] B. Brookes, *Abortion in England, 1900–67* (London, 1988), 144–9; *U.*, 9 Nov. 1951, p. 1; *SU*, 28 Oct. 1955, p. 8.

[93] Col. E. S. Sinnott to Fisher, 11 Jan. 1954 (enclosing extract on Chesser's views from *The Western Daily Press*, Bristol), FP 126, fo. 320; D. S. Bailey, *Homosexuality and the Western Christian Tradition* (London, 1955), and *Sexual Offenders and Social Punishment* (Church of England Moral Welfare Council, London, 1956); anonymous review of *Homosexuality and the Western Christian Tradition* (*CT*, 14 Oct. 1955, p. 4). Cf. Dr C. G. Learoyd to Fisher, 8 June 1956, FP 188, fos. 173–7; Mrs Monica Nunnus to Fisher, 2 July 1956, ibid., fos. 78–80.

[94] Letter from Major-General Douglas Wimberley, *LW* (Mar. 1958), 93.

and heterosexual instincts and the practical implications of this equality.

Some who had been traditionalist became much more liberal on the subject. Archbishop Fisher was among these. He was in correspondence with Dr R. D. Reid, a homosexual ex-headmaster who had personally felt the weight of the law on the matter and had written to Archbishop Lang about the question in the 1930s. Reid was now seeking Fisher's support for reform of the law.[95] In 1953 Fisher wrote to him in very conventional, discouraging fashion:

> Homosexuality is against the Christian law of morals and is rightly regarded as a social menace if it becomes in any sense widespread . . . Quite obviously society must protect itself against this as against any other anti-social moral perversion . . . I hope that all homosexuals will start at once to realize that whatever their physical infirmities or their natural tendencies any indulgence of them is against Christian morals and the public welfare. They should seek priest and psychiatrist for help.[96]

But four years later Fisher acquiesced in the proposals of the Wolfenden Commission—though he emphasized that, while homosexual acts between consenting adults should be decriminalized, they would remain sinful.[97] Among those who thanked Fisher were Peter Wildeblood (homosexual author of *Against the Law*), Sir John Wolfenden, and Dr Reid—though the latter would have liked more sympathy from the Archbishop and other Church leaders towards 'the tragic lot of these people in this country'.[98]

The Church of England Moral Welfare Council (soon to become the Board of Social Responsibility) welcomed the Wolfenden Commission's proposal on homosexual acts; and the National Assembly of the Church of England decided (though only by 155 votes to 138) to accept the recommendation.[99] Majority approval was also given by the Methodist Conference in July 1958.[100] The

[95] Reid to Fisher, 27 Oct. 1953, FP 126, fos. 293–4.

[96] Fisher to Reid, 3 Nov. 1953, FP 126, fo. 298 (quoted in Machin, 'British Churches and Social Issues', p. 362). Cf. Fisher to Col. E. S. Sinnott, 14 Jan. 1954, FP 126, fos. 322–3.

[97] FP 194, fos. 155–6. Cf. Norman, *Church and Society*, 411–12; P. Stanford, *Lord Longford, a Life* (London, 1994), 289–90.

[98] Wildeblood to Fisher, 5 Dec. 1957, FP 194, fo. 195; Wolfenden to Fisher, 24 Sept. 1957, ibid., fo. 159; Reid to Fisher, 24 Sept. 1957, ibid., fo. 157.

[99] Fisher to Wolfenden, 18 Nov. 1957, ibid., fo. 180; Wolfenden to Fisher, 19 Nov. 1957, ibid., fo. 181; O. Chadwick, *Michael Ramsey, a Life* (Oxford, 1990), 145–6.

[100] *MR*, 17 July 1958, p. 16.

Roman Catholic Advisory Committee on Prostitution and Homosexual Offences favoured acquiescence, having made a statement to the Wolfenden Commission that 'penal sanctions are not justified for the purpose of attempting to restrain sins against sexual morality committed in private by responsible adults'.[101] On the other hand, the Church and Nation Committee of the Church of Scotland General Assembly concluded a long and searching report on the question by saying that the proposed legal change could not be advocated;[102] and a committee recommended to the Free Church of Scotland that the change should not be supported.[103] The Church of Scotland report stated:

> In our opinion there are certain forms of behaviour that are so contrary to Christian moral principles, and so repugnant to the general consensus of opinion throughout the nation that, even if private and personal, they should be regarded as both morally wrong and legally punishable.

Thus the official recommendations of Churches or Church committees differed on the question. A Conservative MP, Cyril Black, said that the Homosexual Law Reform Society was mistaken in claiming that there was overwhelming support from the Churches for the Wolfenden Report:

> the Church of Scotland, the Church of Ireland and the Salvation Army have all expressed themselves against this recommendation. My own Church, the Baptist Church, is certainly not in favour of it . . . I think that the leaders of the various Churches have shown themselves to be more or less equally divided on the subject.[104]

There was clearly much ecclesiastical diversity of opinion on the recommended change in the law, and a great deal of division was shown in Parliament until the proposed reform was finally carried ten years after the Wolfenden Report appeared.[105]

The question of permitted limits in publications, theatre and cinema shows, and broadcasting did not, in the fifteen years from 1945, achieve the social prominence it was to attain in the much more

101 HC Deb., 26 Nov. 1958, 596, 389, 395–6.
102 *RGACS* (1958), 359.
103 *PAGAFCS* (1958), 461–2.
104 HC Deb., 26 Nov. 1958, 596, 461–2, also 463–5.
105 S. Jeffery-Poulter, *Peers, Queers and Commons: The Struggle for Gay Law Reform from 1950 to the Present* (London, 1991), 28–89.

libertarian era of the 1960s. Nevertheless there was considerable concern in the 1950s that standards were slipping in all of these respects, indeed that libertarianism was already taking too firm a hold on society. The preservation of public morality did not concern the Churches alone, and differences of opinion on this matter did not coincide with differences of belief. But public morality—whether this entailed attempting to prevent change or agreeing with modifications of attitude—remained a prominent matter among the Churches' concerns in the mid-twentieth century and later.

The cinema declined from a supremely dominant position in entertainment in the later 1940s to one in which television had largely usurped its role ten years later. A record figure of 1,635 million cinema admissions was reached in 1946, and the number of cinemas was also at its highest point, at just over 4,700.[106] But from 1950 the attendance figures showed consistent decline, at least until the 1980s. In 1955 the annual figure for admissions was 1,182 millions, in 1960 it was 501 millions, and in 1980 ninety-six millions; the number of staff employed at British cinemas halved between 1955 and 1965.[107] During the 1950s the rapid rate of cinema closure (the number of cinemas declined from 4,660 in 1950 to 3,034 in 1960) became a frequent subject in parliamentary questions to government ministers. The reason for the decline was not revulsion from the cinema as such—the opening of new areas of realism in film production by the late 1950s, including social mobility in films such as *Room at the Top*, attracted a good deal of attention—but rather competition from television, the small screen within the home. The news broadcasts on television eliminated the appeal of the 'news theatres' which were common about 1950, and the appeal of entertainment television programmes sharply reduced that of the ordinary entertainment film shown in a cinema. Corresponding with the drop in cinema attendance was a sharp rise in the number of television sets owned. Television licences increased from nearly 344,000 in 1950 to nearly ten and a half million in 1960, and to 18,284,865 in 1980.[108] By the mid-1950s, previous statements emphasizing the universal importance of the

[106] Rowntree and Lavers, *English Life and Leisure*, 228; J. Curran and V. Porter (eds.), *British Cinema History* (London, 1983), 372, 375.

[107] Ibid. 372, 380.

[108] Ibid. 372.

cinema, still being made in the late 1940s, were being transferred to television.

Churches were now used to employing the film as a means of spreading their message. Many religious film societies were at work in these years. Some were denominational (such as the Catholic Film Society, the Cine Projector Committee of the Edinburgh presbytery of the Church of Scotland, the Church of England Film Council, and the Liverpool Diocesan Film Unit), and some were interdenominational (Bible Films, the Scottish Religious Film Society, the British Churches' Film Council). Some were national in scope (the Christian Cinema and Religious Film Society) and some were local (the Tyneside Catholic Film Society, the Northern Provincial Films Commission of the Church of England). The Archbishop of Canterbury dedicated a Church Army mobile cinema van in April 1947;[109] and the Christian Commandos had a mobile cinema to assist their missionary efforts in Scotland in that year.[110] The film magnate J. Arthur Rank, a Methodist, assisted not only his own denomination but the Catholics and others in the distribution of films.[111] Religious films sometimes were shown only to church groups, but sometimes entered the general public circuit and were seen by millions.

The widespread opening of cinemas on Sundays during the war had whetted the appetite for more extensive Sunday opening in peacetime, and the debate on this issue revived in the immediate post-war years. Local polls in 1946 and 1947 usually led to the adoption of cinema-opening, though a good deal of opposition was shown. Attitudes to this matter, as to other forms of entertainment or commercial activity on Sundays, differed widely among Christians, varying from complete opposition to willing acceptance. The latter approach was sometimes based on the view that Sunday films could be an antidote to aimless street-loitering or more dangerous behaviour.[112]

[109] Interim Report of the Archbishop of Canterbury's Film Enquiry Commission, May 1947, FP 28, fos. 178–84; *Year Book of the National Assembly of the Church of England* (1950), 476–8.

[110] *CT*, 11 Apr. 1947, p. 209; *BW*, 6 Nov. 1947, p. 75.

[111] *U.*, 26 Sept. 1947, p. 2.

[112] e.g. *BW*, 24 Jan. 1946, p. 249; 23 May 1946, p. 108; *CT*, 13 Sept. 1946, p. 552; 18 Apr. 1947, p. 227; *BW*, 23 June 1955, p. 13. On other Sunday activities, cf. *PAGAFCS* (1947), 145–6, (1948), 340, (1951), 342–3, (1953), 162–3; Church of Scotland Edinburgh Presbytery Minutes, 6 Mar. 1951, CH2/121/64, p. 233; *BW*, 9 Aug. 1951,

Debates on Sunday observance in the Convocation of Canterbury on 20 and 21 May 1947 produced differing opinions, some related specifically to the opening of cinemas. On 20 May the Bishop of Lichfield (E. S. Woods), who was chairman of the Convocation Joint Committee on Sunday Observance, introduced the Committee's report in full synod and stated that:

The Committee was not prepared to condemn wholesale the opening of cinemas on Sunday, but, where the local community exercised its option in favour of opening, the Committee thought that, so far as possible, better films should be shown, and—perhaps still more important—the hours of opening should be carefully arranged with due consideration for the hours of Sunday Schools and of church services.[113]

A speaker in the Lower House of Convocation, Canon R. H. W. Roberts, was 'very much afraid of the desire that was expressed for a recrudescence of Sabbatarianism'.[114] But it was also emphasized in that House that 'Sunday, being the Lord's Day, is primarily set apart for worship . . . It is a matter of common knowledge that to most people Sunday is nothing more than a convenient kind of extension of Saturday afternoon.'[115] On the other hand, the post-war introduction of the five-day working week caused Canon D. J. Symon to express the view that 'the institution of a second day of rest might well result in shifting on to Saturday the weight of the commercialization and secularization of Sunday, and the Christian Sunday might be regained in a large measure owing to the great bulk of secular activity taking place on Saturday'.[116] As time went on, however, it appeared that the public's insatiable appetite for secular amusement could easily fill up Sunday as well as Saturday; the allocation of Saturday entirely to leisure was not going to fill the pews on Sunday. Church assumptions were no longer having the endorsement of social conventions and habits. Instead, new habits and conventions were arising to challenge them.

In the Upper House of Convocation on 21 May, the Bishop of Derby (A. E. J. Rawlinson) pointed out the dangers of using 'sabbatarian language' in attempting to recall the people to lost ways:

p. 10; FCFC Minutes of the General Purposes Committee, 24 Nov. 1950, bk. 2, p. 193; *CT*, 23 Jan. 1953, pp. 49, 51; 6 Feb. 1953, p. 83.

113 *CCC*, 20 May 1947, ii. 4, p. 42; also pp. 58–82, 96–112.

114 Ibid. 65.

115 Ibid. 69.

116 Ibid. 75.

All could see the reasonableness and the importance of Christians fulfilling the precepts of their religion and recognizing the obligation of Sunday worship; and all could see the value of a weekly day of rest as a priceless social boon. On that double platform, he thought they could go with some hope of success both to the religious constituency and to the external world. But if Sabbatarian language were used and the Sabbatarian standpoint adopted, the effects were likely to be unfortunate. Language of that kind sounded obsolete in people's ears; it was apt to be suggestive of old, unhappy, far-off things, memories of the Victorian Sunday . . . (and to suggest) to the minds of not a few of our people the idea that in the controversies between our Lord and the Pharisees on the subject of keeping the Sabbath, the Church was taking the wrong side.[117]

In the same debate the Bishop of Rochester (C. M. Chavasse) noted that conditions on Sunday were becoming increasingly inimical to churchgoing:

Did their lordships realise that one adult in eight was deprived of the possibility of going to church because of the need of ministering to public pleasure and enjoyment on a Sunday? Did they realise that three million children were kept away from Sunday School because of the lure of the cinema? Had they seen the 'bus queues of village children waiting to be taken to the cinema at the nearest town? Did they realise the threat to Sunday by cadet corps and A.T.C. training, and that [*sic*] some of their brightest boys were taken out of choirs and from church attendance for this training? . . . In Kent they were faced with the novelty of Sunday cricket matches on village greens. Such counter-attractions were disastrous to Sunday worship and religious instruction.[118]

A view of Sunday cinema-opening as having more positive benefit was, however, given by the Bishop of Worcester (William Cash):

The police were thankful for the cinemas, and the opportunity they afforded to draw people off the streets, and it must be admitted that the Church was doing little or nothing for this type of person who had no home comforts . . . the agitation for closing cinemas entirely on Sundays was perplexing people, because many found them an asset in dealing with the problems of the day. Had the Church an alternative? If we came forward with a big plan for handling the problem of the younger generation, many of whom have no real homes at all, we might take a stronger line about the Sunday cinema . . . The day had gone for a rigid insistence on Sabbatarian lines of Sunday observance.[119]

[117] *CCC*, 21 May 1947, ii. 4, p. 100.
[118] Ibid. 103.
[119] Ibid. 104–5.

Sabbatarian condemnation of the heiress to the throne and her recently espoused husband, for enjoying themselves in a secular as well as a religious sense on a Sunday in Paris in 1948, received a ready rebuttal from the Roman Catholic *Universe*:

Princess Elizabeth and her husband did no wrong and gave no cause for scandal when on their visit to Paris they went on Sunday to the races, to the opera, and to a dance at a night club. We must distinguish between sanctity and a long, mournful face . . . The Princess and her husband went to church—twice, we believe—that Sunday. What a fine example to us all. If we all followed that example, England—and Scotland—would be in a better state . . . Catholic churches are full to overflowing. Many non-Catholic churches are empty because their clergy give false ideas of God and His glory, making Him dour and unhappy and terrible to the young . . . These people empty the churches. The actions of the Princess and her husband on that Sunday in Paris are calculated to fill them.[120]

Worrying displays of sex and violence in films seem to have remained uncommon before the 1960s, but there was considerable comment in the religious press about such matters. The *Universe* condemned the British Board of Film Censors for merely cutting instead of rejecting the notorious *No Orchids for Miss Blandish* in 1948: 'This film calls not for cuts but for complete rejection. The whole thing is conceived in such a spirit of lasciviousness and brutality that the deletion of a dozen offensive incidents would not make it wholesome . . . No decent Catholic man will take his wife or his girl to see it.'[121] The *Church Times* wrote on this subject:

With a remarkable unanimity the press has denounced the film *No Orchids for Miss Blandish*, one critic suggesting that a special certificate, D for disgusting, should be granted. In fact, the Board of Film Censors has placed it in the A category; in contradistinction to films granted a H certificate, children in the company of adults may witness this film. The British press as a whole cannot be accused of Puritanism or squeamishness. And its judgment on the film must raise serious doubts as to whether the Board of Film Censors is performing the function for which it is appointed . . . Mr [Tom] Driberg raised the question of the value of the censorship in the House [of Commons]. Surely this is also an occasion which gives scope for inter-denominational councils of religious bodies to justify their existence by effective intervention.[122]

[120] *U.*, 28 May 1948, p. 6.
[121] Ibid., 16 Apr. 1948, p. 3; 23 Apr. 1948, p. 6.
[122] *CT*, 23 Apr. 1948, p. 227. Cf. FCFC Minutes of General Purposes Committee, 30 Apr. 1948, bk. 1, p. 143.

The depiction on the screen of more sophisticated vice than the basic cut and thrust of *No Orchids for Miss Blandish* was scarcely less to be condemned. *Salome*, described as a 'vulgar' and 'utterly unworthy' distortion of Scripture, was the subject of concern at a meeting of representatives of the Mothers' Union, the Board of Catholic Women, and the Free Church Women's Council.[123] *Forever Amber*, said the *Universe*, was 'an elaborate and expensive depiction of lechery' ending with 'a phoney moral'.[124] The Scottish edition of this paper said in 1955 that *I am a Camera* was 'addressed to the relatively small group of intelligent, amoral sophisticates who find it unsmart to be shocked by vice if it is dished up with surface charm'.[125] In 1961 Canon John Collins, best known for his campaigning against nuclear weapons, wanted to ban the film *Lolita*, and in consequence the playwright John Osborne wrote accusing him of 'moral bullying'.[126] On a lighter note concerning clerical reactions to cinema shows, the Bishop of Matabeleland told Archbishop Fisher in 1957 that he was going to complain to Ealing Studios that their celebrated film *Kind Hearts and Coronets* contained a comic character with the same title as himself. The clash had perhaps occurred because there was no Bishop of Matabeleland when the film was made in 1948. Ealing Studios refused to meet the bishop's request that the film be withdrawn, and Fisher advised him to 'grin and bear it': it was 'part of the rough and tumble of life you have to take'.[127]

The British Broadcasting Corporation maintained in this period the traditions of Sir John Reith, seeing its national mission as culturally elevating and even religious. Religious broadcasts continued to be plentiful, encouraging the expression of a wide range of views, including non-Christian ones.[128] The broadcast services of worship, however, were restricted to the two established Churches, the Roman Catholic Church, and the major Nonconformist de-

[123] Mrs B. C. Roberts to Archbishop Fisher, 24 and 31 July 1953, FP 129, fos. 16, 18; Fisher to Mrs Roberts, 27 July 1953, ibid., fo. 17.

[124] *U.*, 9 July 1948, p. 3.

[125] *SU*, 14 Oct. 1955, p. 4.

[126] Osborne to Collins, 15 May 1961, Collins Papers 3298, fos. 16–17. Cf. Cardinal Godfrey's private secretary to Collins, 23 May 1961, ibid., fo. 26; *BW*, 18 May 1961.

[127] Bishop of Matabeleland to Fisher, 18 May 1957, FP 190, fo. 124; Fisher to the bishop, 27 May 1957, ibid., fo. 130 (quoted in Machin, 'British Churches and Social Issues', 366).

[128] *CT*, 21 Mar. 1947, p. 160.

nominations. In the mid-1950s it was estimated that 30 per cent of the adult population every week watched or heard at least one of the broadcast Sunday services.[129] In 1948 the Director-General of the BBC, Sir William Haley, told the British Council of Churches that the corporation was deliberately Christian in attitude.[130]

The Churches were generally satisfied with the way this attitude was shown in BBC broadcasts. But Roman Catholics said they were allowed insufficient time on the air; and there were complaints about some programmes on both radio and television which could be construed as disrespectful towards religion or even blasphemous.[131] A series of broadcasts entitled 'Morals without Religion', advocating humanist, non-Christian morality, was delivered in January 1955 by Mrs Margaret Knight, a Lecturer in Psychology at Aberdeen University. These broadcasts caused a great deal of controversy in the press, and the BBC received more letters than ever before on a single subject.[132] Religious concern was also shown over the prospect of diluted standards in commercial broadcasting. From 1953 it was being proposed to establish an Independent Television Authority, and commercial television started broadcasting in September 1955. Although the Government undertook not to permit sponsored television, fears were none the less expressed that the firms which advertised on independent television, and therefore financed it, might be able to influence the programmes. Among other religious bodies, the central committee of the FCFC and the executive committee of the British Council of Churches expressed alarm over this matter. The latter declared in December 1953 that it was 'entirely unconvinced that the present policy of the Government will not in practice leave the decisive influence on programmes with the advertisers who finance them'.[133] A letter from the General Secretary of the Lord's Day Observance Society

[129] B. Paulu, *British Broadcasting: Radio and Television in the United Kingdom* (Minneapolis, 1956), 200.

[130] Ibid. 144, 195–202.

[131] *PAGAFCS* (1952), 416, (1955), 424–5, 561, (1956), 149; *RGACS* (1955), 311; *CT*, 13 May 1955, p. 3.

[132] Paulu, *British Broadcasting*, 176; Margaret Knight, *Morals without Religion, and Other Essays* (London, 1955); *PAGAFCS* (1955), 425, 561.

[133] *LW* (Mar. 1954), 63. Cf. *RGACS* (1955), 310; *CT*, 3 July 1953, p. 483; FCFC Minutes of General Purposes Committee, 3 July 1953, bk. 1, p. 258; 27 Nov. 1953, bk. 1, p. 265.

(H. J. W. Legerton) in the *Church of England Newspaper* in March 1954 urged all Christians to appeal to their MPs that the bill to establish an Independent Television Authority should not be permitted to allow television advertising on Sundays. 'We would, of course, prefer a clause which would close down television altogether on the Lord's Day, but, as there is no hope whatsoever for this, we feel strongly [that] we should press for the exclusion of commercialism.'[134] Safeguards against any suggestion of sponsoring were included in the Act, and there were no suggestions later that these were being contravened.

But, even if this danger proved illusory, there was considerable unease in the later 1950s about the growing elements of sex and violence in some programmes, and considerable doubt about whether the Christian basis of broadcasting was being maintained. The BBC was suspected of being ready to abandon the spirit of Reith, and ITV had not demonstrated that it clearly espoused it. Not only specific scenes on television, but the amount of broadcasting time allowed to those who were sceptical of Christianity, received condemnation.[135] A Sheffield vicar, writing in his parish magazine in 1958, was in no doubt of the menace of Sunday television to Christian spirituality: 'Parents, I implore you, turn off the television on Sundays and keep it off, unless you want to see your children grow up as heathens in a Christian land.'[136] Lord Pakenham, later Earl of Longford, told the House of Lords in June 1959 that 'the British people today have a right to insist . . . that the Christian moral code and the basic religious beliefs of Christianity should be supported and fostered by public services such as the BBC and publicly supervised services such as those of Independent Television'.[137]

Not only films and broadcasts, but publications and theatre productions, could cause worries over moral effects. The danger of pornography and erotic stimulation in the newspaper press and in novels was small at this stage compared with the much greater freedom developed in the 1960s. But imported 'horror comics' in the early 1950s appalled many people. They were described by the Nonconformist *British Weekly* as being 'devoted to every horror

[134] *CEN*, 26 Mar. 1954, p. 13.
[135] e.g. ibid., 22 Mar. 1957, p. 2; *CT*, 6 Dec. 1957, p. 3.
[136] *CEN*, 11 Apr. 1958, p. 1.
[137] *U.*, 12 June 1959, p. 1. Cf. *BW*, 11 June 1959, p. 6; *SU*, 6 Dec. 1957, p. 4.

and corruption of mind and body known to the unoriginal sin of man'.[138] Comics with a strong Christian element were also brought onto the market, however, and did very well.[139] In the theatre, nude shows and other demonstrations of eroticism aroused some strong adverse reactions. In 1954 the Alliance of Honour protested to the Lord Chamberlain (who remained the censor of stage productions until 1968) about 'the indecent and sacrilegious character' of a play on the Edinburgh Festival fringe.[140] In 1957 the drama critic for the *Church of England Newspaper* considered, on the basis of John Osborne's *The Entertainer*, Tennessee Williams's *Camino Real*, and Jean Genet's *The Balcony*, that 'the legitimate theatre is becoming one of the dirtiest places in London'.[141] It was objected in the correspondence columns of the paper that the critic was making Christian values seem 'identical with self-obsessed prudery'. The critic replied that his Christian values prevented him from 'looking with tolerance on such things as nudity, obscenity, and blasphemy in the theatre'. But the correspondent rejoined that the critic was not helping Christianity by giving the impression that 'it is not really sin that worries him but sex as such'.[142] Thus the question of permissiveness on the stage was heralding the more openly 'liberated' claims and actions of the 1960s.

Differing religious reactions were also seen over three other important social questions of the period—abolition of the death penalty for murder, women's work outside the home, and the treatment of coloured immigrants. A Royal Commission came very near to recommending abolition of the death penalty in 1953, and this aim received some encouragement from the passing of the Homicide Bill in 1957. This bill established 'degrees of murder'—capital murders (which would still be subject to the death penalty) being separated from others which would be regarded as less culpable and punishable by life imprisonment. Archbishop Fisher enthusiastically supported the measure, but Bishops Bell and Ramsey strongly disagreed with it as an inadequate

[138] *BW*, 30 Sept. 1954, p. 6. Cf. *PAGAFCS* (1957), 298.

[139] *CT*, 2 Nov. 1951, p. 750.

[140] Church of Scotland Edinburgh Presbytery Minutes, 1 June 1954, CH2/121/65, p. 275. Cf. *BW*, 19 Aug. 1954, p. 12.

[141] *CEN*, 3 May 1957, p. 4. Cf. J. Johnston, *The Lord Chamberlain's Blue Pencil* (London, 1990), 218.

[142] *CEN*, 10 May 1957, p. 10; 17 May 1957, p. 4; 24 May 1957, p. 10.

reform.[143] Before the death penalty was abolished in 1965, both Convocations of the Church of England voted in favour of abolition in 1962.[144]

Over the question of abolition, differing viewpoints occurred within each Church. When the House of Commons considered the question in April 1948, ten Catholic MPs voted for abolition, three voted against, and seven abstained. The cross-party nature of the question was also indicated by this vote: both Labour and Conservative members were among the Catholics who voted for and among those who voted against.[145] The Anglican prelates were frequently in disagreement on the issue.[146] The evangelical *Church of England Newspaper* favoured abolition in the following terms:

> Advocates of the death penalty argue as if it were only an extreme form of punishment. But they are wrong. It is highly questionable whether death is a punishment at all. Rather it is removal from the sphere of punishment, a forestalling. Punishment is directed against a person's mind or body . . . Capital punishment is a blot on the British legal system . . . Every desperate writhing of ratiocination in the attempt to rescue the death penalty from universal abomination enhances its irrationality and its loathsomeness.[147]

The correspondence columns of religious newspapers often showed different opinions from those in the leading articles. The *British Weekly* supported abolition of the death penalty, but a correspondent berated it for not looking 'long and carefully at both sides of an issue':

> Isn't it about time that you devoted a little space to answering a few of the 'hard' questions which, understandably, some Christians have not yet resolved in such a way as to lead them to move for suspension or abolition of the death penalty? . . . Perhaps one of the experts will explain through your columns, for example, on what evidence the principle and practice of C.P. [capital punishment] may be regarded as so alien to the mind of God that we must reject *in toto* . . . the command in Genesis 9, 6, 'Whoso sheddeth man's blood, by man shall his blood be shed; for in the image of God made He man.'[148]

[143] H. Potter, *Hanging in Judgment: Religion and the Death Penalty in England* (London, 1993), 153–9, 178–9.
[144] Ibid. 193–8.
[145] *U.*, 23 Apr. 1948, p. 4.
[146] *CT*, 1 Mar. 1957, p. 16; Potter, *Hanging in Judgment*, 179.
[147] *CEN*, 2 Oct. 1953, p. 2; also 22 July 1955, p. 1; 5 Aug. 1955, p. 10.
[148] *BW*, 25 Aug. 1955, p. 9.

A completely different view, also grounded on scriptural foundations, was expressed by a correspondent of the *Church Times*:

When the issue of marriage or divorce claims the attention of the public, Churchmen of all kinds and ranks rush into the fray to defend and command the Church's teaching on the subject. When the issue of capital punishment comes up, no one would suppose the Church had any teaching on the subject at all. Yet our Lord's condemnation of this barbarous practice stands out far more clearly from the pages of the gospels than his teaching on divorce.[149]

A Church of Scotland minister supported the abolitionist cause in the following terms in *Life and Work*:

I believe that no matter what the dispensers of justice, the custodians of public morals, or some theologians say, man even at his worst is not utterly and totally depraved ... He may have sunk to abysmal depths, but the divine image has not been completely obliterated. A feeble spark, a tiny point of flame, is still there struggling for life amid the dross and ashes of his brutalized nature, and society has no right to extinguish it. The most depraved and abandoned of men can experience the miracle of regeneration. To deny this is to contradict the New Testament ... Life-imprisonment may sound harsh and cruel, but at least it leaves the door open to the change that may eventually occur.[150]

A rise in the number of women at work outside the home occurred after the Second World War. This was the continuance of a trend of the 1930s rather than being a development originated by the war.[151] At a time of nearly full employment in the country, the Government deliberately encouraged the post-war trend in women's work in order to increase industrial output and boost exports. Government policy in this respect, however, caused protests from some religious organizations, including the ICF and the Catholic Women's League, on the grounds that home and family life would be undermined.[152] The *Scottish Universe* noted in 1955 that 'the hand that used to rock the cradle is now becoming increasingly indispensable in the operation of machinery in factories'. This paper said that no mother of young children should go out to work

[149] *CT*, 25 Nov. 1955, p. 9.
[150] *LW* (Feb. 1956) 33.
[151] H. L. Smith, 'The Effect of the War on the Status of Women', in H. L. Smith (ed.), *War and Social Change: British Society in the Second World War* (Manchester, 1986), 208–29, especially 218–19; Summerfield, 'Women in the Two World Wars', 5.
[152] *CT*, 11 Apr. 1947, p. 209; *U.*, 17 Oct. 1947, p. 7.

simply in order to obtain the money to buy luxuries: 'the Catholic mother has a duty to stay at home, even if limited finances should compel her to read a book while her neighbours watch television.'[153] Women's equality in regard to pay, and the elimination of discrimination over employment, had made no progress during the war in spite of efforts in these directions.[154] After the war, no great urge was shown to advance these matters until the 1960s, when successes were at last attained.

The official role of women in the Churches was also under scrutiny in these years. Beginning in 1917, women had been ordained to the ministry in some Nonconformist Churches. The Methodist Church decided to admit women to its ordained ministry, under quite stringent personal conditions, at its conference at Nottingham in July 1945.[155] No other major Church, however, extended ordination to its women members until 1968, when the Church of Scotland did so. There were moves in the 1950s to adopt female ordination in that Church. The presbytery of Edinburgh resolved in December 1959 by ninety-five votes to forty-eight that 'the time has now come when the Church of Scotland should favour the admission of women to the ministry of the Word and Sacraments'.[156]

From 1948 there began to be a sizeable increase in the coloured inhabitants of Great Britain. Previously there had been only small pockets of these inhabitants in seaports, usually settled there for generations. But the demand for labour in the expanding British post-war economy, and the inadequacy of work opportunities and living conditions in their own countries, encouraged a rise in immigrants. By 1959 about 200,000 West Indians, Pakistanis, and Indians had entered the country.[157] In the following decade it was thought desirable to restrict the influx by means of Commonwealth Immigration Acts.

The immigrants began to alter the religious complexion of the country. Whereas Jews—numbering some 350,000 in the 1950s—

[153] *SU*, 7 Oct. 1955, p. 8 (quoted in Machin, 'British Churches and Social Issues', 368). Cf. *U.*, 24 Oct. 1947, p. 1.

[154] Smith, 'Effect', 223–5.

[155] *BW*, 26 July 1945, p. 230.

[156] Church of Scotland Edinburgh Presbytery Minutes, 1 Dec. 1959, CH2/121/67, pp. 133–4.

[157] P. Fryer, *Staying Power: The History of Black People in Britain* (London, 1984), 372–3; J. A. G. Griffith, *Coloured Immigrants in Britain* (London, 1960), 166; B. Maan, *The New Scots: The Story of Asians in Scotland* (Edinburgh, 1992), 98–150, 168ff.

had been the only sizeable non-Christian minority, the settlement of Indians and Pakistanis added many Hindus and Muslims to the population. By the 1970s this fact was underlined by the spread of temples and mosques. Friction with members of the white majority was unavoidable. In the 1950s the immigrants encountered discrimination over appointments to jobs, obtaining accommodation, receiving service in restaurants and public houses, and in other ways. Overt discrimination of this kind probably lessened later, partly because of the passage of anti-discriminatory legislation in the 1960s.

In the 1950s there were only abortive attempts to carry such legislation against racial discrimination. The first race riots in the country (apart from an outbreak in 1919 against negro seaport workers) took place in 1958 at Notting Hill (London) and Nottingham. Among religious attempts to heal the growing division was a suggestion by a prominent Methodist, Donald Soper, that Christians should run community centres for the coloured population—'this is the coffee bar age; we need a place where races can mix and learn to understand'.[158]

Private opinions and actions no doubt varied, but public statements and resolutions give the impression that Christian attitudes were thoroughly against racial discrimination.[159] This attitude did not preclude consideration of limiting the incoming numbers in order to restrict the growth of unemployment—a matter which was also debated in Parliament in the later 1950s. Any such suggestions were opposed by those who wished to maintain full freedom of entry on principle.[160] There were also differences between Christians on the matter of racial integration through intermarriage and the consequent birth of children. The Government was condemned as racialist in 1950 by a variety of religious newspapers—the *Church Times*, the *British Weekly*, and the *Church of England*

[158] *MR*, 30 July 1959, p. 8; *Together in Britain: A Christian Handbook on Race Relations* (Church Assembly Board for Social Responsibility, London 1960), 3–5, 16–17.

[159] e.g. resolution 43 of the Lambeth Conference, 1948, British Council of Churches conference, Liverpool, Apr. 1951, *CT*, 6 Apr. 1951, p. 225; *CCC* (1953), i. 3, pp. 114–24.

[160] Debate in Lower House of Canterbury Convocation, 13–14 Jan. 1959, *CCC* ii. 9, pp. 53–63, 103–8. Cf. J. Williamson, *Father Joe: The Autobiography of Joseph Williamson of Poplar and Stepney* (London, 1963), 135–6; *CEN*, 19 Mar. 1954, p. 2; 28 Nov. 1958, p. 1.

Newspaper—for preventing Seretse Khama returning to Africa to take up his position as chief of his tribe in Bechuanaland. The reasons for the Government's action were that Seretse's marriage in this country to a white Englishwoman was opposed in his tribe, and it was feared that neighbouring South Africa (committed to apartheid) might take over the tribal territory.[161]

The boldly liberal opinion of Father Neville Palmer, an Anglican, in 1951 was that 'it would be all to the good in this country if in a generation or two there was a noticeable change in the colour of the skin of the population from white (so called) to varying degrees of brown!'[162] But this view was far from universal among Christians. It was countered by the much more cautious view of the *Church Times* that, while 'no Christian can condemn racial inter-marriage as always and necessarily wrong', neither was there 'anything specifically Christian in the idea of wholesale racial inter-mixture. The deep differences of racial background and temperament must be counted as part of the divine order of Providence.'[163] A letter in this paper expressed amazement at Father Palmer's apparent wish to 'abolish both races and replace them with a coffee-coloured crowd. Such an idea is completely shocking.'[164]

The Protestant Churches preserved reasonable stability in the post-war years up to 1960, but did not achieve collectively a revival of numbers and influence to the levels of three or four decades before. Sharper numerical decline was to come in the 1960s, and the period 1945–60 has something of the appearance of calm before a storm, in regard both to Church fortunes and to social change. Apart from reactions to the Welfare State, the social and moral concerns of the Churches in the 1950s were much the same as they had been in the 1930s. Prosperity developed much more widely in the 1950s, causing the Churches to warn frequently against its dangers, including the perennial ones of drinking and gambling. There was also continuing wariness in regard to plays, films, and broadcasts. There

[161] R. Hyam, 'The Political Consequences of Seretse Khama: Britain, the Bamangwato, and South Africa, 1948–52', *Historical Journal*, 29 (1986), 21–47; R. Pearce (ed.), *The Political Diaries of Patrick Gordon Walker, 1932–71* (London, 1991), 23–7, 187–9; *BW*, 16 Mar. 1950, p. 8; *CEN*, 17 Mar., p. 2; *CT*, 17 Mar., p. 203.

[162] *CT*, 20 Apr. 1951, p. 269 (quoted in Machin, 'British Churches and Social Issues', 369).

[163] *CT*, 27 Apr. 1951, p. 279.

[164] Ibid. 285.

was continuing controversy over artificial contraception and the extension of divorce facilities, and new controversy over the legalization of homosexual practice and abortion, and over the use of artificial insemination. In 1959 the *British Weekly* claimed that the country was sinking into worship of the trivial and the sensual:

> The trivial is magnified into importance by its constant repetition on the television screen . . . There are signs that the country may soon have to pay heavily for its easy going attitude to the public display of pornography, to the exploitation of sex in advertisement and magazine and to the playing down to the primitive in music and entertainment.[165]

In spite of these fears, it was not until the 1960s that the new urge towards permissiveness—natural in a society that was built on democratic freedom of choice, popular prosperity, and the questioning and critical approach encouraged by widespread education—came to fruition in the form of legislative enactments. The coming developments were foreshadowed in the 1950s—for example, in parliamentary discussions on divorce reform and the Wolfenden Report. An important measure passed in 1959, the Obscene Publications Bill, introduced new legal provisions which enabled the full text of *Lady Chatterley's Lover* to be published, after a trial in the law courts, by Penguin Books in 1960. This was, appropriately, at the start of the permissive decade which saw the opening of betting shops; legalization of abortion and homosexual practice; divorce reform and the questioning of marriage; widening use of a new contraceptive pill; the abolition of censorship of plays; and much more freedom of exhibition and speech in the cinema, theatre, broadcasting, books, magazines, and newspapers.

Collectively, these changes produced a fundamental moral and social reorientation which had pronounced effects throughout the remainder of the twentieth century. The reorientation came from such an overwhelming combination of forces—political democracy, material prosperity, scientific innovation, concern to alleviate the position of minorities—that it was very difficult to resist. Members of the Churches reacted in a variety of ways which had marked them previously in dealing with social thought and social change. They showed by no means complete opposition; indeed to some extent they acknowledged the value of change in moral attitudes. But the traditional Christian emphasis on individual purity was

[165] *BW*, 11 June 1959, p. 6.

assailed by the new developments, as was the desire to maintain marriage and family unity. It became increasingly difficult to claim that the teaching of the Churches was at the root of the new developments. Rather the Churches in the new decade seemed to be tossed about by conflicting traditional and innovatory forces, not sure which way to turn in their efforts to calm the relentless tides.

6
Churches and Moral and Social Change, 1960–1970

The fortunes of the economy and of popular prosperity were rather less certain in the 1960s than in the previous decade. The 'stop–go' cycle continued, devaluation of the pound took place in 1967, and from that year the rate of unemployment (at over half a million) was higher than it had been since 1940. In the 1960s, however, there was nothing resembling the sharper and longer slumps and booms which were to be experienced from the 1970s to the 1990s. To most people in the country, the economic developments of the 1960s probably represented a slight intensification of the problems of the 1950s but not great infringement on the economic benefits of that time—generally full employment, steadily rising real wage levels, increasing consumption, and growing home ownership. But there remained the problems of decline in traditional industries and the detrimental effects this had on the districts where they were situated; the removal of significant numbers of people from some parts of the country to areas of greater prosperity; and the corresponding need to revive the economies of some areas. All these matters were of concern to Church bodies, as was the major government social innovation of the decade—the adoption of widespread comprehensive education.[1]

But the overwhelming social question of the decade was the concentrated growth in permissive or libertarian attitudes and behaviour, amounting collectively to so wide and penetrating a development that it brought about a pronounced change in public and private morals. The change was partly the result of scientific inventions, notably the contraceptive pill. But it was also the delayed consummation of demands for reform going back in some cases for several decades, even to the beginning of the century. Censorship, gambling, abortion, homosexual practice, and divorce

[1] e.g. *RGACS* (1960), 318–21, (1963), 370–2, 383–4, 393–4, (1965), 275–8, (1967), 173–80; *PAGAFCS* (1966), 157; *CT*, 19 Feb. 1965, p. 3.

received liberating reforms which had long been advocated. Such was the volume of change that morality was in some ways set on a new course. This included the moral attitudes and responses in Churches, though there was no uniformity in this respect either between Churches or between the members of a single Church.

The new moral permissiveness or relativism which marked the 1960s was not simply a matter of piecemeal change in connection with different aspects of behaviour. These changes were intended by liberal moral reformers to have a common basis, and to represent a different way of judging and assessing human behaviour. Old moral dogma was to be replaced by new moral relativism. Christians who accepted this view moved closer to 'humanist' (non-believing) morality, which did not have a religious basis. Christian moral reformers, however, wished to retain the religious basis of morality by altering its terms and sanctions.

'The wind of change here is a gale', wrote one of the chief proponents of moral change, John Robinson (Bishop of Woolwich) in *Honest to God*, his controversial and influential treatise of 1963.[2] This book aroused at least as much concern by questioning orthodox Christian doctrine as by questioning established morality.[3] It attacked what Robinson described as 'supranaturalist theology' and 'supranaturalist ethics'. The latter were seen by Robinson as the morals of the Ten Commandments, set in tablets of stone and, after endorsement by Christ, intended to rule the conduct of Christians for evermore.[4] Robinson disliked this moral framework as being too rigid and unadaptable in dealing with individual circumstances. He believed that it 'subordinated the actual individual relationship to some universal, whether metaphysical or moral, external to it'. On this basis, moral decisions were not reached, as he believed they should be, on 'the empirical realities of the particular concrete relationship between the parties concerned'.[5] 'Nothing can of itself be labelled as "wrong",' he wrote. 'One cannot, for instance, start from the position "sex relations before marriage" or "divorce" are wrong or sinful in themselves . . . They

[2] J. A. T. Robinson, *Honest to God* (London, 1963), 105.

[3] See, e.g., D. L. Edwards, *The Honest to God Debate: Some Reactions to the book 'Honest to God'* (London, 1963); J. I. Packer, *Keep Yourselves from Idols* (London, 1963); K. Hylson-Smith, *Evangelicals in the Church of England, 1734–1984* (Edinburgh, 1988), 302–6.

[4] Robinson, *Honest to God*, 106–7.

[5] Ibid. 112.

are not intrinsically so, for the only intrinsic evil is lack of love.'[6] This opened up the whole question, however, of how fairly 'love' was being applied in each case—whether what seemed like 'love' could not itself be blind, selfish, and forgetful of persons involved in the case. To exercise 'love' fully could be a complex and demanding procedure, beyond the capacity of most mortals.

Contemporary inclinations towards a more empirical ethic, the development of a 'new morality', were welcomed by Robinson. His opinions received support in some other Christian publications, notably from the contributors to *Towards a Quaker View of Sex* (published in 1963), who 'rejected almost completely the traditional approach of the organized Christian Church to morality'. The contributors were anxious to preserve marriage and family life, but:

> We think it our duty, not to stand on a peak of perfectionism, asking for an impossible conformity while the tide of human life sweeps by us, but to recognize, in compassion, the complications and bewilderment that love creates and to ask how we can discover a constructive way in each of an immense variety of particular experiences.[7]

These opinions were intensely debated.[8] Many Christians, though by no means all, were strongly opposed to the reforming moral opinions of the time, such as those of Robinson, of the contributors to *Towards a Quaker View of Sex*, and of Canon Douglas Rhymes of Southwark.[9] Pope Pius XII had denounced the 'new morality' in 1952—perhaps anticipating a lot more moral change than was occurring at that date.[10] The pronounced social change and moral shift of the 1960s naturally produced much division among Christians, as they were challenges to the body of

[6] Ibid. 117–18. See also J. Lewis, 'Public Institution and Private Relationship: Marriage and Marriage Guidance, 1920–68', *Twentieth Century British History*, 1/3 (1990), 258–60.

[7] A. Heron (ed.), *Towards a Quaker View of Sex* (London, 1963), 39–40. Cf. J. Weeks, *Sex, Politics, and Society: The Regulation of Sexuality since 1800* (London, 1981), 261; G. I. T. Machin, 'British Churches and Moral Change in the 1960s', in W. M. Jacob and N. Yates (eds.), *Crown and Mitre: Religion and Society in Northern Europe since the Reformation* (Woodbridge, 1993), 223–4.

[8] e.g. *CCC*, 3 Oct. 1961, iii. 6, pp. 486–97.

[9] *CEN*, 29 Mar. 1963, p. 3; 5 Apr. 1963, p. 14; 19 Apr. 1963, p. 5; *CT*, 28 June 1963, p. 12 (letters from Revds J. Slade and A. Burrell); *Daily Telegraph*, 9 Jan. 1964.

[10] E. R. Norman, *Church and Society in England, 1770–1970* (Oxford, 1976), 378–9; *RGACS* (1946), 316–17; G. Gorer, *Exploring English Character* (London, 1955), 94, 113, 116; J. Costello, *Love, Sex, and War: Changing Values, 1939–45* (London, 1985), 356–7.

traditional morality developed over the centuries. The Ten Commandments, however, managed in general to escape the challenge, and to remain an accepted guide even in the conditions of the 'new morality'—adultery, for example, continuing to be frowned on much more than premarital sex. None of the Ten Commandments was directly challenged by the new moral view, though the general tendency of the latter was that they should not be accepted as flatly as perhaps they were previously. The beleaguered Fourth Commandment, to keep the Sabbath holy, had long been subject to a variety of interpretations and encroachments, and did not receive any fresh challenge from the new morality. The Seventh Commandment, forbidding adultery, seemed to be somewhat challenged by Bishop Robinson when, defending Penguin Books at their famous trial in 1960 for publishing the full version of *Lady Chatterley's Lover*, he said that adultery might not invariably be sinful. But Robinson of course was not advocating adultery, and there was no widespread or effective support of adultery in the 1960s or later. Despite the beginning of a reduction in the popularity of marriage, and an increase in living together out of wedlock, adultery continued to be deprecated after premarital sex had become widely accepted. Somewhat ironically, therefore, in the conditions of the 'new morality' the Ten Commandments continued for the most part to provide accepted rules.

The British Churches also survived the tempestuous 1960s, though they had to face not only challenges to traditional morality but sharp decreases in membership and attendance. There was not only a hastening of the well-established decrease in Nonconformist membership, but a marked decline in Easter communicants in the Church of England. The membership of the Church of Scotland continued the decrease which had commenced in 1957 and has run consistently up to the late 1990s. In 1970 the estimated number of Roman Catholics in Great Britain showed its first drop since the eighteenth century—another beginning of a continuing trend. Only some small unorthodox Churches showed increases during the decade.[11] Because of the combination of moral change, decline in

[11] Detailed figures showing these changes are in R. Currie, A. Gilbert, and L. Horsley (eds.), *Churches and Churchgoers: Patterns of Church Growth in the British Isles since 1700* (Oxford, 1977), 31–2, 121–9, 135, 144, 151, 153, 158; *BW*, 8 Mar. 1962, pp. 10, 13. See also A. Hastings, *A History of English Christianity, 1920–85* (London, 1986), 549–52.

numbers, and the growth of alternative pursuits encouraged by increasing prosperity, the Churches were having to face as never before the challenge of secularization. Though unbelief and scepticism might have been growing, the main challenge to the traditional expression of Christianity by church attendance continued to be the 'privatization' of religion. This was the maintenance of belief without church membership or witness, perhaps partly sustained by watching services on television and belonging to a worship and discussion group, a progenitor of the 'house churches' of the 1970s.

Christians in Britain, like their society as a whole, did not respond in a united way to the moral changes of the 1960s. Long experience of developing liberalism, and the gradual extension of democracy, had accustomed the population to evolving and expressing diverse opinions on such questions. None of these questions was unfamiliar before the 1960s, though they now appeared in more concentrated and challenging form. In some respects there was probably a fair degree of consensus among Christians about moral questions—for example, the alarming rise in crime from the late 1950s.[12] There were combined Christian protests against the sale of pornographic literature at Wigan in 1968.[13] When the Roman Catholic Archbishop of Cardiff, John Murphy, said in 1967 that the affluent society was in danger of becoming the 'effluent society', the *Church Times* said: 'There are thousands of Christians outside the Roman Church who must have said "three cheers for the Archbishop" on reading of this protest made in the common Christian cause against the excesses of fashionable moral anarchy.'[14]

The Roman Catholic Church differed from Protestant Churches, however, over divorce, abortion, and artificial birth control. There also continued to be a more pronounced moral puritanism among some smaller Protestant Churches, such as the Free Church of Scotland, than in larger Protestant Churches. The Free Church of Scotland's Committee on Public Questions reported in 1965 that:

[12] A rise delineated, for example, in D. J. V. Jones, '"Where did it all go wrong?": Crime in Swansea, 1938–68', *Welsh History Review*, 15/2 (1990), 240–74, esp. 246, 251, 256, Cf. *PAGAFCS* (1966), 159–60.
[13] *CT*, 16 Feb. 1968, p. 11.
[14] Ibid., 3 Mar. 1967, p. 3.

the moral and ethical standards of the nation have never been lower since the Reformation of four centuries ago than they are to-day. The obsession with sex, which is so glaringly evident in the increasing output of pornographic or near-pornographic literature; in the materials of the screen and stage; and even in the very advertisements which appear on the hoardings and in our magazines, bodes no good for the future of our nation. Our young people to-day are being exploited in ways that were almost unknown to their parents, and our judgements of them must be tempered by a recognition of that fact.[15]

The same committee deplored in the following year that it was now

denied that there can be any such thing as a permanent, fixed, authoritative standard of morals. Ethical conduct is relative. As [an instance] of this, fornication condemned in Scripture as morally wrong, is condoned if not also defended by 'responsible' public authority on the grounds that 'charity' comes before 'chastity'.[16]

The Church and Nation Committee of the Church of Scotland would have agreed with much of this viewpoint, but its report of 1967 gave the reminder that 'earlier days had their own narrow and limited concepts, their moral blind spots and deficiencies . . . we [ought] to remain open to new insights and be ready to study every enlightened approach'.[17]

Much of the debate in Church assemblies and in the publications of Christian thinkers on ethical attitudes and standards was on a generalized intellectual plain. But the realities of day-to-day behaviour were an inescapable part of the controversy over morals. Michael Ramsey (who had succeeded Fisher as Archbishop of Canterbury in 1961), when asked about the short-lived 'topless-dress' craze of the summer of 1964, warned that Christians should be careful before appearing to be shocked.[18] But a letter he received on the subject indicated that some Christians were indeed shocked by such public nudity, and could relate this reaction to wide religious and moral considerations:

As a Christian I have been taught to believe that my body is a temple for my immortal soul, and therefore should be treated with every reverence and respect, and to flaunt it in this way can only cause real distress to many

[15] *PAGAFCS* (1965), 147.
[16] Ibid. (1966), 157.
[17] *RGACS* (1967), 502.
[18] *Guardian* (formerly *Manchester Guardian*), 1 July 1964; extract in RP 68, fo. 191.

of my sex . . . Therefore, might I plead that the whole Church and State speak with one voice now, and condemn the new evil, which, if allowed to snowball, can become a real danger to our society.[19]

Ramsey's secretary replied, on Ramsey's behalf, that 'the Archbishop feels that a tremendous drive of disapproval against topless dresses might have exactly the opposite effect of what is intended'.[20]

The continued growth in popular prosperity and a marked overall decline in churchgoing in the 1960s helped to produce a sustained demand to extend the entertainment opportunities of the 'continental Sunday' during that decade. This brought no comfort to those who wished to maintain a sabbatarian tradition which was already greatly eroded. Diversity of opinion over this matter caused the occasional conflict between Churches. This occurred, for example, when the Free Church of Scotland (whose opposition to ferry services between the Scottish mainland and Hebridean islands was prominent in the 1960s[21]) deplored the 'softness' of the Church of Scotland, and especially its Church and Nation Committee, for showing a liberal attitude to Sunday recreation.[22] The report of that committee in 1960, endorsed by the General Assembly, had stated:

For the great majority of Christian people, worship and Christian service cannot take up the *whole* of the day; some form of physical recreation on Sunday is naturally legitimate. If they join in corporate worship with fellow Christians they may rightly and profitably use some part of the day for enjoyment, whether in walking, driving, sailing, swimming, or in playing of games . . . To frown on such activities is to ignore the need for physical as well as spiritual recreation, and to be guilty of a moralistic legalism from which Christ has set his followers free. The decision on such matters must be left to the conscience of the individual Christian . . . The same may be said of certain other forms of amusement. In an age when many church members look at a television film or a play on Sunday evening in their own homes, is it consistent for the Church officially to set its face against the opening of cinemas, recreation rooms, or restaurants?[23]

[19] Doris Kerr to Ramsey, 3 July 1964, RP, 68, fos. 192–3.
[20] R. Beloe to Doris Kerr, 13 July 1964, ibid., fo. 199.
[21] *PAGAFCS* (1966), 163.
[22] Ibid. (1965), 147.
[23] *RGACS* (1960), 302.

Such opinions were by no means universally popular in the Church of Scotland. An elder of thirty years' standing in that Church wrote about these views that 'thinking men and women will look elsewhere for guidance and leadership rather than to some of the leaders of the Church of Scotland . . . The Free Church of Scotland and the Lord's Day Observance Society are more faithful guardians of our precious heritage.'[24]

The spread of gambling, not only on Sundays when opportunity offered but throughout the week, was of continuing concern to the Churches in a decade which commenced with the Betting and Gaming Act of 1960 and ended with proposals to establish a national lottery. Some marked denominational differences existed, however: a survey of 1965 indicated that 76 per cent of Methodists but only 23 per cent of Anglicans disapproved of football pools (and the gap between them was even greater over support of total abstinence from alcohol). The Betting and Gaming Act legalized cash betting off the course, thus allowing bingo halls and betting shops to open in vast numbers. Apprehensions about the Act were expressed by Church assemblies and newspapers.[25] Later, it was said in 1968 by a committee of the Church of Scotland's Board of Social and Moral Welfare that

> since 1960 about 1,000 gaming clubs have been established in Britain, and about 2,000 bingo clubs . . . We agree with Mr Roy Jenkins [Chancellor of the Exchequer], who said that 'this country has become a gambler's paradise and this has led to a growing connection between gaming clubs and organized crime, often violent crime, in London and other big cities'.[26]

Opponents of gambling received some solace from the passing of a Gaming Bill in 1968, which aimed to carry out a large reduction in the number of clubs.

'Gambling', said a committee of the Free Church of Scotland General Assembly in 1964, 'is morally wrong, socially undesirable, and economically disastrous'.[27] The gambler was suspected as a person who might be trying to bypass an age-old correlation

[24] Letter from W. H. Cooper, Ross-shire, in *BW* (Scottish edition), 7 July 1960, p. 11.

[25] *CEN*, 29 Apr. 1960, p. 1; *BT*, 8 Sept. 1960, p. 5. For the survey mentioned, see A. Wilkinson, *Dissent or Conform?: War, Peace, and the English Churches* (London, 1986), 60.

[26] *RGACS* (1968), 498.

[27] *PAGAFCS* (1964), 130.

between honest toil and monetary reward in order to gain a lot in return for little expense. It seemed that, to this end, increasing numbers of people were playing a mean pinball in the 1960s. 'His motive is to get much for little', reported the Committee on Temperance and Morals to the Church of Scotland General Assembly. 'The Football Pool, the Bingo Club, the Totalisator, the Premium Bond, the bookmaker's odds, all seek to exploit this motive. Such an outlook is a denial of the Christian's true calling.'[28] To the list might have been added the church raffle. There were obvious differences of opinion and practice in churches over raffling.[29] Warnings continued to be given against engaging in this small and well-intentioned flutter on the grounds that it could be a harmful example, encouraging more ambitious risk-taking. 'Mild gambles' were also seen as financial rivals to the church collection: 'comparatively small sums may be spent weekly by many who indulge in a mild gamble, but then "comparatively small sums" are usually about twice the average giving of the church member to the cause of Christ.'[30]

A bill to establish a national lottery was brought into the House of Commons by James Tinn, Labour member for Cleveland, and received a second reading (by a majority of sixty-nine votes to twenty-seven) on 2 February 1968. The bill, however, was ultimately unsuccessful, to the gratification of a number of Church bodies and newspapers.[31] A national lottery was not established for another twenty-six years.

There were continuing anxieties about the growth in alcohol consumption, not least in relation to road accidents as the number of cars continued to mount rapidly. 'A special responsibility rests upon the Church to be the agent of reform' in this sphere, said a report by the Church of Scotland General Assembly Committee on Temperance and Morals in 1961.[32] In the 1960s many Church bodies opposed a desire to extend public-house opening hours, and occasionally voiced a wish to reduce them. Early in 1960 the Ayr

[28] *RGACS* (1963), 406–17 (quoted in Machin, 'British Churches and Moral Change', 227). Cf. *RGACS* (1965), 350ff.; *PAGAFCS* (1962), 162, (1963), 141.

[29] *RGACS* (1960), 342; Church of Scotland Edinburgh Presbytery Minutes, 10 Jan. 1961, CH2/161/67, p. 330.

[30] *RGACS* (1967), 504 (quoted in Machin, 'British Churches and Moral Change', 227); (1968), 500.

[31] *BW*, 7 Mar. 1968, p. 6, 28 Mar. 1968, p. 1; *RGACS* (1968), 499, (1969), 512.

[32] *RGACS* (1961), 450.

presbytery of the Church of Scotland wanted all public houses in Scotland to close at 9.30 p.m., and strongly defended the continuance of closure on Sundays.[33] A correspondent urged in the *British Weekly* at this time that there should be a campaign for Sunday closing in England as well.[34] Concern was aroused when the new supermarkets of the early 1960s intended to seek licences for the 'off-sale' of intoxicating liquor. Arthur Davies, Secretary of the TCCC of England and Wales, wrote to Archbishop Ramsey, Cardinal Godfrey (Archbishop of Westminster), and others about this matter.[35] But his concern did not obtain full episcopal support, as was shown by a letter from Gerald Ellison, Bishop of Chester:

> Parliament must have had in mind the possibility of the supermarket applying for an off-licence, and I cannot really think that this is any more undesirable than the practice at the present time of alcohol being sold in an ordinary grocer's shop. Children go into grocers' shops as much as they do into Woolworths, and whereas the glamour in Woolworths may be rather more marked, yet children have always had the opportunity of seeing alcoholics [*sic*] for sale. Nor do I think that there is any more danger of alcoholics being sold to people under eighteen in Woolworths than anywhere else; in any case the police will be watching this very carefully, and it would not be in the interest of Woolworths or any of the supermarkets to allow juveniles to buy alcoholics.[36]

Abstention from drinking before driving was also often urged, as for example by the Archbishop of Wales, Edwin Morris, who told the Governing Body of the Church in Wales at Llandrindod Wells in 1960 that it was 'beyond question sinful' to risk the lives of others through thoughtless drinking. He argued, against the strict abstentionist line, that the example of Christ had shown that Christians were free to engage in moderate drinking; but they should always recognize the danger of excess, and should abstain at appropriate times.[37]

The 1960 annual assembly of the Congregational Union of England and Wales recommended, on the basis of a pamphlet published by the Christian Economic and Social Research Foundation, that in

[33] *BW* (Scottish edition), 10 Mar. 1960, p. 3. Cf. *RGACS* (1960), 338, (1961), 445, 450–1, (1968), 496.
[34] *BW*, 3 Mar. 1960, p. 15 (letter from A. E. Jones).
[35] Revd A. C. Davies to Ramsey, 12 Dec. 1961, RP 27, fo. 313; Godfrey to Davies, 14 Dec. 1961, ibid., fo. 321.
[36] Ellison to R. Beloe (private secretary to Ramsey), 11 Jan. 1962, ibid., fo. 316.
[37] *CT*, 22 Apr. 1960, p. 7. Cf. *RGACS* (1961), 449.

order to encourage abstention before driving a blood test or a 'breathing apparatus for measuring alcohol-concentration in the body' should be used.[38] This idea was supported by the *Baptist Times*, and the *British Weekly* said that 'the Christian conscience, like the public conscience, rebels at the thought of the massacre of the roads . . . Propaganda and punishment must be organized to ensure that drink and driving never go together.'[39] The Church of Scotland Committee on Temperance and Morals gave warm approval to the Road Traffic Act of 1962, which contained firm provisions with regard to the drink-and-driving problem.[40] The Congregational Union annual assembly welcomed a government announcement in 1965 that a law would be introduced making it an offence to drive with more than a certain amount of alcohol in the blood.[41] In 1968 the Church of Scotland General Assembly strongly approved of the recent introduction of the breathalyser test, by a Road Safety Act, in October 1967. It had already been shown, it was stated, that the test was having a good effect; and it was hoped that 'the country . . . will not be put off by the high-powered publicity against the test being adopted by the Licensed Trade'. In regard to the need for care and attention while driving, the 1969 General Assembly recommended that all drivers should seek to reach 'the standard demanded in the test of the Institute of Advanced Motorists or the Automobile Association's Advanced Driving Course'.[42]

There was also concern over drug-taking and excessive tobacco-smoking, issues which became prominent in the 1960s. Growing addiction to 'soft' drugs such as cannabis and marijuana, and 'hard' drugs such as heroin and LSD, was repeatedly remarked on by Church bodies, which called on the Government to take more action.[43] The Misuse of Drugs Act was passed in 1964 as a deterrent to non-medicinal drug-taking—almost the only non-permissive Act of the decade—but this measure was not at all easy to enforce. The Congregational Union annual assembly in May 1967 resolved to welcome

[38] Resolution of 19 May 1960, *CYB* (1961), 82.

[39] *BT*, 23 June 1960, p. 5; *BW*, 28 July 1960, p. 6. Cf. proceedings of Methodist Conference, 1960, resolution by Revd Kenneth Greet, *MR*, 14 July 1960, p. 5; Church of Scotland Edinburgh Presbytery Minutes, 7 Feb. 1961, CH2/161/67, p. 340.

[40] *RGACS* (1963), 399.

[41] *CYB* (1963–6), 88.

[42] *RGACS* (1968), 496 (cf. ibid. (1967), 504, (1969), 203).

[43] *RGACS* (1965), 348, (1967), 507–8.

the much greater activity being shown by Her Majesty's Government to combat the dangerous and rapid increase in drug addiction, especially among young people, but believes that more needs to be done. All possible steps should be taken to check the illicit trade in dangerous drugs and to provide more adequate facilities for the treatment and cure of addicts.[44]

A desire to take drugs might even indicate spiritual hunger, which the Churches should try to assuage by means utterly different from the provision of psychedelic crutches. The *Church of England Newspaper* stated that 'the LSD cult and the urge for psychedelic experience indicate a groping awareness of "a country far beyond the stars". We must show that the Gospel of our Lord Jesus Christ is able to put a new song into men's mouths and fire them with the hope of glory.'[45] One Anglican society, the Mothers' Union, tried in Blackburn to educate parents in the dangers of drug-taking amongst their teenage children.[46] Kenneth Leech, curate of St Anne's in Soho, wrote a pamphlet on *The Drug Subculture*, published in 1969 by the Church of England Council for Social Aid. The pamphlet saw the spread of drug-taking as 'one part of a many-sided social revolution, in which rebellion against authority plays its part', and called for determined efforts to penetrate 'the loneliness and alienation of the addict'.[47]

Frequent cigarette-smoking first began to be regarded seriously as a cause of lung cancer after the publication of a report on 'Smoking and Health' by the Royal College of Physicians in 1962. The Methodist Conference in that year reaffirmed its advice that

a causal connection between cigarette smoking and lung cancer and other diseases, should be seriously considered by Methodists. In particular, the evidence should be presented, and guidance given, to young people. This was a matter for personal decision, but young Methodists should be advised not to take up smoking.[48]

Similar interest in this matter was shown by other Church assemblies.[49] In 1965 the Church of Scotland's Temperance and Morals Committee urged the Government to act immediately in order to

[44] Resolution of 17 May 1967, *CYB* (1967–8), 86.
[45] *CEN*, 7 July 1967, p. 1.
[46] *CT*, 23 Mar. 1967, p. 15.
[47] Ibid., 2 May 1969, p. 10. Cf. *RGACS* (1968), 496–7, (1969) 501–3; *PAGAFCS* (1967), 137.
[48] *MR*, 12 July 1962, p. 3.
[49] e.g. *RGACS* (1960), 343, (1967), 507.

implement proposals in the College of Physicians' report; and welcomed as a first step the Government's declared intention to stop cigarettes being advertised on commercial television.[50]

The morality of public output in the form of books, newspapers, plays, films, and television and radio programmes was another concern of the Churches in the 1960s, as it was of society at large. This was inevitable in a decade when the frontiers of permissiveness were sharply extended and censorship was weakened or (in the case of plays) abolished. Differing opinions among Christians and non-Christians were shown in response to these changes.[51]

Legal permission to publish the full version of *Lady Chatterley's Lover*, after an epoch-making trial in 1960, showed these differing viewpoints. This was the case not least in the Anglican hierarchy, where Archbishop Fisher was in conflict over the matter with Bishop Robinson. The latter, who wrote in a book ten years later that the Church 'had reparation to make' as regards 'reinstatement of the genuinely erotic as a subject of beauty and delight', had appeared at the trial and defended the book. In his speech in court he had advised Christians to read it and made the highly contentious statement that it portrayed 'the love of a woman in an immoral relationship, so far as adultery is an immoral relationship'.[52] Robinson was accused of rejecting the Seventh Commandment, which forbade adultery.[53] He was not doing this, but he was saying that the terms of the Commandment were in certain circumstances open to question. He was seeking to make relative what appeared to be absolute.

Fisher could have none of this. After warning Robinson in a letter that 'I cannot defend you, of course, at all',[54] he rebuked him publicly at a diocesan conference at Canterbury two days later, on 5 November 1960:

[50] Ibid. (1965), 351.

[51] A. Aldgate, *Censorship and the Permissive Society: British Cinema and Theatre, 1955–65* (Oxford, 1995), 151–2; J. Richards and A. Aldgate, *Best of British: Cinema and Society, 1930–70* (Oxford, 1983), 131–43.

[52] Newspaper cutting in FP 246, appended to fos. 158–9. See J. A. T. Robinson, *Christian Freedom in a Permissive Society* (London, 1970), 73–6; and E. James, *A Life of Bishop John A. T. Robinson, Scholar, Pastor, Prophet* (London, 1989), 93–6.

[53] Revd L. H. Cuckney to Col. R. J. A. Hornby (Chief Information Officer, Church House, Westminster), 29 Oct. 1960, FP, fo. 158.

[54] Fisher to Robinson, 3 Nov. 1960, ibid., fo. 160.

Anyone must know that in this sexually self-conscious and chaotic age, to speak pastoral wisdom in public on particular questions is extremely dangerous. The bishop exposed himself to this danger. The Christian fact is that adultery . . . is always a sin, and at present a very prominent, even all pervasive sin. The good pastor will teach his people to avoid both the fact of and the desire for sex experience of an adulterous kind and of fornication also, from the plain undeviating teaching of the Bible, both Old and New Testament . . . In my judgement, the Bishop was mistaken to think that he could take part in the trial without becoming a stumbling block and a cause of offence to many ordinary Christians.[55]

This statement was widely published, and aroused differing reactions among Christians. Fisher was congratulated by Enid Blyton, the children's author, and strongly criticized by Valerie Pitt, a Lecturer in English at Woolwich Polytechnic.[56] Even stronger criticism came from Mrs Daphne Laing of Dundee, who wrote to him:

I am one—and I am sure there are thousands more—who are horrified at the narrow and moralistic view you express . . . I am certain that Jesus must squirm at this sort of pitifully inadequate action. You—and not the Fine Christians like Dr John Robinson—are the one who is driving people out of the Church.[57]

In defence of his action Robinson wrote to Fisher as follows:

The whole tenor of the book is clearly against promiscuity in sexual relationships . . . Properly read it can be both a liberating and a humbling experience . . . It is a monstrous irony, when sex is commercialized on all sides, that the State should have proceeded against one of the few authors of our generation who have protested bitterly against its prostitution and perversion.[58]

Leading Christians who favoured the publication included Edward Wickham, Bishop of Middleton, who thought that *Lady Chatterley's Lover* could have 'a profound value'; and the President of the Methodist Conference, Edward Rogers, who did not think the book was obscene.[59] Another prominent Methodist, Donald

[55] Fisher's speech at the conference, ibid., fo. 162. *The Times*, 7 Nov. 1960.

[56] Blyton to Fisher, 6 Nov. 1960, FP 246, fo. 168; Pitt to Fisher, 6 Nov. 1960, ibid., fo. 169; James, *Life*, 103–4; Fisher to Pitt, 10 Nov. 1960, FP 246, fos. 193–5; Fisher to Blyton, 17 Nov. 1960, ibid., fo. 204.

[57] Daphne Laing to Fisher, 6 Nov. 1960, ibid., fo. 172 (quoted in Machin, 'British Churches and Moral Change', 229); cf. David Holbrook to Fisher, 6 Nov. 1960, FP 246, fos. 170–1.

[58] Robinson to Fisher, 8 Nov. 1960, ibid., fos. 178–80.

[59] *Sunday Dispatch*, 6 Nov. 1960.

Soper, told 300 people at Speaker's Corner in Hyde Park that he was delighted that the book had been legally reprieved: 'it is an excellent piece of literature and . . . a sincere attempt by the author to present one side of married life.'[60] But opponents of the book included Monsignor Gordon Wheeler, Administrator of Westminster Cathedral; A. M. Renwick, Moderator of the General Assembly of the Free Church of Scotland; and the Temperance and Morals Committee of the Church of Scotland, which condemned the book unequivocally as 'pernicious, pornographic, and in some passages positively blasphemous'.[61]

One forthright enemy of *Lady Chatterley's Lover* was Basil Buckland, Rector of Longton, Stoke-on-Trent, whose wife was celebrated a few years later as the partner of Mary Whitehouse in her campaign to 'clean up' television. Buckland believed that everyone in the Church of England 'ought to be bitterly ashamed that we, largely through the advocacy of one of our bishops, but also by our own flabbiness, have allowed a book which glorifies adultery and unrestrained lust to be approved for general reading'.[62]

Securing legal acceptance of the publication of *Lady Chatterley* was like the removal of a boulder which released an avalanche of markedly permissive fictional writing and uninhibited pictorial display in magazines and newspapers. Much of this was of the 'soft-pornographic' kind which was not likely to be prosecuted under the Obscene Publications Act. But it aroused fierce disputes in which denunciations came from religious periodicals and other quarters. Publicity to launch the magazine *Penthouse* in Britain in 1965, claiming that it led 'the struggle for moral and intellectual freedom', was described by the *British Weekly* as 'diabolical drivel' and as 'one of the first major steps in a cataclysmic flood of planned pornography'.[63] This periodical welcomed only with strong reservations the ending of the Lord Chamberlain's powers of stage censorship by an Act of 1968. On the one hand, said the *British Weekly*, pressure for freedom of expression in the arts 'comes, genuinely, from creative thinkers, writers, and producers'; on the other hand, 'it also comes from pornographers and perverts, anxious to cash in on the permissive society, happy to corrupt if it means commercial

[60] *The Times*, 7. Nov. 1960.
[61] Ibid.; *Sunday Dispatch*, 6 Nov. 1960; *RGACS* (1961), 447.
[62] *Sunday Dispatch*, 6 Nov. 1960.
[63] *BW*, 11 Feb. 1965. p. 1.

gain'.[64] Disputes over the new freedom for publication and entertainment have continued to erupt up to the end of the century. In many ways the permissive society, for all its good intentions, has brought not peace but a sword.

The television set, ensconced as a prize possession in most British households by the 1960s, was described in 1967 as 'the most powerful medium of propaganda that mankind has yet invented'.[65] Naturally the mighty medium was carefully watched for signs of undue permissiveness. By the early 1960s many television broadcasts seemed to be adopting moral permissiveness, especially in the case of *avant garde* discussions and 'experimental' plays. The satirical programmes which flourished at this time were sometimes construed not as harmless fun but as damagingly mocking religion and symbolizing a sick and decadent society.[66]

Television was especially vulnerable to criticism by Christians and others because of the large amount of time that children spent watching it, and the difficulty of ensuring, even by careful timetabling, that they would not see some highly unsuitable material. A Catholic memorandum was written jointly by John Heenan (Archbishop of Liverpool), Monsignor George Tomlinson, and Father Agnellus Andrew, and submitted to a government committee on broadcasting in 1961. The memorandum complained of deteriorating standards and of frequent 'complete lack of restraint and reticence' in programmes which could seriously infringe 'both modesty and morality'.[67] The Church and Nation Committee of the Church of Scotland said in this year (as it was to do on later occasions) that plays and films that 'appeared to question the sanctity of marriage and family life' should not be broadcast; that all forms of blasphemy should be banned from the air; and that programmes should not display any encouragement of drinking and gambling.[68]

Protests of this kind from Church bodies and individual Christians were liable to be regarded by 'progressive' broadcasting authorities as routine minority complaints, and consequently

[64] *BW*, 3 Oct. 1968. p. 6.

[65] Peter Kirk, reviewing Mary Whitehouse's book, *Cleaning Up TV*, *CT*, 24 Feb. 1967, p. 5.

[66] e.g. *Daily Herald*, 14 Jan. 1963; *Daily Mirror*, 14 Jan. 1963.

[67] Copy of memo. (Feb. 1961) in FP 261, fo. 313. Cf. 'The Future of Broadcasting', a statement by the Church of England Radio and Television Council, 5 Dec. 1960, ibid., fos. 236, 323–33; *LW* (June 1964), 211.

[68] *RGACS* (1961), 430. Cf. ibid. (1965), 300ff.

ignored. In the case of television especially, however, a novel popular movement appeared which compelled the authorities to pay some attention. Mrs Mary Whitehouse, a teacher, and Mrs Norah Buckland, wife of a clergyman—both of whom were attached to Moral Rearmament and the Mothers' Union—launched a 'Clean Up TV' campaign in 1964. Their manifesto stated: 'We call upon the BBC for a radical change of policy and demand programmes which build character instead of destroying it, and encourage and sustain faith in God and bring Him back to the heart of our family and national life.'[69]

Their *bête noire* was the Director-General of the BBC, Sir Hugh Greene. Mrs Whitehouse wrote later: 'If you were to ask me who, above all, was responsible for the moral collapse which characterized the sixties and seventies, I would unhesitatingly name Sir Hugh Carleton Greene.'[70] But Greene was no anti-Christian crusader: it was on his suggestion that the still-running (in 1997) *Songs of Praise*, the most popular of all religious broadcasts in Britain, was launched in 1961.[71]

'Clean-Up TV' broadened into the National Viewers' and Listeners' Association, founded early in 1965.[72] The association commenced with the unexpectedly large figure of 300,000 supporters, including about 100 MPs from different parties. Members of the working committee included a Roman Catholic vicar-general and a leading Methodist minister, Kenneth Greet. But the initial appearance of solidarity began to wane somewhat when Greet withdrew his support on the grounds that the expressions of the association were too negative.[73] A clerical opponent of the association, C. D. Westbrook, wrote to the *Church Times* that he could not give his support because his religion compelled him to defend 'the priceless value of freedom of speech; a freedom which it has taken centuries

[69] M. Whitehouse, *Cleaning up T.V.: From Protest to Participation* (London, 1967), 23.

[70] Quoted in A. Briggs, *The History of Broadcasting in the United Kingdom*, v (Oxford, 1995), 309.

[71] Ibid. 335 n.

[72] Whitehouse, *Cleaning up T.V.*, 19, 23 ff.; *BT*, 3 Sept. 1964, p. 12, 24 Sept., p. 1. For Mrs Whitehouse's motivation and campaigns, see also Weeks, *Sex, Politics, and Society*, 277–81.

[73] *CT*, 5 Mar. 1965, p. 1; 12 Mar. 1965, p. 3; *BW*, 18 Mar. 1965, p. 6; *T.*, 24 Sept. 1965 (letter of R. J. Snell); Whitehouse, *Cleaning up T.V.*, 52–3. Cf. D. W. Bebbington, *Evangelicalism in Modern Britain: A History from the 1730s to the 1980s* (London, 1989), 264.

to secure and which has too often been denied and brutally suppressed in the name of religion'. In contrast to this, a Birmingham doctor wrote to the same paper that Mrs Whitehouse 'deserves the support of all Christians who have the future of our nation at heart'; and the Church of Scotland General Assembly said, in relation to current broadcasting policy, that 'democracy and society can be damaged as much by a decadent morality as by subversive politics'.[74] The Free Church of Scotland's Public Questions Committee suggested in 1966 that there might be a conspiracy in broadcasting 'to overthrow the Christian moral standards accepted in this country at least since the Reformation'.[75]

The National Viewers' and Listeners' Association had to run the gauntlet of objection and ridicule, but it had a certain success. It did not appear to alter broadcasting policy fundamentally, but it was claimed by 1967 that the moral standard of television broadcasts was becoming more acceptable.[76] Nevertheless the expression of different views on Mrs Whitehouse's aims showed that by no means all Christians agreed with her association and its mission. It also became clear eventually that the struggle over questions she emphasized was not likely to end in victory for one side or the other, but only in compromise.

Representations of homosexuality and lesbianism in television drama were among the aspects which were questioned by many supporters of Mrs Whitehouse. But the Wolfenden Report of 1957, advocating the legalization of homosexual acts between consenting adults, had won wide though by no means universal acquiescence among Christian leaders and Church assemblies. Such supporters of legalization, however, were by no means usually prepared to regard the homosexual orientation as equivalent to the heterosexual one. They were not, in many cases, prepared to abandon the traditional view that homosexuality was unnatural. Consequently they did not as yet express an overt desire—such as has been expressed by some leading Christians since the 1970s—that homosexuals should enjoy the same freedom and rights as heterosexuals—for example, the right to live as a married couple after a

[74] Letter in *CT*, 19 Mar. 1965, p. 14; letter from Dr Robert Browne, ibid., 3 Mar. 1967, p. 7; *RGACS* (1965), 247, 300ff.

[75] *PAGAFCS* (1966), 159.

[76] *RGACS* (1967), 162.

church or a civil wedding. Parliament debated the non-party question of legalizing homosexual acts on several occasions in the years after the Wolfenden Report.[77] Finally there was passed in 1967 a private member's bill introduced by Leo Abse (Labour MP for Pontypool), which provided for legalization.[78] Thus the long-debated reform became one of the major liberalizing measures of that notable year for permissiveness, 1967. After the legislation had gone through, however, Christians continued to hold differing views on the subject, and for various reasons the subject has remained a prominent matter of debate up to the present.

Agreement with homosexual law reform could be conceded by diluting a traditional moral assumption. In the 1960s there was no sign of a widespread willingness among Christians to abandon another traditional moral assumption, that sexual relations should be limited to marriage. Indeed the signs were that the latter view was still being firmly upheld.[79] During the decade, however, this belief began to be strongly challenged by the invention and widespread adoption of the relatively 'safe' contraceptive pill. The force of this crucial medical circumstance, added to the developing multitude of auxiliary challenges arising from broadcasts, films, publications, and fashions in dress, made it very difficult to maintain opposition to premarital sex. By the 1970s and 1980s there seemed to be a widespread tendency among Christians to acquiesce tacitly, not in promiscuity and certainly not in adultery, but in premarital sexual relations between a couple firmly attached to each other. 'The teaching of Jesus', it was stated in a report to the Church of Scotland General Assembly in 1963, 'gives no express command concerning pre-marital intercourse'.[80]

In 1962 the incongruously named (in this context) Reith Lectures, given by Professor G. M. Carstairs on the radio, stated that premarital sexual intercourse should be condoned. This resembled the opinions expressed by some recent writers, notably Eustace Chesser in his controversial book of 1960, *Is Chastity Outmoded?* Carstairs, a humanist in personal viewpoint, was a medical scientist

[77] See O. Chadwick, *Michael Ramsey, a Life* (Oxford, 1990), 146–9; correspondence in RP 78, fos. 25–225; *CEN*, 18 Feb. 1966, p. 2.

[78] L. Abse, *Private Member: A Psychoanalytically Orientated Study of Contemporary Politics* (London, 1973), 145–58.

[79] e.g. *CT*, 3 Sept. 1965.

[80] *RGACS* (1963), 411.

and son of a Church of Scotland minister. His lectures were published by Penguin Books, under the title *This Island Now*. The third lecture, on questions arising in adolescence, included this highly controversial statement:

> It seems to me that our young people are rapidly turning our society into one in which sexual experience, with precautions against conception, is becoming accepted as a sensible preliminary to marriage; a preliminary which makes it more likely that marriage, when it comes, will be a mutually considerate and mutually satisfying partnership.[81]

To many Christians this statement must have seemed a highly unwelcome example of the new morality, and it received considerable condemnation. The Church of Scotland Temperance and Morals Committee acknowledged that the lecture was 'a timely and able analysis of adolescence', but entirely rejected the commendation of premarital sex. Carstairs, said the Committee in its report to the General Assembly of 1963, had produced no evidence that 'unchastity is a better preparation for marriage than the exercise of self-restraint'. Carstairs had not said, however, as the report tended to assume, that 'sexual harmony' was the only basis needed for a successful marriage.[82] The General Assembly, in its deliverance on this report, stressed that 'chastity before marriage and fidelity after marriage remain the true ideal for the Christian'.[83] Carstairs received letters both for and against his statement; those who wrote letters against included the Baptist Union, the Free Church of Scotland presbytery of Glasgow, a Catholic Women's Group, and the clergy of the rural deanery of York.[84]

Reactions against Carstairs's broadcast opinion were naturally influenced by worries that premarital sexual activity was increasing. Statistics produced in 1960 had shown that venereal disease was growing among teenagers. The *Church Times* said that this was because of laxity by parents and teachers, and perhaps also by the Churches, in giving children the correct moral instruction:

[81] G. M. Carstairs, *This Island Now: The BBC Reith Lectures, 1962* (Harmondsworth, 1964), 49–50, 103–12 (quoted in Machin, 'British Churches and Moral Change', 233–4).

[82] *RGACS* (1963), 410–11. Cf. *LW*, Feb. 1963, p. 53; *CT*, 31 May 1963, p. 4.

[83] *RGACS* (1963), 419. Cf. ibid. (1967), 509, (1969), 505; *PAGAFCS* (1963), 143, (1968), 132.

[84] Carstairs, *This Island Now*, 108.

The responsibility lies supremely on all those parents and teachers who have so lightly discarded the whole Christian scheme of things. It is no use expecting to pluck the fruits of purity when they have cut the roots of faith . . . The Church ought to be asking itself whether any of the blame lies at its own door . . . Has it been courageous enough in fighting those who, on fashionable moral grounds, call good evil, and evil good?[85]

Teachers, for their part, claimed that it was difficult to inculcate a high standard of morality when the output of the media was repeatedly undermining their efforts.[86]

Deteriorating sexual morals were held to be exemplified by a well-publicized extramarital affair in high places in 1963. The Secretary for War, John Profumo, resigned after first denying and then admitting having had an adulterous relationship with Christine Keeler (the current Cold War espionage worries also being exemplified by the allegation that she was a security risk, as she was currently also friendly with a Soviet emissary). The scandal 'encouraged the belief abroad that Britain is finished, not only as a military power but as a moral power', said the *British Weekly*.[87] Religious newspapers rebutted claims by some politicians that the moral issue had no bearing on the Minister's public role. The *Church Times* declared:

Christians cannot regard moral decadence and corruption in public life as matters of no public concern. Rottenness in high places, lying, sexual licence and the widespread social acceptance of adultery cut at the roots of the nation's life, because they are contrary to the law of God.[88]

A letter in this paper stated that 'the present climate of this country and the tragedy of Mr Profumo both rise up in judgment against . . . [those] who reject the law of God and with it the morality of society in favour of a morality of self-development and social selfishness'.[89] The *Church of England Newspaper* saw the scandal as resulting from the spreading influence of the new morality:

Reflecting on the whole affair, the Christian may wonder whether this is not just the fruits of relativism in dogma that transmits itself easily to morals and in which absolute standards based on biblical truth are

85 *CT*, 29 Apr. 1960, p. 3.
86 *T.*, 30 Apr. 1960, p. 403.
87 *BW*, 13 June 1963, pp. 1, 6.
88 *CT*, 14 June 1963, p. 3. Cf. ibid., 21 June, pp. 19–20; *BW*, 27 June, p. 9.
89 *CT*, 14 June 1963, p. 14 (letter of George Goyder). Cf. Machin, 'British Churches and Moral Change', 233–5.

dismissed as naïve. Simplicity is an offence that we must be ready to accept.[90]

Differences between Protestants and the Roman Catholic Church over contraception became harder by the 1960s, following clear statements by the Lambeth Conference in 1958 and the Church of Scotland General Assembly in 1960 permitting the use of artificial methods. Birth-control methods were rendered more effective by the new contraceptive pill. The chairman of the Lambeth Conference's Family Planning Group, Bishop Stephen Bayne, said in March 1960 that he could see no reason why the new invention should be regarded as 'an offence to Christian conscience', and he 'welcomed the news that women in Britain were being invited to share in the experiments to test its trustworthiness'.[91] About two years later, however, worries were being expressed that the new pill might become available to the unmarried as well as the married.[92]

Official discouragement continued to be given by the Catholic Church to all artificial methods of contraception. Archbishop Fisher, in a letter of December 1960, complained about Catholic 'attacks on liberty' in this connection.[93] But in the reforming atmosphere of the 1960s there was gathering dispute between conservative and liberal Catholics on the subject. This was indicated in various publications, including the *Tablet*, which presented 'the Conservative case' and 'the arguments for reform' in successive issues in the spring of 1967.[94] Conservatives argued that the Church could not reverse its long-lasting condemnation of artificial contraception without causing a general loss of confidence in its teaching; but liberals argued that worldwide forces in favour of contraception had recently become so powerful that this loss of confidence need not occur.

[90] *CEN*, 14 June 1963, p. 8. Cf. *CT*, 28 June 1963, p. 12 (letter of George Goyder); Benjamin Corbyn to Archbishop Ramsey, 27 June 1964, RP 62, fos. 307–8; *BW*, 14 Mar. 1968, p. 8.

[91] *BW*, 31 Mar. 1960, p. 1.

[92] R. Beloe to Revd G. R. Dunstan (member of Church of England Council for Social Work), 22 Feb. 1962, RP 18, fo. 331; Dunstan to Beloe, 23 Feb. 1962, ibid., fo. 332.

[93] Fisher to Lord Hailsham, 14 Dec. 1960, FP 241, fos. 308–10.

[94] *T.*, 29 Apr. 1967, pp. 478–85, 6 May, pp. 510–13; T. D. Roberts (ed.), *Contraception and Holiness* (London, 1965); *BT*, 27 Apr. 1967, p. 7 (article by 'Miss R.', a Roman Catholic).

If the Catholic Church seemed clearly divided on the question by this time, it did not become more unified by a papal effort at direction on the subject. This was the issue of the famous encyclical *Humanae Vitae* in July 1968. Resulting from lengthy consideration by the supposedly liberal Pope Paul VI, the encyclical demonstrated a wish to maintain the official position in the face of both the permissive movement of the age and the current concern about a world population explosion. The encyclical issued clear advice against the use of artificial contraceptive methods. As an encyclical, however, it was part of 'ordinary' papal teaching and did not have the status of an infallible decree pronouncing an article of faith. The Pope always refused to describe the encyclical as infallible, and before it was issued he had removed any reference to the commitment of 'mortal sin' by disobeying it. Moreover, he said that his advice 'invited' the assent of the faithful.[95] There was thus room for decision through the exercise of individual conscience on the matter—though, from a worldwide economic perspective, there was the serious question whether such personal consideration and decision would be exercised by those who most needed to exercise it.

In the existing circumstances the encyclical, despite its qualifications, was inflammatory. Apart from the unfavourable opinions of Protestants,[96] there was a storm of reaction from liberal Catholics, indicating serious strain in the Catholic body. A group initially called the Catholic Renewal Movement, and later Catholics for a Changing Church, resisted the papal injunction. Fifty-five Roman Catholic priests signed a letter to *The Times* on 2 October 1968 declaring that 'they could not in conscience give loyal internal and external obedience to the view that all such [artificial] means of contraception are in all circumstances wrong'.[97] A Catholic historian has written:

> [there was] not only immediate confusion, including scuffles on the steps of Westminster Cathedral between rival groups, but an immense and lasting decline in ecclesiastical morale. A majority of at least middle-class Catholic, married people were probably already using the pill . . . and few now

[95] P. Hebblethwaite, *Paul VI, the First Modern Pope* (London, 1993), 517–18.

[96] e.g. Robinson, *Christian Freedom*, 114–17 (essay on 'The Ecumenical Consequences of *Humanae Vitae*').

[97] See also *The Times*, 1 Apr. 1967, pp. 339–40; P. Coman, *Catholics and the Welfare State* (London, 1977), 101–4.

pulled back. Priests found themselves caught between laity and bishops: publicly they were in trouble if they dissented from the encyclical, privately and in confession they could say what they really thought. The whole situation was demoralizing. Few even of its supporters argued for the infallible character of what the pope had said, but what was clear was a resultant sharp decline in respect for papal authority and the emergence of a strange feeling among even many loyal Catholics that they were now, and would hereafter remain, somehow 'against' the pope.[98]

The Protestant reaction to *Humanae Vitae* was generally unfavourable, but it was not uniform. There continued to be diversity of viewpoint among Protestants, even among members of the same Church. A televised discussion in July 1963 brought strong objections (not only from Catholics) because it seemed weighted towards the view that contraception had eliminated the need for premarital chastity.[99] The advertising and propagating of birth-control techniques remained a cause of controversy, especially as the matter of bestowing contraceptives on the unmarried was involved.[100] Permission for this to be done legally was included in an Act of 1967 concerning the contraceptive advice which could be given by health clinics. In consequence the Anglican Bishop of Portsmouth, John Phillips, resigned from the presidency of his local Family Planning Association. Chastity, he said, appeared to be at a discount in the new Act. This measure, he stated, 'assumed that only pregnancy or contraception were open to young people, and nowhere was there any sign that a third choice—chastity—should be considered'.[101] The firm resolution in favour of artificial contraception at the Lambeth Conference in 1958 by no means won the acquiescence of all Anglicans. A letter appearing in the *Church Times* on 1 May 1960 said that 'we have no right to "plan" the entry of an immortal soul into the world. What we should plan is the wise, temperate, and reverent use of the procreative instinct, instead of mutilating and interfering with God's work of creation.'[102] Another letter in this paper gave a different view, by congratulating the Church on having

[98] Hastings, *History*, 575–7.
[99] Revd I. N. Miller to Sir Arthur Fforde, 15 July 1963, RP 33, fo. 151.
[100] e.g. *RGACS* (1968), 492.
[101] *CT*, 8 Mar. 1968, p. 1. Cf. *RGACS* (1968), 492, 501–2, (1969), 503–8.
[102] Letter from Mrs Frances Edwards, *CT*, 13 May 1960, p. 13. Cf. letter from Revd D. J. G. Davies, ibid., 3 Sept. 1965, p. 12.

sufficient humility and courage to review the situation regarding family planning . . . If the principle of family planning is once conceded (as by use of the 'safe period'), why not make the best use of all God has given us, and accept the findings of medicine and science and use them in the cause of ignorant, suffering humanity?[103]

Over the question of legalizing abortion, divergence between Catholic and Protestant opinion did not become as clear-cut as the division over artificial contraception, and it appeared much later. Indeed, it is unclear to what extent the leadership of Protestant Churches acquiesced in abortion when it was legalized in 1967. The decision remained personal and individual. An Anglican commission in 1964 declared that the foetus was sacred and therefore should not be destroyed: only if the life or health of the mother were seriously endangered should abortion be permitted.[104] Archbishop Ramsey went beyond this in making concessions to opinion which was in favour of abortion. At a session of the full synod of the Canterbury Convocation on 17 January 1967, he proposed that abortion should be permitted if the child was likely to be seriously deformed or defective; if conception occurred because of rape; or if the mother were judged 'totally incapable' of rearing a child.[105] He could not give full agreement, however, to David Steel's Termination of Pregnancy Bill, introduced into Parliament in 1966 after previous abortion bills had been debated in the 1960s.[106] In some ways this bill proposed to grant more than Ramsey's proposed conditions, in other ways less. The bill would allow abortion to take place, through either the National Health Service or private medical facilities, within twenty-eight weeks of conception, provided that two doctors agreed either that there was risk to the mother's life, or that there was risk to the health of the mother or of children she already had, or that the unborn child was likely to be seriously handicapped.[107] Although Archbishop Ramsey could not support the bill, some bishops voted for it in the Lords, and the measure passed in 1967.

[103] Ibid., 27 May 1960, pp. 11–12.
[104] Chadwick, *Ramsey*, 154.
[105] *CCC*, 17 Jan. 1967, iv. 6, pp. 3–6.
[106] *CEN*, 1 Apr. 1966, p. 9. See correspondence in RP 70, fos. 171–241.
[107] *CT*, 26 May 1966, p. 1; FCFC Minutes, 23 Sept. 1966, bk. 2, pp. 288–9; B. Brookes, *Abortion in England, 1900–67* (London, 1988), 155–6.

In the oppositon shown to Steel's bill there appeared a combined effort by Anglican and Roman Catholic clergy in the Shrewsbury area, who jointly petitioned their MP against the measure as being 'unacceptable to Christian conscience'.[108] The General Assembly of the Church of Scotland recommended in May 1966 conditions for abortion which were similar to those enacted in 1967: abortion should be permitted when the mother's life was at risk or if her health might be seriously affected, or if physical or mental abnormality of the child was very likely. The Methodist Conference's report on abortion in July 1966 went beyond these conditions in adding as justifications for abortion the occurrence of pregnancy as a consequence of rape and the serious unlikelihood of the mother being able to bring up a child. The Free Church of Scotland, however, resembled the Roman Catholic Church (to which it was generally so strongly opposed) in objecting to any liberalizing of the abortion law, describing any such move as 'another slide down the slope of the permissive society'. A Catholic statement issued by Cardinal Heenan (Archbishop of Westminster) after a meeting of bishops in October 1966 declared that abortion was an 'abominable crime' like infanticide and should on no account be permitted. This official view was supported by many Catholic organizations, such as the Guild of Catholic Doctors. Probably the majority of Catholic opinion was strongly against abortion; but *Slant*, the journal of Catholic Marxists, argued that abortion was justified in some cases as life only became 'social and meaningful' after birth.[109] The Earl of Longford, a Roman Catholic, spoke and voted against David Steel's bill, even though it was encouraged by the Government in which Longford was a Cabinet Minister. Barbara Castle wrote in her published diary about a Cabinet meeting in July 1967: 'Longford gave us his usual bleat about our giving time for the abortion bill. I'm afraid he just sounds comical.'[110]

The Society for the Protection of the Unborn Child, which was formed in January 1967 to resist the abortion bill, was largely Roman Catholic in composition but included members of other Churches. Norman St John Stevas, a leading Catholic layman, ap-

[108] *CT*, 3 Mar. 1967, p. 17.

[109] L. J. F. Smith, 'The Abortion Controversy, 1936–77: A Case Study in Emergence of Law', Ph.D. thesis (Edinburgh, 1979), 143–6.

[110] P. Stanford, *Lord Longford, a Life* (London, 1994), 343–4, 357–8; *T.*, 22 July 1967, p. 790.

pealed in March to Anglicans to sign a petition drawn up by the new society against the abortion bill. The petition stated that 'we fully accept the need for a moderate measure of abortion law reform, but we feel that the present proposals amount to abortion on demand and constitute a threat to the principle of the sanctity of human life'.[111]

At the end of the 1960s—that decade of limited but distinctive social revolution—came a radical reform of the divorce law. Divorce through 'breakdown of marriage' in addition to 'proved matrimonial offence' was proposed in a private member's bill (the Matrimonial Causes and Reconciliation Bill) introduced in 1963 by Leo Abse—the central figure in obtaining both homosexual and divorce reform in the 1960s. Church leaders responded unfavourably. On the initiative of Aubrey Vine, General Secretary of the FCFC, interdenominational negotiations took place.[112] In consequence, the bill was opposed by what the *Church Times* described as 'an unprecedented essay in Christian co-operation'—a combination of the Roman Catholic hierarchy, the National Federation of the Free Churches, and Anglican leaders. These insisted that the existing legal requirement of a 'matrimonial offence' should continue to be the sole means of divorce.[113] A joint statement was issued on 3 April 1963 by the Archbishops of Canterbury, York, and Wales; the Archbishop of Birmingham (on behalf of the Roman Catholic hierarchy of England and Wales); and the Moderator and General Secretary of the FCFC. These welcomed the proposals in the bill to attempt reconciliation between the parties to a marriage, but continued:

There is, however, great concern about one clause which would add a new ground for divorce of such a kind as to introduce a dangerous new principle into our marriage laws. It is the clause which would allow divorce after seven years' separation, whether or no a matrimonial offence has been

[111] *CT*, 10 Mar. 1967, p. 14.

[112] Vine to Archbishop Ramsey, 14 Feb. 1963, RP 43, fo. 60; Ramsey to Vine, 15 Feb. 1963, ibid., fo. 64; memo. by R. Beloe (Ramsey's secretary), ibid., fos. 101–2; Monsignor Derek Worlock to David James, MP, 19 Mar. 1963, ibid., fos. 105–7; Ramsey to Most Revd Donald Coggan, Archbishop of York, 27 Mar. 1963, ibid., fos. 116–17; R. Beloe to Moderator of FCFC, and to Archbishop of Wales (separate letters), 1 Apr. 1963, ibid., fos. 124–7.

[113] *CT*, 10 May 1963, p. 3; cf. *CEN*, 5 Apr. 1963, p. 1; *T.*, 6 Apr. 1963, p. 380, subsequent discussion in letters and memos., RP 43, fos. 130–207; *PAGAFCS* (1963), 141.

committed against the petitioner. Until now the State laws of marriage in this country have been framed on the assumption that marriage is a lifelong covenant not to be terminated solely by the wish of the partners . . . we believe . . . that it would help to undermine the basic understanding of marriage as a lifelong union if the principle were introduced that a marriage could be terminated by the desire of the partners to terminate it.[114]

This stand was deplored by reforming laymen and clerics such as Canon Douglas Rhymes, who wrote: 'It looks as though the Church prefers the sordid to the decent way of ending marriage.'[115] When the bill failed to get through Parliament, reformers complained that clerical obstruction had succeeded. Humanists said that the Christian 'minority' had no right to enforce its views on the non-Christian 'majority' in society.[116]

Soon afterwards, however, there was a marked change in the official Church of England attitude to the divorce law, moving in the direction of Leo Abse's bill. In April 1964 an Anglican commission on the law of divorce, appointed by Archbishop Ramsey, commenced its proceedings.[117] The Bishop of Exeter (R. C. Mortimer) was chairman, and in 1966 the commission produced a radical report entitled *Putting Asunder*. This proposed that 'breakdown of marriage' rather than 'the matrimonial offence' should become the permitted ground of divorce in a law court, provided that serious attempts at reconciliation had been made. The report also proposed that a divorce settlement should include provisions for the custody of children and for the regular payment of alimony.

The proposal for 'breakdown of marriage' in *Putting Asunder* received the general support of the Church of Scotland, the Methodist Church, and some other Protestant Churches.[118] Ramsey defended the proposal in the House of Lords; a report of the Law Commission entitled *The Field of Choice* supported the change; and the National Assembly of the Church of England gave its

[114] *CEN*, 5 Apr. 1963, p. 1; *T.*, 6 Apr., p. 380.

[115] *Daily Telegraph*, 9 Jan. 1964; FCFC Minutes, 3 May 1963, bk. 2, pp. 207–8.

[116] See Abse, *Private Member*, 159ff.

[117] Draft letter by Ramsey to persons invited to serve on the commission, RP 43, fos. 32–3: 'I feel it would be right to examine any possible changes in the Law of Divorce which could remove the bad features of the present system, and yet avoid the concept of divorce by consent.' See also correspondence, ibid. 82, fos. 106ff.

[118] Chadwick, *Ramsey*, 151–2; *RGACS* (1968), 481–9, (1969), 523–4; *BW*, 1 May 1969, p. 10; *CYB* (1968–9), 92.

approval by a majority vote in February 1967.[119] This did not mean, however, that 'divorce by consent' was being accepted: the proposal was that the court would have to be satisfied that a marriage was irretrievable before it would grant a divorce. Nor did it mean that Protestant Churches were relaxing their disapproval of divorce. The thirty-year-old resolutions of the Convocations of the Church of England that marriage of a divorced person should not take place in church remained unchanged, despite the wish of some clergy to remove them.[120] The Archbishop of Wales, Edwin Morris, said in a visitation charge to the clergy of Monmouth diocese in April 1967 that 'the Church would gain a lot of cheap publicity if it agreed to marry divorced persons, but we are not here to be popular or to accept the world's standards in place of those of our Lord'.[121]

The Church of Scotland General Assembly resolved in May 1968 to accept 'a quite radical departure from the standpoint . . . accepted by the General Assembly of 1958':

> We are unanimously resolved that divorce should now be granted on the grounds of breakdown of marriage as over against the need to prove certain matrimonial offences . . . [which] are often the outcome rather than the cause of a deteriorating marriage. An accusatorial principle of divorce tends to encourage matrimonial offence, increasing bitterness, and widen the rift that is already there. Separation for a continuous period of at least two years, consequent upon a decision of at least one of the parties not to live with the other, should act as the sole evidence of marriage breakdown. This . . . would give time for the opportunity of reconciliation through the application of all sorts of private, family, social, and religious influences. It would ensure that divorce could not be obtained so quickly that a mistake in the heat of the moment or at the height of hurt pride should lead on to an action to be regretted for a life-time afterwards.[122]

Ramsey made it clear that he was against taking reform so far as to allow divorce by consent.[123] Leo Abse, doubtless encouraged by *Putting Asunder*, commenced another parliamentary effort in 1968. He then introduced a Divorce Reform Bill, which was eventually

[119] *CT*, 24 Feb. 1967, p. 16; *CCC*, 11 Oct. 1967, iv. 7, p. 269.
[120] *CCC*, 10 Oct. 1967, iv. 7, pp. 244–56; *CT*, 3 May 1968, p. 1.
[121] *CT*, 14 Apr. 1967, p. 9.
[122] *RGACS* (1968), 487–8.
[123] Chadwick, *Ramsey*, 151–2; *CT*, 24 Feb. 1967, pp. 12, 16.

carried in 1969.[124] Ramsey said in the Lords that the bill's provision that divorce could take place after five years of separation, even though one of the parties objected, was too liberal a concession; and similarly that the proposed divorce after two years of separation, by the consent of both parties, allowed too short a period. It was said at an FCFC committee meeting that this was 'the first bill to reform the law on divorce which had received its initiative from the Churches',[125] and there was considerable truth in this. Nevertheless, Ramsey thought the measure went beyond what the Church of England should concede. He did not vote on the second reading of the bill in the Lords on 30 June 1969, but the bishops who voted divided five to three in favour of the measure.[126] Ramsey's strictures on the bill were far exceeded by Lord Longford, who in the Lords debate described parts of the bill as utterly evil.[127] Contributing to the Anglican opposition to the measure was the *Church Times*, which said that it struck 'at the root of the institution of marriage as a lifelong and monogamous union' and would 'make marriage a temporary contract, dissoluble at will'.[128] The Mothers' Union also declared itself officially against the bill, but this view was challenged by some of its members.[129]

It is difficult to assess how far the Divorce Reform Act of 1969, which was applied from 1 January 1971, enabled the ensuing steep rise in divorces to take place (the rate more than doubled in England and Wales between 1970 and 1986). It is probably true that increased pressure to obtain divorces by proving a matrimonial offence (not least by the well-tried means of faking adultery) would have been present without such an Act.[130] Nevertheless the great easing of the law which the Act brought about, and the wide publicity attending the measure, probably played a large part in encouraging the unhappily married to seek divorce.

[124] Abse, *Private Member*, 172 ff.; L. Stone, *Road to Divorce: England, 1530–1987* (Oxford, 1992), 407–9.

[125] FCFC Minutes, 24 Nov. 1967, bk. 3, p. 20.

[126] *CEN*, 4 July 1969, p. 1.

[127] Chadwick, *Ramsey*, 152–3.

[128] *CT*, 16 Feb. 1968, p. 12. Cf. ibid., 24 Feb. 1967, p. 12; *CEN*, 16 May 1969, p. 10 (letter of J. S. Battie).

[129] *CT*, 16 Feb. 1968, p. 14 (letters from Mrs Janet Bernard and Mrs Ruth Webb); 15 Mar. 1968, p. 9 (letters from Mrs Marjorie Lush and Mrs Elizabeth Barlow); 22 Mar. 1968, p. 14 (letter from Mrs Phyllis Bretherton).

[130] Chadwick, *Ramsey*, 153.

Other social questions of notable concern during the decade were female equality, capital punishment, and racial discrimination. There was much controversy over the first of these, and of course women were deeply involved over the issues of abortion, contraception, divorce, and homosexual activity, all of which notably affected their personal behaviour (the last of them as being linked to lesbianism). Another measure of female liberation was the Equal Pay Act of 1970, abolishing differences in payment between the sexes for the same work, but its operation was postponed on financial grounds until 1975. The Homicide Act of 1957 had reduced the application of the death penalty, retaining it for only six types of killing. But the Act was very difficult to operate, and the demand for complete abolition of capital punishment gathered pace in the early 1960s. Christian opinion was sharply divided over this matter, as it long had been. Mervyn Stockwood, Bishop of Southwark, was supported by all his fellow-bishops in the Province of Canterbury when he moved in Convocation that the penalty be abolished for an experimental period in January 1962; on a similar vote in the Convocation of York only one bishop voted against abolition.[131] After a bill abolishing the death penalty had passed the Commons in 1965, Ramsey was urged to introduce it in the Lords. Initially he intended to do this, but withdrew in favour of a less prominent role in support of the measure, which was carried (no bishop voting against) later that year. The new Act was to operate for five years, and was extended in 1970.[132]

Racial questions received a good deal of attention from Church leaders, assemblies, and newspapers. Delegates at a conference held by Christian Action in 1965 were urged that various policies should be adopted against racial prejudice. These included the initiation of educational campaigns by religious leaders 'to make the Churches a positive force for inter-racial harmony'; and requesting the Migration Committee of the British Council of Churches, in conjunction with the Roman Catholic Church, to consider employing more chaplains among immigrant groups.[133] In the same year the annual assembly of the Congregational Union of England and Wales stated that:

[131] Ibid. 159.

[132] Ibid. 160–2; H. Potter, *Hanging in Judgment: Religion and the Death Penalty in England from the Bloody Code to Abolition* (London, 1993), 198–203.

[133] *CT*, 12 Feb. 1965, pp. 1, 3.

there are no valid grounds for an attitude of racial superiority in individuals, or groups, or races ... We feel that race relations in Britain have reached a crucial stage and that the situation demands the active concern of the whole population. We therefore call upon all men of goodwill to work for the creation of a harmonious multi-racial community.[134]

Although coloured immigration was the most inflammatory domestic issue of the 1960s, anti-Semitism promoted by neo-Nazi groups was equally to the fore at the very beginning of the decade. In the full synod of the Canterbury Convocation in January 1960, the Bishop of Lichfield (Ambrose Reeve) carried a motion deploring

recent outbreaks of anti-semitism in various countries including our own ... England had its failings, but normally violent anti-semitism had not been one of them. Therefore, it was most perturbing when anti-semitism was found rearing its head here ... it was to his mind incredible that anybody anywhere should [now] glory in the swastika.[135]

The anti-Semitic outbreaks had not started in this country, he continued, but at least fifty of our towns had been affected by them. 'Their duty clearly as Christians was to work for the best possible relationships between the various races.'[136] The Archdeacon of Oxford, seconding the motion, urged all members of Convocation to support the work of the Council of Christians and Jews (founded in 1942) which operated both on a national basis and through local branches.[137]

But racial concerns in the 1960s were usually towards the recent Commonwealth immigrants, of whom the *Baptist Times* said in 1964: 'generally the immigrants have settled down well; they have proved to be reliable workers and citizens.'[138] Before this, however, the Government had become convinced that restriction of immigrant numbers was necessary for economic and social reasons, including housing conditions and the availability of jobs. Consequently the Commonwealth Immigration Act—the first of three

[134] Resolution of 20 May 1965, *CYB* (1965–6), 86–7.
[135] *CCC*, 19 Jan. 1960, iii. 1, pp. 12, 13.
[136] Ibid. 13.
[137] Ibid. 17.
[138] *BT*, 1 Oct. 1964, p. 5.

such measures in the course of the decade—had been passed in 1962, accompanied by a rather toothless Race Relations Act which was the first in a series of anti-discrimination measures. Ramsey acknowledged the good intentions behind the new policy to restrict immigration. Nevertheless he said the immigration bill had come as 'a great shock', though he said that the shock should spur the country on 'to attack with far greater vigour those [living] conditions which have created any case for this proposal'.[139]

In October 1964 Ramsey accepted from the new Labour Government the chairmanship of their National Committee for Commonwealth Immigrants (NCCI), because 'he wanted to do all he could for racial harmony in a Britain which now was bound to be multi-racial'.[140] Ramsey found his new job a lot more difficult than he had probably expected, however, for during the next five years the immigration issue reached its peak of intensity, British opinion dividing sharply for and against the idea of a multiracial society. Christians were by no means all in favour of encouraging a multiracial society. There were Christians in white racial groups which sprang up, such as the National Front; Christians also in Parliament, such as Enoch Powell, who urged repatriation of immigrants. Two clergymen in Sussex helped to found a Racial Preservation Society advocating subsidized repatriation of coloured immigrants.[141] The *Tablet* called moderately for restrictions on immigration:

> The worst enemies of a better social climate, who play straight into the hands of the 'Keep Britain White' people, are those who press for a greater extension of coloured immigration. It is in proportion as immigration is controlled and limited that it is reasonable to expect the social climate to improve.[142]

The view of the Church and Nation Committee of the Church of Scotland in 1967 was on similar lines:

> There is a natural reluctance among our people to restrict the entry of Commonwealth citizens into Britain, but at the same time, in view of the large increase in the number of such immigrants and of the problem

[139] Newspaper extract in RP 18, fo. 285; P. Ely and D. Denney, *Social Work in a Multi-Racial Society* (Aldershot, 1987), 23.
[140] Chadwick, *Ramsey*, 166.
[141] Ibid. 168–71.
[142] *T.*, 29 Apr. 1967, p. 459.

created thereby, there is also a considerable amount of fear lest the country should no longer be able to support all the people who want to live in it.[143]

Two years later this committee said: 'the answer to racial discrimination must lie . . . in the spiritual and moral teaching of the Church and in the practical day to day witness of Christians in our society.' The committee welcomed the Race Relations Act of 1968, and recommended support for the Community Relations Commission which this measure established in place of the NCCI.[144]

To add to the tension created by self-consciously white organizations, there were black power organizations attempting to counterbalance them. The victory of Peter Griffiths, a Conservative who advocated repatriation, at Smethwick in the general election of 1964 was criticized by local clergy and ministers. This led a local Conservative councillor to call for a public boycott of the churches in Smethwick on one Sunday, in protest against 'the intolerable position of clergymen continually criticizing everything the Conservatives in Smethwick seem to do'.[145]

The Government, having already passed a second Commonwealth Immigration Bill in 1965, rushed through a third in 1968 to try and stem a flood of Asian immigrants who had been expelled from Kenya. The bill involved breaking agreements and making special provision for white immigrants, and has been described as 'blatantly racialist'.[146] Ramsey spoke in the Lords against the bill, and was strongly supported by Lord McLeod, an ex-Moderator of the General Assembly of the Church of Scotland, but the measure was carried on second reading by a majority of twenty-four. Lord Soper voted against the bill, and Bishop Robinson resigned from the Labour Party on account of his opposition to it.[147] The NCCI, thoroughly opposed to the government action, decided only under strong protest to remain in being. Many members resigned from the central committee or from subcommittees.[148]

Ramsey's views on immigration were impugned as 'exactly and diametrically wrong' by Enoch Powell in his dramatic speech on 20

143 *RGACS* (1967), 171. Cf. *CYB* (1965–6), 87.
144 *RGACS* (1969), 141, 203–4.
145 *BT*, 29 Oct. 1964, p. 3.
146 Ely and Denney, *Social Work*, 28.
147 *BW*, 7 Mar. 1968, p. 1.
148 Chadwick, *Ramsey*, 72–3.

April 1968 at Birmingham. The speech envisaged 'rivers of blood' if immigration was not almost entirely stopped and a policy of repatriation adopted. In the furore which followed Powell's dismissal from the Conservative shadow cabinet on account of this speech, bodies of workers and members of the National Front held demonstrations on his side; an Anglican rector described him as a saviour of his country; and there was a march on Lambeth Palace directed against Ramsey. When Powell made a similar speech in November, Ramsey commented in a formal statement:

> Mr Powell's policy is a counsel of despair. He may consider that his plans are motivated by humane principle, but they entirely rule out any possibility of harmonious racial integration . . . What is needed is a programme of education and the exercise of those basic Christian beliefs in the equality of man to which this country is pledged through its support of human rights year and the United Nations Charter.

An address delivered by Ramsey in December 1968 against discrimination was interrupted for some ten minutes by members of the National Front.[149] The cleavages caused in society by the immigration issue continued to display themselves thereafter. Religious opinion was as divided as the rest of society, but the leadership of the Churches generally advocated policies of limited immigration and elimination of discrimination.

Within a century in which the Churches had to face and adapt to an unprecedented amount of social change, the 1960s provided the most intense concentration of innovation and challenge. Members of the Churches reacted to this in the diverse ways which had marked their response to previous social change. The new morality found supporters and opponents in the Churches, as well as some who were undecided. On the one hand, it found a champion in Bishop Robinson, and, on the other, was described by the Public Questions Committee of the Free Church of Scotland as 'the process which is devaluing, dehumanizing, and brutalizing human life'.[150] Widely differing approaches were seen in reaction to all the practical manifestations of the moral changes—the relaxation of censorship and the licence shown in publications, films, plays, and television broadcasts; the legalization of abortion and homosexual

[149] Ibid. 173–6. Cf. *CT*, 26 Apr. 1968, pp. 1, 24.
[150] *RGACS* (1968), 129, (1969), 125.

acts; a notable liberalization of the divorce law; and the growth of premarital and extramarital sexual activity through the adoption of the contraceptive pill, among other reasons. The controversy over the treatment of coloured immigrants had involved Church leaders as much as any other members of society. These developments all happened in the 1960s, but their effects remained to be worked out over many years. Only near the end of the century can we look back and see something of their full impact. The Churches not only had to respond to this avalanche of change which contravened their traditional and established moral positions, but they had to do this when they were going through a period of obvious weakening in their membership numbers. This weakening has not been effectively reversed since the 1960s, but its impact on the position of the Churches remains a lot more ambiguous than the clear effects of the permissive Sixties on contemporary British society.

7
Churches and Social Questions, 1970–1996

The British Churches had been subject to marked challenge, attack, and numerical decline in the 1960s. In the years since then, the Churches have experienced more stability, but only at the lower level of influence to which secularization and indifference had reduced them by 1970. The Roman Catholic Church had to face declining numbers, as all major Protestant Churches had previously had to do and continued to do.[1] There were one or two brief periods when the traditional Churches showed increased attendance (as in the later 1980s), but these signs were transient.[2] The only sectors of religion which have experienced convincing growth are the pentecostal ('charismatic') Christian groups and the non-Christian religions, especially Muhammadanism and Hinduism.

The relative stability of the post-1970s years has not excluded controversy and upheaval in the Churches. There have been continuing theological battles between liberal and conservative opinion, especially in the 1970s; there has been notable conflict over social policy between those of a 'consensus' and those of a 'Thatcherite' persuasion. One of the chief examples of controversy and disruption has been the twenty-year conflict over ordaining women in the Church of England and other Anglican Churches in the British Isles.[3] The issue was naturally linked to the broader, prominent social question of women's liberation.

Female ordination was introduced into the major non-episcopal Churches at various points from 1917 to 1968. The impetus towards women's ordination in Anglican Churches increased when the American Episcopal Church decided to ordain women in 1976. In

[1] A. Hastings, *A History of English Christianity, 1920–85* (London, 1986), 602–5; *LW* (May 1988).

[2] *The Times*, 11 Oct. 1989.

[3] Cf. E. Luscombe, *The Scottish Episcopal Church in the Twentieth Century* (Edinburgh, 1996), 47–53.

1989 the Synod of the Church of Ireland voted in favour of female ordination. In the Church of England the matter was resolved by votes in the General Synod (a body which had replaced the National Church Assembly in 1970 and had more power of self-government than the latter body, though not complete freedom from parliamentary control in religious matters). After a first clear vote in favour in the General Synod in 1984, the step was given final approval by the Synod in November 1992. A similar resolution was carried in the General Synod of the Scottish Episcopal Church in 1994 and in the Governing Body of the Church in Wales in 1996. In the Church of England the momentous change brought soreness and division, no major schism but a significant number of individual secessions. It also brought criticism from the Church of Rome, and increased conviction that reunion between Rome and Canterbury (a hopeful prospect in the 1970s and early 1980s, but fading since then) was not likely for the foreseeable future.[4]

Two decades previously, in 1972, the attempt to reunite Anglicans and Methodists had failed in the General Synod; so by the early 1990s the isolation of the Church of England was doubly emphasized within two decades. Further removed from the State by its own enlarged self-government (an example of this was the increased influence it acquired in the appointment of bishops by a measure of 1977), it still wanted to retain the appearance of an established national Church. Calls for disestablishment in order to achieve complete self-rule were occasionally heard, but they did not develop into an effective movement (in the case of the Church of Scotland they were not heard at all, because this was a self-governing establishment).[5] Although shrinking in the 'real' terms of attendance and other figures, the Church of England retained a high profile, partly because of its ancient establishment trappings but more so because of the outspoken collisions between its most prominent leaders and the Government, especially in the 1980s.

Ecumenicalism seemed first to advance and then to retreat in the two decades following the only post-1945 inter-Church union in England, that between the Congregational and Presbyterian Churches in 1972 to form the United Reformed Church (there had

[4] *The Times*, 29 Nov. 1991, 5 Nov. 1994, 28 Jan. 1995.

[5] Ibid., 9 Nov. 1974, 5 July 1976, 28 July 1982, 3 Mar. 1983 (leading article, 'Citizen Benn in the Pulpit').

been a small Presbyterian union in Scotland in 1958).[6] British church attendance did not recover in the 1970s from its sharp overall drop in the previous decade. Adult attendance at church, it has been stated, declined to only 11 per cent of the English population by 1979, to 13 per cent of the Welsh population by 1982, and to 17 per cent of the Scottish population by 1984.[7] By the mid-1980s there were some signs of greater stability in church membership and attendance, but these produced little if any sustained definite increase. During the 1970s the charismatic groups, often meeting as 'house churches', provided the main signs of renewal among Christians.[8] In the later 1980s and early 1990s the revival of a rather more traditional Evangelicalism has been added to the advancing features in British religion.

During the 1970s and later the Churches had to confront the growing effects of the permissive developments of the 1960s—a steadily rising divorce and abortion rate, a steady increase in cohabitation, and a steady increase in illegitimate births.[9] The 1970s, however, were a decade when permissiveness was being widely questioned as well as widely accepted. In the 1980s the questioning, though seeming to decline and narrow in general scope and expression, became more pronounced in the case of homosexual acts because of the gradual spread of the AIDS disease. Society continued to become on the whole more prosperous—by 1988 a record 73 per cent of households had central heating—but also to be increasingly free and unconventional in personal behaviour. Annual revelations of social statistics usually showed a rise in material possessions and a rise in permissive behaviour going together.

Neither the Churches in general, nor a single denomination, presented a homogeneous reaction to these developments. By the 1980s the Churches were often criticized for acquiescing in, or compromising with, permissiveness. But Christians took a lead in the public protests, prominent in the early 1970s, against some of the effects of permissiveness. In 1971 Lord Longford, a Roman

[6] A. Macarthur, 'The Background to the Formation of the United Reformed Church (Presbyterian and Congregational) in England and Wales in 1972', *Journal of the United Reformed Church History Society*, 4/1 (Oct. 1987), 3–22.

[7] D. W. Bebbington, *Evangelicalism in Modern Britain: A History from the 1730s to the 1980s* (London, 1989), 250.

[8] A. Walker, *Restoring the Kingdom: The Radical Christianity of the House Church Movement* (London, 1985; rev. edn., 1988).

[9] Cf. Hastings, *History*, 597.

Catholic Labour peer who was by no means absolutely opposed to the permissive society, conducted investigations into the availability of pornography and campaigned against it. His actions helped to centralize concern which had been shown over some dramatic productions since the Lord Chamberlain's censorship had ended in 1968. Longford was supported by Evangelicals such as the Archbishop of York (Donald Coggan) and Donald Soper, and by others outside his own Church as well as by fellow-Catholics. But the support of Christians was far from being universal. Archbishop Ramsey, for one, felt lukewarm towards his effort.[10] Longford's report, published in September 1972, was widely read.[11] A recent convert to Christianity, the well-known journalist and broadcaster Malcolm Muggeridge, christened a nationwide campaign for traditional morality in 1971–2 'the Festival of Light'. Participants in the Festival ignited beacons across the country as symbols of the rays of light they hoped to shed, and the Festival culminated in a rally and march in London in September 1972. Five years later a follow-up rally was held. The Nationwide Festival of Light had become a permanent organization, and later branched into the Care Trust (to conduct research into moral attitudes and behaviour) and Care campaigns (for pressure-group action).[12]

Sunday observance, in the sense of 'keeping Sunday special' for worship and rest, had been deeply encroached on by 1970. But resistance continued to be shown, usually unsuccessfully, to extension of the permitted secular uses of the Sabbath. Examples of such resistance were to the opening of public houses in Scotland in 1973; to the extension of Sunday ferry sailings in the Western Isles in 1989; and to the increase of shop-opening hours on Sundays in 1985–6, when, it has been noted, the opposition 'extended well beyond Evangelical ranks and, remarkably, intended government legislation was defeated by a revolt of backbench Conservative MPs'.[13] The Sunday traders and shoppers had their way later, how-

[10] O. Chadwick, *Michael Ramsey, a Life* (Oxford, 1990), 162–5.

[11] Earl of Longford (Francis Pakenham), *Pornography: The Longford Report* (London, 1972); P. Stanford, *Lord Longford, a Life* (London, 1994), 400–27; Bebbington, *Evangelicalism*, 265; *The Times*, 26 Aug. 1970 (article by Sir Alan Herbert, President of the Society of Authors); J. C. Robertson, *The Hidden Cinema: British Film Censorship in Action, 1913–75* (London, 1989), 134–75.

[12] J. Capon, . . . *and there was Light: The Story of the Nationwide Festival of Light* (London, 1972); Bebbington, *Evangelicalism*, 265.

[13] Bebbington, 265. On Sunday ferry sailings, see *The Times*, 22 May 1989, 6 Jan. 1991 (articles by Kerry Gill).

ever, as did those who wanted to allow horse racing, accompanied by full betting opportunities, on the Sabbath. In connection with the latter question, a leading article in *The Times* on 30 May 1988, referring especially to sport on Bank Holiday weekends, described thus the state of affairs over the preceding three decades:

Thirty years ago prominent [sporting] events were restricted to the Saturday and Monday, with Sunday observed as a day of rest and worship. In recent years, top-class professional events have increasingly been staged on Sundays throughout the year . . . Thus yesterday [Sunday, 29 May] saw the final day of the three-day equestrian event at Windsor, an international swimming meeting at Leeds, a football competition at Wembley, and a full programme of Sunday League cricket, and today the professional golf tournament at Wentworth has its finale after the third round yesterday. The one sport that the public could not watch yesterday was horse-racing . . . [which] depends on gambling, and this is governed by the Gaming and Lotteries Act, which forbids both on-course and off-course betting on Sundays (although credit card betting by telephone is possible all day). There are no easy ways to circumvent this law.

The article noted regretfully that current attempts to allow horse-racing, with unrestricted betting, on Sundays were meeting obstruction in the House of Commons, and summarized the general situation as follows:

opponents of the change—including the Keep Sunday Special Campaign and the Transport and General Workers' Union—believe that this is the first step towards racing being permitted on most [Sundays] or even every Sunday of the year, disrupting family life and society by forcing more people to work regularly on a Sunday. Yet many public facilities are already open on a Sunday, thus obliging people to work. These include historic houses and garden centres, bingo halls and casinos. It is inconsistent not to allow betting shops also to be opened on afternoons when racing is taking place. Increasing dissatisfaction with the position of professional sports events on Sundays, and of horse racing in particular, reflects the deeper changes—above all the decline of church going—which bit by bit have been changing the character of Sunday. The successful moves to liberalize Sunday drinking laws, and the so far unsuccessful attempts to sort out the absurdities of our Sunday trading laws are part of the moves to allow everyone a greater choice of activities at the weekend. In the long run, it is unlikely that these trends can be stopped.[14]

[14] *The Times*, 30 May 1988. Cf. ibid., 16 Feb. 1989.

For the first time since the 1930s, high unemployment developed in the mid-1970s, and has lasted until the late 1990s. This did not cause noticeable decreases in the large amounts spent on drinking and gambling. The rising real wages of the employed continued to encourage spending on these and other objects of leisure and on consumer goods. In the 1980s there was considerable worry over the influence of alcohol and drugs in producing a rapidly escalating crime rate and growing hooliganism at football matches. Drink consumption continued to increase, and it was estimated at the end of the decade that over five million men and about one million women drank above medically recommended levels.[15] The Church of England's National Council for Social Aid condemned the amounts of money spent on alcohol: 'it is a national disgrace that so much is spent on manufacturing, distributing, and consuming alcohol and so little is spent on responding to the problems generated.'[16] Religious attempts to curb drink had become more concerned to inculcate the necessity for temperate consumption rather than to preach abstinence. From the 1960s, for example, candidates for the Methodist ministry were no longer required to declare themselves total abstainers.[17]

Religious approaches to gambling were now also directed to curbing excess rather than trying to prevent the pursuit altogether. On a visit to the Towcester Races in May 1991 (accompanied by sixty of his clergy) to celebrate the 450th anniversary of the founding of his diocese, the Bishop of Peterborough (William Westwood) said of betting: 'It is like drinking. It is objectionable only if people drink too much. I just enjoy life.'[18] In 1992 it was proposed that gambling should be allowed, on a strictly limited basis, in Methodist church halls.[19] This more relaxed attitude had doubtless resulted in part from the sheer relentless force of the national dedication to 'having a flutter'—shown for example by the estimated five million regular bingo players in Britain in 1989 (about half a million of whom, the great majority of them women, played each day);[20] and by the huge regular participation in the National Lottery after it was finally launched in November 1994.

[15] *Dundee Courier and Advertiser*, 2 Feb. 1989 (leading article).
[16] *The Times*, 24 June 1988.
[17] Ibid., 29 Nov. 1990, p. 23.
[18] Ibid., 25 May 1991, p. 24.
[19] Ibid., 28 May 1992.
[20] Ibid., 5 Jan. 1989.

Church leaders, and Christians in general, held differing opinions on the Lottery. But among Church leaders there was a general tendency to condemn the huge prizes that could, exceptionally, be won. A 'double roll-over' draw on 6 January 1996 produced a forty-two million pound jackpot, shared by three winners. In consequence it was planned that an ecumenical delegation, led by David Sheppard, Bishop of Liverpool, would meet the Heritage Secretary in the Government, Mrs Virginia Bottomley, in order to express fears about the encouragement to cupidity, irresponsible use of money, and fractious human relations, arising from the Lottery.[21] The General Assembly of the Church of Scotland in 1995 and 1996 was firm in its resolution—despite the expression of differing views—that churches under its authority should not apply for funding from National Lottery proceeds, though in 1996 it was agreed that two committees should consider the matter further.[22]

The effect of the various social changes of the 1960s on marriage produced a rate of one in three marriages ending in divorce by the 1980s (the highest in the then European Community and the cause of a large rise in single-parent families).[23] The rate continued slowly to increase thereafter. A report early in 1996 indicated that

> forty-one per cent of current marriages are expected to break down, against an estimate of thirty-seven per cent in 1987 and thirty-four per cent in 1980. The proportion is rising, by about one per cent a year, even though the number of divorces has fallen because of the increase in people choosing to cohabit rather than marry.[24]

The steep rise in divorce since the 1960s has been described as

> perhaps the most profound and far-reaching social change to have occurred in the last five hundred years. A gigantic moral, religious, and legal revolution has accompanied and made possible the shift from a system of marriage prematurely terminated by death to a system of marriage prematurely terminated by choice.[25]

The visible crumbling of marriage as a lifelong commitment naturally aroused great concern in the Churches, one of whose central and agreed traditions was the maintenance of marriage as a

[21] *Dundee Courier and Advertiser*, 24 May 1996, p. 9.
[22] Ibid.
[23] *The Times*, 14 Dec. 1987.
[24] Ibid., 20 Mar. 1996.
[25] L. Stone, *Road to Divorce: England, 1530–1987* (Oxford, 1992), 422.

permanent bond. The provisions of the 1969 Divorce Act, coming into effect on 1 January 1971, prompted a debate in the full synod of the Canterbury Convocation on 13 October 1971, introduced by Canon P. A. Welsby, who moved 'that this Synod, having in mind the present climate of opinion, reasserts the sanctity of marriage and the family'. It was necessary to counter the opinion of 'a small but vocal minority who assume or assert that marriage and family are outmoded and, indeed, undesirable institutions'. This could be done, said Welsby, by drawing attention to the continuing popularity of marriage. The new divorce law, in substituting 'breakdown of marriage' for 'matrimonial offence' as the allowable reason for divorce, could be seen as strengthening marriage by stressing its 'relational' characteristics.[26] Welsby's seconder, Canon G. R. Sansbury, noted that

> it is our belief and experience that the Christian *mores* of sex, marriage, and the family, in fact work best and are conducive to the general happiness, whereas the permissive society has produced an unprecedented crop of unhappiness, breakdown, and misery. It is not that our contemporaries take sex too seriously; they do not take it seriously enough.[27]

In the new General Synod and its commissions there was repeated discussion of removal of the Convocation ruling against the marriage of divorced people in church. The Synod rejected removal in 1973 and 1978, supported it in 1981, but rejected it in 1985, and the ruling has remained.[28] A majority of opinion in the Church of England at large seemed in favour of abolishing the ruling: a gallup poll in October 1984 suggested that 55 per cent of regular Anglican churchgoers were of this view.[29]

The British people had carried through something of a revolution in their sexual and family patterns without apparently wanting, in the case of many of them, to have such a revolution. Many divorces seemed to occur without the parties really wanting them:

[26] *CCC*, 13 Oct. 1971, v.1, pp. 43–6.
[27] Ibid. 48.
[28] Hastings, *History*, 610; J. S. Peart-Binns, *Bishop Hugh Montefiore* (London, 1990), 175–82; *CT*, 10 and 24 July 1981 (protests against the reform in letters from Revd R. Giles, Peterborough, and Revd M. Warchus, Selby).
[29] G. Heald and R. J. Wybrow, *The Gallup Survey of Britain* (London, 1986), 222.

having approached a lawyer, they were often swept along by a legal process which was strong in provision for separation but weak in provision for encouraging reconciliation. A study of divorcees in 1988 found that 51 per cent of divorced men and 29 per cent of divorced women would rather have stayed married. This report stated that 'some couples have sought legal advice in response to what they regard as a marital crisis rather than a breakdown', and that 'many people simply do not know whether their marriage is at an end; indeed they may be using the legal system as a way of finding out'.[30] *British Social Attitudes*, a survey produced annually from 1983 by Social and Community Planning Research, found in 1986 that there was profound and widespread support for marriage as an institution. There was concern over the fact that many were sidestepping marriage in order to cohabit, or, if they entered on marriage, regarded it as something that could be broken easily and quickly.[31]

Thus, when Church leaders called for revival of a stronger commitment to marriage, they were speaking for large numbers of people who could not realistically be numbered amongst their flocks. In 1988 the National Campaign for the Family called for a much longer period to occur before a marriage could be ended in divorce, and for more State money to be spent on licensed marriage counselling services. A change in the marriage law was proposed in 1995 by the Lord Chancellor, Lord Mackay, and remains under sharp debate at the time of writing (not least among Mackay's Conservative colleagues). The proposed reform seeks in some ways to strengthen marriage by instituting conciliation procedures for those contemplating divorce, but at the same time to provide a quick 'no-fault' divorce procedure. Mackay had made it clear that he was concerned to 'save saveable marriages' as much as to ease the 'trauma and bitterness' of divorce.[32] But the Roman Catholic bishops of England and Wales, at their annual post-Easter Low Week meeting in April 1996, declared that 'to strengthen marriage it is not enough to reform divorce', and called for statutory avowals that marriage was a lifelong commitment to be included in the proceedings at registry office weddings. Cardinal Hume, Archbishop of Westminster, said after the meeting: 'we think we should

[30] *The Times*, 14 Jan. 1988, 19 June 1995.
[31] Ibid., 29 Oct. 1987.
[32] Ibid., 27 Apr. 1995. See also ibid., 19 June 1995 (leading article).

make the entrance to marriage more difficult and not something that people just drift into.'[33]

While repeatedly reaffirming their ideal of marriage as a lifelong, irreversible commitment, the Churches felt bound to exercise realism and compassion in the face of rising divorce rates. Various innovations or changes in attitude were adopted or suggested. 'Divorce services'—religious ceremonies to mark the end of a marriage—were commenced by the United Reformed Church. This Church conducted a well-publicized ceremony for a divorce at Sheffield in November 1995. Subsequently some similar services were held by Anglican clergymen. One of these, who had conducted a divorce ceremony and written a text for such services, explained that it was 'a service of healing to help someone come to terms with what has happened to them. It helps them realize that God still loves them and releases them from the hurt.' The text of the service began with the following words: 'We have gathered here today to support [somebody] who was recently divorced. God's word instructs us that marriage is a life-long commitment. We have come together to support her and ask God to release her from the guilt and fear.' There followed scriptural readings, and prayers for the divorced person, any children from the marriage, and the former spouse.[34]

In 1988 the Church of England General Synod proposed to permit divorcees who had remarried to receive ordination (ordained clergy who had divorced and remarried were allowed to retain their livings). This measure was passed by the required majorities in all three houses in the Synod (bishops, clergy, and laity), but was rejected by the Ecclesiastical Committee of Parliament (consisting of members of both Lords and Commons). It was the first time that parliamentary rejection of a measure had occurred since the Synod began in 1970. Rejection took place on the grounds that the principle of the indissolubility of marriage was being abandoned in order to comply with current trends in behaviour.[35] In 1989 the measure was passed by the Lords but narrowly defeated in the Commons, and in November of that year all three houses of the Synod voted in favour of resubmitting the measure to the Com-

[33] *The Times*, 20 Apr. 1996. Cf. ibid., 25 Apr. 1996; *Dundee Courier and Advertiser*, 25 Apr. 1996.

[34] *Sunday Telegraph*, 14 Apr. 1996 (article by Catherine Elsworth).

[35] *The Times*, 19 May 1988.

mons in 1990, when it was passed.[36] Among other aspects of the religious position of the divorced was the question of easing the entry of divorced persons to communion. In 1995 the Methodist Conference set up a small committee to recommend an official position on the admission of divorced persons to communion, as a substitute for individual decision by the minister, which had prevailed hitherto.

Marriage was not only becoming more fragmented by the much greater use of divorce proceedings. It was being bypassed by increasing numbers of people who chose to live together out of wedlock and perhaps to have illegitimate families. The 1988 issue of *Social Trends*, a government statistical survey, showed that the illegitimacy rate increased from under 5 per cent of total births in the late 1950s to 21 per cent in 1986; that two-thirds of the illegitimate births in 1986 were to couples who were not married but living together in a 'stable relationship'; and that between 1979 and 1985 the number of women who were unmarried but cohabiting doubled.[37] *The Times* reported in December 1993 that 'last year [1992] more than three quarters of all births outside marriage were jointly registered and almost three quarters of those were registered by men and women living at the same address and presumed to be cohabiting'.[38]

The Churches could not sanction cohabitation without notably weakening their valuation of marriage, and they showed no signs of doing the latter—as is indicated by the wording of the divorce services that have been introduced to some extent. All they could do in face of the rise of cohabitation to a large and openly confessed place in society was to treat it with sympathetic forbearance, something they were perhaps partly encouraged to do by the fact that many of the cohabitees were avowed Christians. Statements by religious organizations about cohabitation clearly differed between Churches by the mid-1990s. In June 1995 a Church of England report, *Something to Celebrate*, said that people should no longer

[36] Ibid., 9 Nov. 1989.

[37] *Sunday Telegraph*, 17 Jan. 1988 (article by Geoffrey Wheatcroft); Stone, *Road to Divorce*, 417. Cf. *The Times*, 14 Jan. 1988, where it was reported that 'illegitimacy rates in Britain are comparatively high among black women but the rate of increase between 1971 and 1986 was higher among white women. Illegitimacy rates among Asian women are very low'; and ibid., 29 Apr. 1993, reporting the findings of the *General Household Survey*.

[38] *The Times*, 10 Dec. 1993.

be condemned for 'living in sin' and that the phrase should be abandoned. The day after this report was issued, Cardinal Hume officially launched the Catholic Agency for Social Concern, established by the Catholic Bishops' Conference of England and Wales. He told a press conference held in connection with this event that

> full sexual relationships are only possible inside marriage . . . We [Roman Catholics] are hardliners when it comes to this matter . . . But pastorally we are always compassionate and I think we have quite a good record of being understanding. We never want to drive anyone out of the Church; we want to help them come to terms with the Catholic position.[39]

In September 1992 a survey in Scotland suggested that a majority of both church members and non-church members did not oppose cohabitation, though there was a slight tendency for the former category to be more disapproving than the latter.[40] Such surveys generally returned majorities accepting cohabitation but large majorities opposing adultery. The future of marriage, cohabitation, and the Churches' attitudes towards both will no doubt be a matter of pronounced social interest.

The question of artificial contraception had aroused a great deal of controversy in the years immediately before 1970, but has generated comparatively less heat since then. The issue is a perennial cause of dispute, however, in relation to the instruction given about birth control in schools and elsewhere. There was Roman Catholic concern, for example, over a recommendation by a Department of Education working group in 1988 that birth-control teaching should be made compulsory in schools.[41] The Protestant Churches have generally accepted the use of artificial contraception. The Roman Catholic Church maintains official opposition to it, as was shown in the papal encyclical *Veritatis Splendor* in 1993. But this document, like *Humanae Vitae*, did not claim infallibility;[42] and individual Catholics do or do not meet their Church's ideal in regard to the question.[43]

Abortion is one of the leading social controversies of the 1960s which has retained more prominence than birth control in subse-

[39] *The Times*, 8 June 1995.
[40] *Dundee Courier and Advertiser*, 11 Sept. 1992.
[41] *Independent*, 20 Aug. 1988.
[42] *The Times*, 23 Sept. 1993, 29 Sept. 1993 (correspondence columns).
[43] e.g. ibid., 13 Feb. 1996.

quent years. The Roman Catholic Church has continued to oppose abortion (as, for example, in its Declaration on Procured Abortion in 1974), except in cases where the mother is likely to die through giving birth. Over this issue, the Roman Catholic Church seems to possess the general support of its laity—'anti-abortion petitions collected at the back of the church after Sunday Mass have become a regular feature of local Catholic life', it was stated in 1988.[44] But much of the opposition to abortion comes from outside the borders of Catholicism. The tenth anniversary of the Nationwide Festival of Light in 1981 was celebrated as a 'pro-life' rally in the Methodist Central Hall, Westminster:

> Over a thousand supporters watched as 150,000 white petals drifted down from the roof, each representing an abortion carried out in Britain over the past twelve months . . . the Festival's director, Mr Raymond Johnston—who posed the question 'when did your life begin?'—answered it by declaring that it had to be 'at conception', because at that time a human being was genetically complete, needing only food, oxygen, and time.[45]

The Church of England and the Church of Scotland, in declarations of 1983 and 1986 respectively, favoured abortion only on fairly strict conditions—for example, in cases where the birth would involve serious risk to the health of the mother. Methodists and other Nonconformists tend to be more liberal, though there are differing opinions within their ranks. While the attempts to revise or repeal the Abortion Act of 1967 have come largely from Roman Catholics, they have had considerable Protestant support. It was noted in 1988 that 'a large section of the population, far wider than the twelve per cent of it which is Catholic, now supports a more restrictive abortion law'.[46]

In 1990, after a parliamentary struggle of several years, David Alton, a Liberal Democrat MP and a Roman Catholic, had partial success when he carried a bill to reduce the permitted period for an abortion from twenty-eight weeks from the time of conception to twenty-four (he had wanted a reduction to eighteen weeks).[47] Debate on the desirability of further changes in abortion law and practice continues—not least over the possible introduction of an

[44] Ibid., 25 Jan. 1988 (article by Clifford Longley).
[45] *CT*, 2 Oct. 1981.
[46] *The Times*, 25 Jan. 1988 (article by Clifford Longley). Cf. *LW*, May 1988.
[47] Cf. *The Times*, 14 Jan. 1988 (article by Ronald Butt), 21 May 1988 (article by David Alton); Peart-Binns, *Bishop Hugh Montefiore*, 264–6.

abortion pill, to be administered in hospitals, which would replace the surgical operation.

The Roman Catholic Church also continues to oppose all artificial means of giving birth, such as artificial insemination by a husband (AIH) and artificial insemination by a donor (AID). The latter practice is also officially opposed by the Church of England and the Church of Scotland, but not the former—though it is not clear whether 'husband' is now taken to include 'permanent partner' or whether the latter is regarded as a 'donor'.

The question of the Churches and their attitudes to homosexual practice was by no means laid to rest by the Sexual Offences Act of 1967. The removal of criminality from homosexual acts by this measure (when committed between consenting adults) was not accompanied by the spread of approval of such decriminalized acts among the population at large. In 1977 *Gay News* was condemned and fined for blasphemous libel, on a prosecution initiated by Mary Whitehouse, after it had published a poem linking Christ with homosexual fantasies. The coming of the frequently fatal AIDS disease in the 1980s (Britain had had over 1,200 cases by 1988), with indications that the disease spread particularly among homosexuals, stiffened society's traditional disapproval of homosexual practice.[48] Even though opinion has softened towards homosexuals more recently, a majority in society seems opposed to accepting homosexual inclinations and actions on the same level as heterosexual ones. Differences of view on this matter no doubt affect every Church. In the Church of England, for example, there is a wide difference between clergy who give church blessings to the unions of homosexual and lesbian couples and clergy who maintain a traditional abhorrence of homosexual practice.[49] In a General Synod debate in November 1987, a call from a rector, Tony Higton, for homosexual clergy to be removed from their posts was overwhelmingly rejected. But a more moderate motion by the Bishop of Chester (Michael Baughen), declaring that homosexual genital acts fell short of the ideal of 'total commitment' to be found in marriage, was carried by a huge majority. Heavily defeated was a liberal amendment to this motion by

[48] *The Times*, 12 Jan. 1988 (article by Ben Pimlott).

[49] Ibid., 10 and 11 Nov. 1987. Cf. J. Dominian and H. Montefiore, *God, Sex, and Love: An Exercise in Ecumenical Ethics* (London, 1989), 51–70.

Malcolm Johnson, who was rector of a church (St Botolph's, Aldgate, London) which was then the base of the Lesbian and Gay Christian Movement founded in 1976 (and who later declared his homosexuality).[50]

The passing of Baughen's motion gave more satisfaction to the traditionalists on the question of homosexual behaviour than to the progressives. A few bishops—beginning with the Bishop of Ripon (David Young), who was supported by the Bishops of Truro (Peter Munford) and Norwich (Peter Knott) and by the Archbishop of Canterbury (Robert Runcie)—declared that, in accordance with traditional practice, they were banning known practising homosexuals from ministering in their dioceses.[51] Richard Kirker, an Anglican clergyman who was General Secretary of the Lesbian and Gay Christian Movement, said that the Bishop of Ripon was inviting people to 'snoop and pry' and to 'threaten and harass' those in stable, responsible, loving relationships.[52] The whole matter of the Anglican Church's attitude to homosexuality remained a matter for re-examination and debate, as occurred, for example, in a conference of Anglican prelates from different countries at Windsor in March 1995.[53] Further airing of the subject was anticipated at later important Anglican gatherings.

There were marked differences among Methodists at the end of 1987 over the appointment of a declared homosexual as a probationary minister at the Methodist West London Mission.[54] In July 1988 the Methodist Conference unanimously rejected a motion that 'practising homosexuals shall not be received into full connection or ordained into our ministry', but voted to establish a commission to study the question of ordaining practising homosexuals. The commission, however, was unable to reach agreement, except on the point that homosexual orientation, as opposed to practice, was no reason for refusing ordination. The commission's report recommended that the decision on accepting a candidate for ministerial training should be left to 'the discretion of those appointed to make such judgement'. Otherwise, the report advised a Church which

[50] *The Times*, 12 Nov. 1987 (including article by Bernard Levin); ibid., 16 Nov. 1987 (article by Clifford Longley); *Sunday Telegraph*, 28 Jan. 1996.

[51] *The Times*, 30 and 31 Dec. 1987. Cf. ibid., 7 Sept. 1996, p. 1.

[52] Ibid., 31 Dec. 1987, 1 Feb. 1988; *Sunday Telegraph*, 3 and 10 Jan. 1988.

[53] *The Times*, 17 Mar. 1995.

[54] *Sunday Telegraph*, 3 Jan. 1988.

was very divided on the matter to try and tolerate the different opinions within it.[55]

As well as necessary involvement with the continuing and varying manifestations of moral change, many Church leaders became known from 1980 as outspoken critics of government economic and social policy. They have appeared as defenders of the former party political 'consensus' and the State interventionist attitude to social policy which was condemned by the Thatcherite, 'New Right', free-enterprise approach in the late 1970s and 1980s.[56]

Opposition to Thatcherism has been by no means universal among clergy and ministers. According to surveys of political preferences among Anglican clergy, about a third favoured the Conservative Party in the early 1980s.[57] Some (in different denominations) have spoken clearly in favour of Thatcherism, and some of these are of high standing in their Churches. But there was not the consistent opposition from a minority of bishops to collectivism that had appeared in the inter-war years. There was distinctly less than there had been among Church leaders at that time to counteract the voices of such leaders in the 1980s as the Anglican Bishops David Sheppard and David Jenkins, Professor James Whyte of the Church of Scotland, and the Roman Catholic Archbishop Derek Worlock. On the other hand, many leading laypeople, including Margaret Thatcher herself, have been both Thatcherite and Christian. Thatcher at times overtly based her politics on her religious upbringing, when she imbibed Methodist principles of a *laissez-faire* and not a collectivist kind. The Catholic *Pro Fide* movement contained a strand of right-wing political Conservatism.[58]

In the 1980s the rather odd spectacle occurred, for a country in which Christianity was supposedly in recession, of a battle taking place over social policy between two sides, both of which contained in their foremost ranks many ardent Christians who openly used their Christianity as a justification of their thought and policy. This

[55] *The Times*, 10 May 1990.

[56] For a summary of the New Right arguments, see D. Harris, *Justifying State Welfare: The New Right versus the Old Left* (Oxford, 1987), 7–8, 22–8.

[57] K. Medhurst and G. Moyser, *Church and Politics in a Secular Age: The Care of the Church of England* (Oxford, 1988), 227, 230ff.

[58] Hastings, *History*, 636–9; see also pp. 651–2.

religious battle was occasionally face to face, as when Mrs Thatcher delivered a celebrated defence of her policies to the General Assembly of the Church of Scotland in May 1988.[59] The spectacle was even odder when Mrs Thatcher presented herself as a would-be moral reformer who was getting inadequate support from the very religious leaders who should strongly concern themselves with moral issues.[60]

The clash between Church leaders and the Government over social policy came to a head in the early 1980s, when unemployment (at its highest for fifty years) and deprivation were highlighted by street rioting in parts of Bristol, Liverpool, London, Manchester, and Birmingham. Some of the rioting contained racial ingredients, for the first time in over twenty years. There were varied religious responses to the riots, some attaching little responsibility to government policies and others giving them most of the blame. The Bishop of Southwell (Denis Wakeling) ascribed the riots mainly to 'moral weakness' arising from inadequate guidance in homes, schools, and churches. In the August 1981 issue of his *Diocesan News* he said: 'It is facile to blame these riots on the Government, or the police, or immigration. Today we are reaping the whirlwind of decades of moral weakness that has resulted in the pursuit of "affluence without responsibility" becoming the religion of the day.'[61] An explanation much less comforting to the Government was given in an article in the *Tablet* by Father Michael Gaine of the Liverpool Institute of Higher Education:

> While I would reject as inadequate any moralistic solution which suggested that what was needed was more discipline, or a greater respect for authority, I do believe that there is a moral issue at the heart of these disturbances. It is sad that it has required violence to force this issue on our attention . . . The issue is for how long our society will allow such gross social and economic inequalities. Unless we have the will to remove them,

[59] *The Times*, 23 May 1988 (leading article); 27 May 1988 (article by T. E. Utley); 1 June 1988 (leading article); 31 Dec. 1987 (article by Ronald Butt). Cf. ibid., 2 June 1989 (article by Brian Griffiths, head of Mrs Thatcher's Policy Unit); 21 Oct. 1991 (article by Revd Professor W. P. Stephens, 'What the Churches can Learn from Thatcherism').

[60] Ibid., 27 Oct. 1987 (leading article); 31 Dec. 1987 (article by Ronald Butt); 13 Feb. 1988 (leading article). Cf. summary of a survey of the moral attitudes of General Synod members, 1990–5 (ibid., 14 Feb. 1996); R. Plant, 'The Church and the Government', in J. C. D. Clark (ed.), *Ideas and Politics in Modern Britain* (London, 1990), 117, 127.

[61] *CT*, 31 July 1981.

and instruct our elected representatives to take the necessary steps to do so, at personal costs to income and accumulated wealth, we must individually bear a share of the moral responsibility for these riots and their accompanying violence.[62]

The Churches probably received at this time more public attention over questions of public social policy than they did over theological issues or questions of personal morality, or than they managed to attract physically by means of holding their ordinary services. It required the compelling and fractious issue of women clergy in the Church of England a few years later to sustain the large degree of attention which had been attained through highly publicized controversy with the Government.

The urban rioting had focused attention on the plight of the inner-city areas, and one of the best-known responses was *Faith in the City* (1985), the report of a commission appointed in 1983 by the Archbishop of Canterbury (Robert Runcie) and consisting mostly of Anglicans, with some members of other Churches. The report was a very practical document. It was curiously like the social surveys of Charles Booth for London and Seebohm Rowntree for York about 1900, in that it concluded that perhaps one in four people in the country as a whole, and a much higher proportion in the 'urban priority areas', was 'forced to live on the margins of poverty or below the threshold of an acceptable standard of living'. The statistical estimates of Booth and Rowntree in this respect were remarkably similar to those of *Faith in the City*. That the report would do nothing to narrow the gulf between Thatcher and many Church leaders was also shown by the specific recommendations of the document. The recommendations applying to government action were unlikely to please a ministry which wanted to reduce State expenditure. The report urged higher public spending on rate support, child benefit, the Urban Programme, the Community Programme, aid for small firms, and aid for job creation. It also recommended that there should be an expanded public-housing programme in the priority areas, including housing provision for the homeless; and that the Government should authorize an independent inquiry to undertake a wide review of the links between

[62] *T.*, 18 July 1981. Cf. *MR*, 16 and 23 July 1981 (statements at Methodist Conference). See also Lord Scarman, *The Scarman Report: The Brixton disorders, 10–12 April 1981* (Harmondsworth, 1981), esp. 157–75 ('The Disorders and Social Policy').

wages, income support, and the taxation system.[63] It was also recommended that the Church of England should raise an Urban Fund for inner-city improvement projects, and this was very successful in gaining contributions over the next few years.[64] By the time that a sequel to the report was produced in 1990, entitled *Living Faith in the City*, the Government had expended much more on the urban priority areas. But it was still criticized in ecclesiastical quarters for not doing enough—for example, by the Roman Catholic Bishops' Conference of England and Wales in a report of 1990 on growing homelessness.[65]

By the late 1980s the economic success of Thatcherism in the middle of the decade began to decline. By the end of 1990 Thatcher had lost office over a variety of issues in which European Community questions were particularly prominent; inflation and unemployment were rising again; and the country was sliding into another recession from which it was only slowly recovering by late 1996. There had not been much time for the 'trickling-down' effect of Thatcherite prosperity to work to the benefit of the poor. When the prosperity faded, there was a growing gap in the country between higher and lower incomes—the negation of the effects of previous 'consensus' politics which most Church leaders apparently wanted to see restored.[66]

Not surprisingly, therefore, the sometimes severe conflicts between Thatcher's Government and Church leaders—for example, a president of the Methodist Conference, Richard Jones, described the 'trickling-down' claim as 'a scandalous attempt to put a veneer of respectability over hurtful social injustice'[67]—had not lessened by the time she left office.[68] Though they became quieter,[69] the

[63] *Faith in the City: A Call for Action by Church and Nation—the Report of the Archbishop of Canterbury's Commission on Urban Priority Areas* (General Synod of the Church of England, London, 1985), 359–66; *The Times*, 14 Nov. 1987 (article by Alan Webster, Dean of St Paul's); ibid., 14 Nov. 1988 (on raising the Church's Urban Fund, as recommended in the report); 13 Feb. 1989 (article by Raymond Plant).

[64] *The Times*, 30 Jan. 1990, 7 May 1991.

[65] Ibid., 30 Dec. 1990 (dealing with the report entitled *Homelessness: A Fact and a Scandal*).

[66] *The Times*, 21 Mar. 1988 (article by Clifford Longley).

[67] Ibid., July 1988; quoted G. Finlayson, *Citizen, State, and Social Welfare in Britain, 1830–1990* (Oxford, 1994), 372.

[68] e.g. *The Times*, 13 Feb. 1989 (report of Commons debate on 'Church, Government, and Moral Values').

[69] Ibid., 4 May 1996 (article by Anthony Howard).

clashes over matters of policy by no means disappeared under Thatcher's successor, John Major. This has been shown, for instance, by an attack by George Carey, Archbishop of Canterbury, in an Easter sermon in Canterbury Cathedral in 1994, on the declining value of the income of the poorest tenth of the population (a decline he estimated at about 14 per cent since 1979). The poorest tenth was 'cut off from a reasonable share of opportunities, hope, status, security and prosperity'.[70] A new Anglican report in 1995, *Staying in the City*, appearing ten years after *Faith in the City*, found that faith in improvement had been little vindicated. Conditions in the inner-city areas were, it stated, at least as bad as a decade before, and 'the gap between rich and poor has grown much wider'. But the Environment Secretary, John Gummer, a former member of the General Synod of the Church of England, said that the new report underestimated 'the enormous amount that had been done' along the lines of the recommendations in the 1985 document.[71]

In the course of the twentieth century, the Churches have been presented with innumerable and unprecedented challenges to their moral and social assumptions. Their responses to these challenges have marked all Churches, even those such as the Roman Catholic Church, which, according to its official pronouncements, has moved not at all. The comparative degree of adjustment between the Churches to this torrent of change is very difficult to assess. Official rules and pronouncements often do not reflect actual practice, which is basically a matter for personal decision and action and certainly differs among the members of each Church. While there have been changes in moral pronouncements and attitudes, the basic moral rules of Christianity, the Ten Commandments, have remained remarkably intact and well respected. One has to make a qualification even here, however, with regard to the Fourth Commandment, 'Remember the Sabbath Day and keep it holy'. The actions of Christians show that they can be trying to keep this day holy only through having remarkably diverse and extended concepts of the term.

The present writer does not pretend to any gifts of prophecy, and will not endeavour to predict the moral and social developments to

[70] *The Times*, 4 Apr. 1994.
[71] Ibid., 17 Nov. 1995.

which the Churches will feel compelled to respond. Nor will he attempt to predict the shape of Christian organizations in years to come. The prospects for a mere continuance of British Churches in their present forms are not very bright, though it may be too early to say whether the powerful and effective revivals of the eighteenth and nineteenth centuries in Britain—Evangelical, Anglo-Catholic, and Roman Catholic—have exhausted their respective influences. Informal Evangelicalism is currently having increasing influence amongst the young;[72] and, looking beyond the boundaries of Christianity alone, inter-faith discussions, strengthened by the growth of non-Christian religions in the country through immigration, are creating a growing amount of interest.

[72] e.g. *The Times,* 6 and 13 Jan. 1996, 11 Apr. 1996.

BIBLIOGRAPHY

I CORRESPONDENCE

British Library
Cecil of Chelwood Papers (Add. MSS 51071–51204)
Marie Stopes Papers (Add. MSS 58493–58560)
Lambeth Palace Library
Bishop Bell Papers
Canon John Collins Papers
Archbishop Davidson Papers
Archbishop Fisher Papers
Bishop Headlam Papers
Archbishop Lang Papers
Archbishop Ramsey Papers
Archbishop William Temple Papers

II MINUTES AND OTHER RECORDS

Baptist Handbook
Church of Scotland Presbytery Minutes (in Scottish Record Office, except where stated): Aberdeen, Dingwall, Dundee (Dundee City Archives), Edinburgh
Chronicle of the Convocation of Canterbury
Congregational Year Book
Dundee United Free Church of Scotland Presbytery Minutes, in Dundee City Archives
Free Church Federal Council Minutes, in Dr Williams's Library
Hansard, *Parliamentary Debates*, 5th series
Industrial Christian Fellowship, *Annual Reports*
National Free Church Council Minutes, in Dr Williams's Library
Official Handbook of the Presbyterian Church of England
Primitive Methodist Year Book
Principal Acts of the General Assembly of the Free Church of Scotland, with the Minutes and Reports
Public Morality Council, *Annual Reports*
Reports to the General Assembly of the Church of Scotland, with the legislative Acts
Year Book of the National Assembly of the Church of England
York Journal of Convocation

III NEWSPAPERS AND PERIODICALS

Baptist Times
British Weekly
Catholic Herald
Christian World
Church of England Newspaper
Church Family Newspaper
Church Times
Daily Express
Daily Worker
Dundee Courier and Advertiser
Evening Standard
Guardian (a Church of England newspaper)
Independent
Industrial Sunday News
Life and Work: The Church of Scotland Magazine and Mission Record
The Link (quarterly journal of the Industrial Christian Fellowship)
Methodist Recorder
Methodist Times
Methodist Times and Leader
New Campaigner: Being the Official Organ of the Temperance Council of the Christian Churches of England and Wales
New Statesman
Newcastle Daily Journal
News Chronicle
The Pilgrim
Scotsman
Scottish Universe
Spectator
Sunday Dispatch
Sunday Telegraph
Tablet
The Times
Universe
Western Mail
Yorkshire Herald
Yorkshire Post

IV REFERENCE WORKS

A Handbook of Catholic Charitable Organizations (Catholic Social Guild, Oxford, 1935).
Church of Scotland Year Book.

Crockford's Clerical Directory.
Handbook of British Chronology, ed. E. B. Fryde, D. E. Greenway, S. Porter, and I. Roy (3rd edn., Royal Historical Society, London, 1986).
The Longman Handbook of Modern British History, 1714–1987, ed. C. Cook and J. Stevenson (2nd edn.; London, 1988).
The Longman Companion to Britain since 1945, ed. C. Cook and J. Stevenson (London, 1995).
Welsh Church Year Book.

V BOOKS, PAMPHLETS, AND ARTICLES

(Place of publication of books and pamphlets is London unless otherwise stated.)

A Brief Record of the War and Social Order Committee (n.d. [1922]).
A Code of Social Principles (Catholic Social Guild Year Book; Oxford, 1929).
Abrams, M., Gerard, D., and Timms, N. (eds.), *Values and Social Change in Britain* (1985).
Abse, L., *Private Member: A Psychoanalytically Orientated Study of Contemporary Politics* (1973).
Aldgate, A., *Censorship and the Permissive Society: British Cinema and Theatre, 1955–65* (Oxford, 1995).
Anderson, O., *Suicide in Victorian and Edwardian England* (Oxford, 1987).
Archbishops' Advisory Board for Spiritual and Moral Work: first report (Maidstone, n.d. [1920]).
Armitage, J. J. R., *Labour: The Next Phase—the Industrial Christian Fellowship, its Aims and Operations* (n.d.).
Artificial Human Insemination (Public Morality Council, 1947).
Aspinall, S., 'Women, Realism, and Reality in British Films, 1943–53', in J. Curran and V. Porter (eds.), *British Cinema History* (1983), 272–93.
Aspinwall, B., 'The Welfare State within the State: the St Vincent de Paul Society in Glasgow, 1848–1920', *Studies in Church History*, 23 (Oxford, 1986), 445–59.
Ayer, A. J., *Language, Truth and Logic* (1936).
Bailey, D. S., *Homosexuality and the Western Christian Tradition* (1955).
—— *Sexual Offenders and Social Punishment* (1956).
Baldwin, S., *On England, and Other Addresses* (1926).
Barnett, C., *The Audit of War: The Illusion and Reality of Britain as a Great Nation* (1986).
Bebbington, D. W., *The Nonconformist Conscience: Chapel and Politics, 1870–1914* (1982).
—— *Evangelicalism in Modern Britain: A History from the 1730s to the 1980s* (1989).

Beck, G. A. (ed.), *The English Catholics, 1850–1950* (1950).
Beddoe, D., *Back to Home and Duty: Women between the Wars, 1918–39* (1989).
Bell, G. K. A., *Randall Davidson, Archbishop of Canterbury* (2 vols.; 1935).
——'The Church and Religious Drama', *Chichester Diocesan Gazette* (1938).
——*Christianity and World Order* (Harmondsworth, 1940).
Binfield, C., *Pastors and People: The Biography of a Baptist Church* (Coventry, 1984).
Birnbaum, N., 'Hope's End or Hope's Beginning? 1968—and After', *Salmagundi*, 81 (Winter 1989), 141–58.
Blaikie, A., *Illegitimacy, Sex, and Society: Northeast Scotland, 1750–1900* (Oxford, 1993).
Bland, L., '"Cleansing the Portals of Life": The Venereal Disease Campaign in the Early Twentieth Century', in M. Langan and W. Schwarz (eds.), *Crises in the British State, 1880–1930* (1985), 192–208.
Boyd, K. M., *Scottish Church Attitudes to Sex, Marriage, and the Family, 1850–1914* (Edinburgh, 1980).
Brake, G. T., *Drink: Ups and Downs of Methodist Attitudes to Temperance* (1974).
Bray, R. A., *Labour and the Churches* (1912).
Braybon, G., and Summerfield, P., *Out of the Cage: Women's Experiences in Two World Wars* (1987).
Breitenbach, E., and Gordon, E. (eds.), *Out of Bounds: Women in Scottish Society, 1800–1945* (Edinburgh, 1992).
Briggs, A., *Social Thought and Social Action: A Study of the Work of Seebohm Rowntree, 1871–1954* (1961).
——*The History of Broadcasting in the United Kingdom* (5 vols.; Oxford, 1961–95).
Bristow, E., *Vice and Vigilance: Purity Movements in Britain since 1700* (Dublin, 1977).
Brookes, B., *Abortion in England, 1900–67* (1988).
Brown, C., *The Social History of Religion in Scotland since 1730* (1987).
Brown, S. J., 'The Social Vision of Scottish Presbyterianism and the Union of 1929', *Records of the Scottish Church History Society*, 24/1 (1990), 77–96.
——'"A Victory for God": The Scottish Presbyterian Churches and the General Strike of 1926', *Journal of Ecclesiastical History*, 42 (1991), 596–617.
——'The Decline and Fall of Kirk-Session Discipline in Presbyterian Scotland, *c.*1830–1930' (unpublished conference paper, Association of Scottish Historical Studies, 1991), 1–22.
——'The Campaign for the Christian Commonwealth in Scotland, 1919–39', in W. M. Jacob and N. Yates (eds.), *Crown and Mitre: Religion and*

Society in Northern Europe since the Reformation (Woodbridge, 1993), 203–21.

Buckle, G. E. (ed.), *Letters of Queen Victoria, third ser., 1886–1901* (3 vols., 1930–2).

Burness, C., 'The Long Slow March: Scottish Women MPs, 1918–45', in E. Breitenbach and E. Gordon (eds.), *Out of Bounds: Women in Scottish Society, 1800–1945* (Edinburgh, 1992), 151–73.

Calder, A., *The People's War: Britain, 1939–45* (1969).

Capon, J., *. . . and there was Light: The Story of the Nationwide Festival of Light* (1972).

Carpenter, E., *Archbishop Fisher, his Life and Times* (Norwich, 1991).

Carpenter, S. C., *Winnington-Ingram: The Biography of A. F. Winnington-Ingram, Bishop of London* (London, 1949).

Carr-Saunders, A. M., and Jones, D. C., *A Survey of the Social Structure of England and Wales* (2nd edn., Oxford, 1937).

Carstairs, G. M., *This Island Now: The BBC Reith Lectures, 1962* (Harmondsworth, 1964).

Carter, H., *Local Option: Shall We Support It?* (n.d. [1920]).

——*The Church and the Drink Evil* (1922).

——*Facts about Greyhound Racing* (1928).

Catterall, P., 'Morality and Politics: The Free Churches and the Labour Party between the Wars', *Historical Journal*, 36 (1993), 667–85.

Caulfield, M., *Mary Whitehouse* (1975).

Chadwick, O., *Hensley Henson: A Study in the Friction between Church and State* (Oxford, 1983).

——*Michael Ramsey, a Life* (Oxford, 1990).

Chesser, E., *Is Chastity Outmoded?* (1960).

Christianity and Industrial Problems, Being the Report of the Archbishops' Fifth Committee of Inquiry (1918).

Clapson, M., *A Bit of a Flutter: Popular Gambling and English Society, c.1823–1961* (Manchester, 1992).

Clark, J. C. D. (ed.), *Ideas and Politics in Modern Britain* (1990).

Clarke, P., *Hope and Glory: Britain, 1900–90* (Harmondsworth, 1996).

Cleary, J. M., *Catholic Social Action in Britain, 1909–59: A History of the Catholic Social Guild* (Catholic Social Guild Year Book, Oxford, 1961).

Clump, C. C., *A Catholic's Guide to Social and Political Action* (Catholic Social Guild Year Book, Oxford, 1939).

Coleman, P., *Christian Attitudes to Homosexuality* (1980).

Coman, P., *Catholics and the Welfare State* (1977).

Comfort, A., *Sexual Behaviour in Society* (1950).

Competition: A Study in Human Motive (1917).

Coote, A., and Campbell, B., *Sweet Freedom: The Struggle for Women's Liberation* (2nd edn., Oxford, 1987).

Cope, G., *Christians in the Class Struggle* (1942).

Co-ordination: A Plea for Closer Co-operation between Diocese, Parish, and Church Societies (1939).

Costello, J., *Love, Sex, and War: Changing Values, 1939–45* (1985).

Cox, J., *The English Churches in a Secular Society: Lambeth, 1890–1930* (Oxford, 1982).

Craig, R., *Social Concern in the Thought of William Temple* (1963).

Crane, P., *Britain's Crisis: A Personal Opinion* (Glasgow, 1947).

Crawford, V. M., *Catholic Social Doctrine, 1891–1931* (Catholic Social Guild Year Book, Oxford, 1931).

Crosby, Travis L., *The Impact of Civilian Evacuation in the Second World War* (1986).

Croucher, R., *We Refuse to Starve in Silence: A History of the National Unemployed Workers' Movement, 1920–46* (1987).

Crowther, A., *British Social Policy, 1914–39* (Basingstoke, 1988).

Cunningham, W., *Personal Ideals and Social Principles: Some Comments on the Report of the Archbishops' Committee on Christianity and Industrial Problems* (1919).

Curran, J., and Porter, V. (eds.), *British Cinema History* (1983).

Currie, R., Gilbert, A., and Horsley, L. (eds.), *Churches and Churchgoers: Patterns of Church Growth in the British Isles since 1700* (Oxford, 1977).

Davenport-Hines, R., *Sex, Death, and Punishment: Attitudes to Sex and Sexuality in Britain since the Renaissance* (1990).

Davie, G., *Religion in Britain since 1945: Believing without Belonging* (Oxford, 1994).

Davies, A., 'The Police and the People: Gambling in Salford, 1900–39', *Historical Journal*, 34 (1991), 87–115.

Davies, C., *Permissive Britain: Social Change in the Sixties and Seventies* (1975).

Davies, G., *The Churches and State Purchase* (repr. from *The Welsh Outlook*, 1918).

Davies, R., George, A. R., and Rupp, G. (eds.), *A History of the Methodist Church in Great Britain* (4 vols.; 1978–88).

De Groot, G. J., *Blighty: British Society in the Era of the Great War* (1996).

Dearmer, P. C. (ed.), *Christianity and the Crisis* (1933).

Demant, V. A., *This Unemployment: Disaster or Opportunity?* (1931).

——*God, Man, and Society* (1933).

——*Christian Sex Ethics, an Exposition* (1963).

Denny, N. D., 'Temperance and the Scottish Churches, 1870–1914', *Records of the Scottish Church History Society*, 23/2 (1988), 217–39.

Dingle, A. E., *The Campaign for Prohibition in England: The United Kingdom Alliance, 1872–95* (1980).

Dominian, J., and Montefiore, H., *God, Sex, and Love: An Exercise in Ecumenical Ethics* (1989).

Duff, E., *The Social Thought of the World Council of Churches* (1956).

Edward [Luscombe], Reminiscences and Reflections (Dundee, 1989).
Edwards, D. L., *The 'Honest to God' Debate: some Reactions to the Book 'Honest to God'* (1963).
Edwards, M., *S. E. Keeble, Pioneer and Prophet* (1949).
Eliot, T. S., *The Idea of a Christian Society* (1939).
Elliott, C., *et al., Christian Faith and Political Hopes: A Reply to E. R. Norman* (1979).
Ely, P., and Denney, D., *Social Work in a Multi-Racial Society* (Aldershot, 1987).
Emsley, C., '"Mother, what *did* policemen do when there weren't any motors?" The Law, the Police, and the Regulation of Motor Traffic in England, 1900–39', *Historical Journal*, 36 (1993), 357–81.
Faith in the City: A Call for Action by Church and Nation—the Report of the Archbishop of Canterbury's Commission on Urban Priority Areas (General Synod of the Church of England, 1985).
Finlayson, G., 'A Moving Frontier: Voluntarism and the State in British Social Welfare, 1911–49', *Twentieth Century British History*, 1/2 (1990), 183–206.
——*Citizen, State, and Social Welfare in Britain, 1830–1990* (Oxford, 1994).
Fisher, G., *Thorny Problems* (PMC booklet; 1943).
——*The Church and Marriage* (1954).
——*Problems of Marriage and Divorce* (1955).
Fletcher, R., *The Family and Marriage in Britain* (Harmondsworth, 1966).
Focus on Drink and Gambling (Temperance Council of Christian Churches of England and Wales, n.p., 1977).
Fogarty, M. P., *Planning and the Community* (Catholic Social Guild Year Book, Oxford, 1942).
——*The Machinery of Town and Country Planning* (Catholic Social Guild, Oxford, 1944).
Forrester, D. B., *Christianity and the Future of Welfare* (1985).
—— and Skene, D. (eds.), *Just Sharing: a Christian Approach to the Distribution of Wealth, Income and Benefits* (1988).
Fox, A., *Dean Inge* (1960).
Fuller, R., and Rice, B., *Christianity and the Affluent Society* (1966).
Fryer, P., *Staying Power: The History of Black People in Britain* (1984).
Garbett, C., *In the Heart of South London* (1931).
——*The Challenge of the Slums* (1933).
Gardner, L. (ed.), *Some Christian Essentials of Reconstruction* (1920).
Garvie, A. E., *The Christian Ideal for Human Society* (1930).
——*Memories and Meanings of my Life* (1938).
Gilbert, A. D., *The Making of Post-Christian Britain* (1980).
Gilley, S., and Shiels, W. J. (eds.), *A History of Religion in Britain* (Oxford, 1994).

Glass, D. V., *Social Mobility in Britain* (1954).
Goldring, R., 'Divorce and Dissent: Free Church attitudes to divorce and remarriage, 1910–37', *Journal of the United Reformed Church History Society*, 5/10 (June 1997), 622–32.
Goldthorpe, J. H., *Class Mobility and Social Structure in Modern Britain* (2nd edn.; Oxford, 1986).
Gore, C., *Christ and Society* (1928).
Gorer, G., *Exploring English Character* (1955).
Gowland, D., and Roebuck, J., *Never Call Retreat: A Biography of Bill Gowland* (1990).
Gray, A. H., *Men, Women, and God: A Discussion of Sex Questions from the Christian Point of View* (1923).
——*Sex Relations without Marriage: A Defence of the Christian Standard* (1928).
Green, P., *Betting and Gambling* (2nd edn.; 1935).
——*The Moral Condition of Great Britain Today* (1943).
Greenslade, S. L., *The Church and Social Order: A Historical Sketch* (1948).
Griffith, J. A. G., *Coloured Immigrants in Britain* (1960).
Griffiths, B., *Morality and the Market Place: Christian Alternatives to Capitalism and Socialism* (1982).
Gummer, J. S., *The Permissive Society* (1971).
Hall, R., *Marie Stopes, A Biography* (1977).
Halsey, A. H., *Trends in British Society since 1900* (1972).
——*Change in British Society* (Oxford, 1986).
Hammerton, H. J., *This Turbulent Priest* [Life of Charles Jenkinson] (1952).
Harris, D., *Justifying State Welfare: The New Right versus the Old Left* (Oxford, 1987).
Harris, J., *William Beveridge, a Biography* (Oxford, 1977).
——*Private Lives, Public Spirit: A Social History of Britain, 1870–1914* (Oxford, 1993).
Hastings, A., *A History of English Christianity, 1920–85* (1986).
Haw, G. (ed.), *Christianity and the Working Classes* (1906).
Headlam, A. C., *The Church and Industrial Questions: A Sermon Preached before the University of Cambridge* (1919).
——*What It Means To Be a Christian* (1933).
Heald, G., and Wybrow, R. J., *The Gallup Survey of Britain* (1986).
Heard, G., *Morals since 1900* (1950).
Heenan, J. C., *Cardinal Hinsley* (1944).
Hebblethwaite, P., *Paul VI, the First Modern Pope* (1993).
Henson, H. H., *Christian Morality: Natural, Developing, Final* (Oxford, 1936).
——*Retrospect of an Unimportant Life* (3 vols.; 1942–50).

Herbert, A. P., *The Ayes Have It: The Story of the Marriage Bill* (1937).
——*Independent Member* (1950).
Heron, A. (ed.), *Towards a Quaker View of Sex* (1963).
Hicks, E. L., *Diaries, 1910–19*, ed. G. Neville (Lincoln Record Society; Woodbridge, 1993).
Highet, J., *The Churches in Scotland Today* (1950).
Hill, C. R., *Horse Power: The Politics of the Turf* (Manchester, 1988).
Holmes, C., *John Bull's Island: Immigration and British Society, 1871–1971* (1988).
Holt, R., *Sport and the British: A Modern History* (Oxford, 1989).
Hornsby-Smith, M. P., *Roman Catholics in England: Studies in Social Structure since the Second World War* (Cambridge, 1987).
Hughes, H. S., *Consciousness and Society: The Reorientation of European Social Thought, 1890–1930* (Brighton, 1988; 1st edn., 1959).
Hunter, A. G., *Christianity and Other Faiths in Britain* (1985).
Hyam, R., 'The Political Consequences of Seretse Khama: Britain, the Bamangwato, and South Africa, 1948–52', *Historical Journal*, 29 (1986), 921–47.
Hylson-Smith, K., *Evangelicals in the Church of England, 1734–1984* (Edinburgh, 1988).
——*High Churchmanship in the Church of England, from the Sixteenth Century to the Late Twentieth Century* (Edinburgh, 1993).
Hynes, S., *The Edwardian Turn of Mind* (Princeton, 1968).
Inge, W. R., *The Social Teaching of the Church* (1930).
Inglis, K. S., *Churches and the Working Classes in Victorian England* (1963).
Ingram, K., *Basil Jellicoe* (1936).
——*Christianity, Right or Left?* (1937).
Iremonger, F. A., *William Temple, Archbishop of Canterbury, his Life and Letters* (1948; new impression, 1949).
Jacob, W. M., and Yates, N. (eds.), *Crown and Mitre: Religion and Society in Northern Europe since the Reformation* (Woodbridge, 1993).
James, E., *A Life of Bishop John A. T. Robinson, Scholar, Pastor, Prophet* (1989).
Jasper, R. C. D., *Arthur Cayley Headlam* (1960).
——*George Bell, Bishop of Chichester* (1967).
Jeffery-Poulter, S., *Peers, Queers, and Commons: The Struggle for Gay Law Reform from 1950 to the Present* (1991).
Jenkins, R., *A Life at the Centre* (1991).
Jeremy, D. J., *Capitalists and Christians: Business Leaders and the Churches in Britain, 1900–60* (Oxford, 1990).
Johnston, J., *The Lord Chamberlain's Blue Pencil* (1990).
Jones, D. J. V., '"Where did it all go wrong?" Crime in Swansea, 1938–68', *Welsh History Review*, 15/2 (1990), 240–74.

Jones, H., *The Working Faith of a Social Reformer, and other Essays* (1910).

Jones, P. d'A., *The Christian Socialist Revival, 1877–1914: Religion, Class, and Social Conscience in Late Victorian England* (Princeton, 1968).

Jones, S. G., *Workers at Play: A Social and Economic History of Leisure, 1918–39* (1986).

——*The British Labour Movement and Film, 1918–39* (1987).

Kaye, E., 'Constance Coltman, a Forgotten Pioneer', *Journal of the United Reformed Church History Society*, 4/2 (1988), 134–46.

Kent, J., *William Temple: Church, State and Society in Britain, 1880–1950* (Cambridge, 1992).

Kenyon, R., *The Catholic Faith and the Industrial Order* (1931).

Kirk, P. T. R., *Industry and Class War* (n.d.).

Knight, M., *Morals without Religion, and Other Essays* (1955).

Knox, W. W., 'Religion and the Scottish Labour Movement, c.1900–39', *Journal of Contemporary History*, 23 (1988), 609–30.

Lacey, T. A., *Marriage in Church and State*, rev. R. C. Mortimer (1947).

Langan, M., and Schwarz, W. (eds.), *Crises in the British State, 1880–1930* (1985).

Leathard, A., *The Fight for Family Planning: The Development of Family Planning Services in Britain, 1921–74* (1980).

Lee, J., *The Social Implications of Christianity* (1922).

Levitt, I., *Poverty and Welfare in Scotland, 1890–1948* (Edinburgh, 1988).

Lewis, D. S., *Illusions of Grandeur: Mosley, Fascism, and British Society, 1931–81* (Manchester, 1987).

Lewis, J., *Women in England, 1870–1950* (Brighton, 1984).

——'Public Institution and Private Relationship: Marriage and Marriage Guidance, 1920–68', *Twentieth Century British History*, 1/3 (1990), 233–63.

——*Women and Social Action in Victorian and Edwardian England* (1991).

Lewis, J., *Christianity and the Social Revolution* (1935).

Lidgett, J. Scott, *The Idea of God and Social Ideals* (1928).

Little, K., *Negroes in Britain* (2nd edn.; 1972).

Lloyd, R., *The Church of England, 1900–65* (1966).

Lockhart, J. G., *Cosmo Gordon Lang* (1949).

Lodge, D., *How Far Can You Go?* (Harmondsworth, 1981).

Longford, Lord (Pakenham, Francis), *Pornography: The Longford report* (1972).

Lowe, R., 'The Second World War, Consensus, and the Foundation of the Welfare State', *Twentieth Century British History*, 1/2 (1990), 152–82.

Luscombe, E., *The Scottish Episcopal Church in the Twentieth Century* (Edinburgh, 1996).

Maan, B., *The New Scots: The Story of Asians in Scotland* (Edinburgh, 1992).

McAleer, J., 'Scenes from Love and Marriage: Mills and Boon and the Popular Publishing Industry in Britain, 1908–50', *Twentieth Century British History*, 1/3 (1990), 264–88.

Macarthur, A., 'The Background to the Formation of the United Reformed Church (Presbyterian and Congregational) in England and Wales, 1972', *Journal of the United Reformed Church History Society*, 4/1 (1987), 3–22.

Machin, G. I. T., *Politics and the Churches in Great Britain, 1869 to 1921* (Oxford, 1987).

——'Marriage and the Churches in the 1930s: Royal Abdication and Divorce Reform, 1936–7', *Journal of Ecclesiastical History*, 42 (1991), 68–81.

——'British Churches and the Cinema in the 1930s', in D. Wood (ed.), *The Church and the Arts* (Studies in Church History, 28; Oxford, 1992), 477–88.

——'British Churches and Moral Change in the 1960s', in W. M. Jacob and N. Yates (eds.), *Crown and Mitre: Religion and Society in Northern Europe since the Reformation* (Woodbridge, 1993), 223–41.

——'British Churches and Social Issues, 1945–60', *Twentieth Century British History*, 7/3 (1996), 345–70.

McIntyre, I., *The Expense of Glory: A Life of John Reith* (1993).

McKibbin, R., 'The "Social Psychology" of Unemployment in Inter-War Britain', in P. J. Waller (ed.), *Politics and Social Change in Modern Britain* (Brighton, 1987), 161–91.

——'Working Class Gambling in Britain, 1880–1939', in R. McKibbin (ed.), *The Ideologies of Class: Social Relations in Britain, 1880–1950* (Oxford, 1991), 101–38.

——(ed.), *The Ideologies of Class: Social Relations in Britain, 1880–1950* (Oxford, 1991).

McLaren, A., *Birth Control in Nineteenth Century England* (1978).

Maclean, D., *The Counter-Reformation in Scotland, 1560–1930* (1931).

McRoberts, D. (ed.), *Modern Scottish Catholicism, 1878–1978* (Glasgow, 1979).

Malvern, 1941: The Life of the Church and the Order of Society, Being the Proceedings of the Archbishop of York's Conference (1941).

Marriage, Divorce, and the Royal Commission: A Study Outlining the Report of the Royal Commission on Marriage and Divorce, 1951–5 (Church of England Moral Welfare Council, 1956).

Marrin, A., *The Last Crusade: The Church of England in the First World War* (Durham, NC, 1974).

Marsh, D. C., *The Changing Social Structure of England and Wales, 1871–1951* (1958).

Marwick, A., *British Society since 1945* (2nd edn., Harmondsworth, 1990).

Mason, M., *The Making of Victorian Sexual Attitudes* (Oxford, 1994).

Mayor, S., *The Churches and the Labour Movement* (1967).

Meacham, S., *A Life Apart: The English working class, 1890–1914* (1977).

——*Toynbee Hall and Social Reform, 1880–1914: The Search for Community* (New Haven, 1987).

Medhurst, K., and Moyser, G., *Church and Politics in a Secular Age: The Case of the Church of England* (Oxford, 1988).

Melching, W., '"A New Morality": Left-Wing Intellectuals on Sexuality in Weimar Germany', *Journal of Contemporary History*, 25 (1990), 69–85.

Meller, H., *Leisure and the Changing City, 1870–1914* (1976).

Men Without Work: A Report Made to the Pilgrim Trust (Cambridge, 1938).

Mews, S. P., 'The Churches', in M. Morris (ed.), *The General Strike* (Harmondsworth, 1976), 318–37.

——'The Sword of the Spirit: A Catholic Cultural Crusade of 1940', in W. J. Sheils (ed.), *The Church and War* (Studies in Church History, 20; Oxford, 1983), 409–30.

Morgan, K., *Rebirth of a Nation: Wales, 1880–1980* (Oxford, 1981).

——*The People's Peace: British History, 1945–89* (Oxford, 1990).

Morris, J. N., *Religion and Urban Change: Croydon, 1840–1918* (Woodbridge, 1992).

Morris, M. (ed.), *The General Strike* (Harmondsworth, 1976).

Mort, F., 'Purity, Feminism, and the State: Sexuality and Moral Politics, 1880–1914', in M. Langan and W. Schwarz (eds.), *Crises in the British State, 1880–1930* (1985), 209–25.

Mortimer, R. C., *Gambling* (1933).

Mowat, C. L., *Britain between the Wars, 1918–40* (1955).

Muir, A., *John White, CH* (1958).

Munby, D. L., *Christianity and Economic Problems* (1956).

——*God and the Rich Society* (1961).

——*The Idea of a Secular Society and its Significance for Christians* (1963).

Murphy, J., *Church, State, and Schools in Britain, 1800–1970* (1971).

National Life (special supplement, n.d.).

National Temperance Convention (1918).

Norman, E. R., *Church and Society in England, 1770–1970* (Oxford, 1976).

O'Brien, R., *et al.*, *Faith in the Scottish City: The Scottish Relevance of the Report of the Archbishop's Commission on Urban Priority Areas* (Edinburgh, 1986).

Oliver, J., *The Church and Social Order: Social Thought in the Church of England, 1918–39* (1968).

Oldmeadow, E., *Francis, Cardinal Bourne* (2 vols.; 1940–4).

Packer, J. I., *Keep Yourselves from Idols* (1963).

Palmer, B., *High and Mitred: A Study of Prime Ministers as Bishop Makers, 1837–1977* (1992).

Parker, O., *For the Family's Sake: A History of the Mothers' Union, 1876–1976* (Folkestone, 1975).

Paulu, B., *British Broadcasting: Radio and Television in the United Kingdom* (Minneapolis, 1956).

Pearce, R. (ed.), *The Political Diaries of Patrick Gordon Walker, 1932–71* (1991).

Peart-Binns, J. S., *Blunt* (Queensbury, Yorks., 1969).

——*Defender of the Church of England: A Biography of R. R. Williams, Bishop of Leicester* (Oxford, 1984).

——*Maurice B. Reckitt, A Life* (Basingstoke, 1988).

——*Bishop Hugh Montefiore* (1990).

Peck, W. G., *The Social Implications of the Oxford Movement* (1933).

Peden, G. C., *British Economic and Social Policy: Lloyd George to Margaret Thatcher* (Deddington, Oxon., 1985).

Peel, A., *Thirty-Five to Fifty* [articles from the *Congregational Quarterly*] (1938).

Pegg, M., *Broadcasting and Society, 1918–39* (1983).

Perkins, E. Benson, *The Problem of Gambling* (1919).

——*Gambling in English Life* (n.d., [1950]).

Perman, D., *Change and the Church: An Anatomy of Religion in Britain* (1977).

Petrow, S., *Policing Morals: The Metropolitan Police and the Home Office, 1870–1914* (Oxford, 1994).

Pickering, W. S. F., *Anglo-Catholicism: A Study in Religious Ambiguity* (1991).

Plant, R., 'The Church and the Government', in J. C. D. Clark (ed.), *Ideas and Politics in Modern Britain* (1990), 116–29.

Popplestone, G., *Social Issues in British Society* (1985).

Potter, H., *Hanging in Judgment: Religion and the Death Penalty in England from the Bloody Code to Abolition* (1993).

Prestige, G. L., *The Life of Charles Gore* (1935).

Priestley, J. B., *English Journey* (new edn., Harmondsworth, 1977; 1st edn., 1934).

Pronay, N., and Croft, J., 'British Film Censorship and Propaganda Policy during the Second World War', in J. Curran and V. Porter (eds.), *British Cinema History* (1983), 144–63.

Prostitution: The Moral Bearings of the Problem (Catholic Social Guild, 1917).

Public Morality Council: Revised Objects and Constitution (1935).

Purcell, W., *Fisher of Lambeth: A Portrait from Life* (1969).

Ramsey, M., *Durham Essays and Addresses* (1956).

Rapp, D., 'The British Salvation Army, the British Early Film Industry, and Urban Working-Class Adolescents, 1897–1918', *Twentieth Century British History*, 7/2 (1996), 157–88.

Rattenbury, J. E., *Six Sermons on Social Subjects* (1908).

Rauschenbusch, W., *Christianity and the Social Crisis* (New York, 1913).

Reason, W., *The Social Problem for Christian Citizens* (n.d. [1913]).

——(ed.), *The Proceedings of COPEC* (1924).

——*A Handbook to the Drink Problem* (1926).

Reckitt, M. B., *The Social Teaching of the Sacraments, being the Report of the Second Anglo-Catholic School of Sociology, 1926* (1927).

——*Faith and Society* (1932).

——*Religion and Social Purpose* (1935).

——*Religion in Social Action* (1937).

——(ed.), *Prospect for Christendom: Essays in Catholic Social Reconstruction* (1945).

——*Maurice to Temple: A Century of the Social Movement in the Church of England* (1947).

——*P. E. T. Widdrington* (1961).

Regulation 33B and the V. D. Situation: A Note to Members of Parliament from the British Social Hygiene Council (1942).

Reith, J. C. W., *Into the Wind* (1949).

Reynolds, D., *Rich Relations: The American Occupation of Britain, 1942–5* (1995).

Richards, J., *The Age of the Dream Palace: Cinema and Society in Britain, 1930–9* (1984).

——and Aldgate, A., *Best of British: Cinema and Society, 1930–70* (Oxford, 1983).

Ridgwell, S., 'South Wales and the Cinema in the 1930s', *Welsh History Review*, 17 (1994–5), 590–615.

Roberts, C. H. (ed.), *The Christian Commando Campaigns: An Interpretation* (1945).

Roberts, E., *A Woman's Place: An Oral History of Working-Class Women, 1890–1940* (Oxford, 1985).

Roberts, R., *The Classic Slum: Salford Life in the First Quarter of the Century* (Harmondsworth, 1973).

Roberts, T. D. (ed.), *Contraception and Holiness* (1965; 1st edn., New York, 1964).

Robertson, J. C., *The Hidden Cinema: British Film Censorship in Action, 1913–75* (1989).

Robinson, J. A. T., *Honest to God* (1963).

——*Christian Freedom in a Permissive Society* (1970).

——*The Place of Law in the Field of Sex* (1973).

Rogers, E. (ed.), *Declarations of [Methodist] Conference on Social Questions* (1959).

Rolph, C. H. (ed.), *The Trial of Lady Chatterley* (1961).
Rose, J., *Marie Stopes and the Sexual Revolution* (1992).
Rowntree, B. S., *Poverty: A Study of Town Life* [York] (1902).
——(ed.), *Betting and Gambling: A National Evil* (1905).
——*Industrial Unrest: A Way Out?* (New York, 1922).
——*The Unemployment Problem: Some Practical Steps towards its Solution* (n.d. [1923]).
——*Society and Human Relations* (1924).
——*The Human Needs of Labour* (1937).
——*Poverty and Progress: A Second Social Survey of York* (1941).
——and Lavers, G. R., *English Life and Leisure, a Social Study* (1951).
Royle, E., *Modern Britain: A Social History, 1750–1985* (1987).
The Rt. Hon. H. H. Asquith, M.P., for Local Veto and against State Purchase (1918).
Sampson, A., *Anatomy of Britain* (1962).
Scannell, P., and Cardiff, D., *A Social History of British Broadcasting*, i (1922–39) (Oxford, 1991).
Scarman, Lord, *The Scarman Report: the Brixton disorders, 10–12 April 1981* (Harmondsworth, 1981).
Scharlieb, M., *Self-Control and Birth Control* (n.d. [1920]).
Sheen, H. E., *Canon Peter Green: A Biography of a Great Parish Priest* (1965).
Slack, K., *George Bell* (1972).
Smith, D. C., *Passive Obedience and Prophetic Protest: Social Criticism in the Scottish Church, 1830–1945* (New York, 1987).
Smith, H. L. (ed.), *War and Social Change: British Society in the Second World War* (Manchester, 1986).
——'The Effect of the War on the Status of Women', in H. L. Smith (ed.), *War and Social Change: British Society in the Second World War* (Manchester, 1986), 208–29.
Smout, T. C., *A Century of the Scottish People, 1830–1950* (1986).
Smyth, C., *Cyril Foster Garbett, Archbishop of York* (1959).
Snowden, Philip, *An Autobiography* (2 vols.; 1934).
Social Thought in the Society of Friends: A Brief Record of the War and Social Order Committee (n.d., [1922]).
Soloway, R. A., *Birth Control and the Population Question in England, 1877–1930* (Chapel Hill, NC, 1982).
Soper, D., *Calling for Action: An Autobographical Enquiry* (1986).
Spencer, M., *The Social Function of the Church* (1921).
——(ed.), *The Kingdom of God in Industry* (1927).
Stanford, P., *Lord Longford, a Life* (1994).
Stevenson, J., *British Society, 1914–45* (Harmondsworth, 1984).
Stone, L., *Road to Divorce: England, 1530–1987* (Oxford, 1992).

Stopes, M., *Married Love* (1918).
——*Wise Parenthood* (1918).
——*A New Gospel to All Peoples: A Revelation of God Uniting Physiology and the Religions of Man* (1920).
——*Contraception: Its Theory, History, and Practice* (1923).
——*Sex and Religion* (1929).
——*Roman Catholic Methods of Birth Control* (1933).
Stuart, C. (ed.), *The Reith Diaries* (1975).
Studdert-Kennedy, G., *Dog-Collar Democracy: The Industrial Christian Fellowship* (1982).
Suggate, A. M., *William Temple and Christian Social Ethics Today* (Edinburgh, 1987).
Summerfield, P., 'Women in the Two World Wars', *Historian*, 23 (Summer 1989), 3–8.
Sutherland, H. G., *Birth Control: A Statement of Christian Doctrine against the Neo-Malthusians* (1922).
Tawney, R. H., *The Acquisitive Society* (1921; rev. edn., 1945).
——*Religion and the Rise of Capitalism, a Historical Study* (1927; 1st edn., 1926).
——*Equality* (1964; 1st edn., 1931).
Temple, W., *Christianity and the Social Order* (Harmondsworth, 1942).
Terrill, R., *R. H. Tawney and his Times* (1974; 1st edn., Cambridge, Mass., 1973).
The Christian Cinema and Religious Film Society (n.d.).
The Church's Guide to Films for Religious Use (1946).
The First Object of the Mothers' Union: To Uphold the Sanctity of Marriage (n.d.).
The Greyhound Racing Calendar for the year 1927 (n.d. [1927]).
The Industrial Christian Fellowship: What It Stands For (1938).
The Methodist Conference, Liverpool 1949 (n.d. [1949]).
The Public Morality Council: Organization and Objects (n.d.).
The Tradition of Sunday (1930).
Thomas, T. (ed.), *The British, their Religious Beliefs and Practices, 1800–1986* (1988).
Thompson, F. M. L. (ed.), *The Cambridge Social History of Britain, 1750–1950* (3 vols.; Cambridge, 1990).
Titmuss, R. M., *Problems of Social Policy* (1950).
Together in Britain: A Christian Handbook on Race Relations (Church Assembly Board for Social Responsibility; 1960).
Towards a New Social Order, Being the Report of an International Conference Held at Oxford, August 20–24 1920 (1920).
Towards a New Social Order: Report of the 'New Town' Conference Held at Oxford, August 24–27 1920 (1920).

Travell, J., 'Leslie Weatherhead, Preacher and Pastor, 1893–1976', *Journal of the United Reformed Church History Society*, 4/7 (1990), 447–50.

Turner, J., 'State Purchase of the Liquor Trade in the First World War', *Historical Journal*, 23 (1980), 589–615.

Urgent and Important: Concerning Regulation 33B (Association for Moral and Social Hygiene; n.d. [1942]).

Verma, G. K., *et al.*, *Ethnicity and Educational Achievement in British Schools* (1986).

Vidler, A. R., *Sex, Marriage, and Religion: A Discussion of Some Modern Problems* (1932).

Wagner, D. O., *The Church of England and Social Reform since 1854* (New York, 1930).

Walker, A., *Restoring the Kingdom: The Radical Christianity of the House Church Movement* (1985; rev. edn., 1988).

Waller, P. J. (ed.), *Politics and Social Change in Modern Britain* (Brighton, 1987).

Walvin, J., *The Negro and English Society, 1555–1945* (1973).

——*Leisure and Society, 1830–1950* (1978).

Ward, W. R., 'The Way of the World: The Rise and Decline of Protestant Social Christianity in Britain', in *Kirkliche Zeitgeschichte*, ii (1988), 293–305.

Warnock, M., *Ethics since 1900* (1960).

Watt, L., *The Natural Rights of Man* (Catholic Social Guild Year Book, Oxford, 1940).

Weatherhead, L., *The Mastery of Sex through Psychology and Religion* (1931).

——*This is the Victory* (1940).

Weeks, J., *Sex, Politics, and Society: The Regulation of Sexuality since 1800* (1981).

Welsby, P. A., *A History of the Church of England, 1945–80* (Oxford, 1986).

Whitehouse, M., *Cleaning up T.V.: From Protest to Participation* (1967).

——*Who Does She Think She Is?* (1971).

——*A Most Dangerous Woman?* (Tring, 1982).

Wicks, B., *No Time to Wave Goodbye* (1988).

Wigley, J., *The Rise and Fall of the Victorian Sunday* (1980).

Wilkinson, A., *The Church of England and the First World War* (1978).

——*Dissent or Conform?: War, Peace, and the English Churches, 1900–45* (1986).

——*The Community of the Resurrection, a Centenary History* (1992).

Williams, G. P., and Brake, G. T., *Drink in Great Britain, 1900–79* (1980).

Williamson, J., *Father Joe: The Autobiography of Joseph Williamson of Poplar and Stepney* (1963).

Withrington, D. J., 'The Churches in Scotland, *c.*1870–1900: Towards a New Social Conscience?', *Records of the Scottish Church History Society*, 29 (1975–7), 155–68.

Wolfe, K. M., *The Churches and the British Broadcasting Corporation, 1922–56* (1984).

Wolffe, J., *God and Greater Britain: Religion and National Life in Britain and Ireland, 1843–1945* (1994).

Wright, A., *British Socialism: Socialist Thought from the 1880s to the 1960s* (1983).

VI UNPUBLISHED THESES

Abendstern, M., 'Expression and Control: A Study of Working Class Leisure and Gender, 1918–39—a Case Study of Rochdale Using Oral History Methods', Ph.D. thesis (Essex, 1986).

Campbell, D. P., 'Methodism and Social Problems in the Inter-War Period, 1918–39', M.Litt. thesis (Oxford, 1987).

Catterall, P. P., 'The Free Churches and the Labour Party in England and Wales, 1918–39', Ph.D. thesis (London, 1989).

Goodfellow, I., 'The Church Socialist League, 1906–23', Ph.D. thesis (Durham, 1983).

Gordon, J. C., 'The Temperance Movement and the Labour Party in Glasgow, 1920–76', MA thesis (Newcastle upon Tyne, 1982).

Higgins, R., 'William Robertson Nicoll and the Liberal Nonconformist Press, 1886–1923', Ph.D. thesis (St Andrews, 1995).

Jones, F. W., 'Social Concern in the Church of England, 1880–1940', Ph.D. thesis (London, 1968).

Moloney, T. W., 'The Public Ministry of Cardinal Hinsley, 1935–43', Ph.D. thesis (London, 1980).

Smith, L. J. F., 'The Abortion Controversy, 1936–77: A Case Study in the Emergence of Law', Ph.D. thesis (Edinburgh, 1979).

Wolfe, K. M., 'Christianity and the BBC, 1922–51: The Politics of Sacred Utterance', Ph.D. thesis (London, 1982).

INDEX

Abbreviations in Index

Abp	Archbishop	Marq.	Marquess
Bp	Bishop	R. C.	Roman Catholic
C. of E.	Church of England	Revd	Reverend
C. of S.	Church of Scotland	Ven.	Venerable (Archdeacon)
Fr	Father	Visct	Viscount
Ld	Lord